CONFESSIONS OF AN INTERNATIONAL BANKER

SEAN HICKEY

Order this book online at www.trafford.com
or email orders@trafford.com

Most Trafford titles are also available at major online book retailers.

Front cover (top left to bottom right)

Pigeon's Rock, Beirut, 1971
Dubai Creek, 1980
Toronto City Hall, 1965
Bab al Yemen, Sana'a, Yemen Arab Republic, 1972
BBME, London head office, 1970 (HSBC Bank Plc)
FBME Nicosia office 1964 (FBME Bank Ltd)
Cessna 206 after the crash, Makete, Tanzania 2009 (Mark Taylor)
An oil rig in the Arabian Gulf
Camels in the Abu Dhabi desert.

Printed in the United States of America.

ISBN: 978-1-4669-7379-4 (sc)
ISBN: 978-1-4669-7378-7 (hc)
ISBN: 978-1-4669-7380-0 (e)

Library of Congress Control Number: 2012924039

 www.trafford.com

North America & international
toll-free: 1 888 232 4444 (USA & Canada)
phone: 250 383 6864 ✦ fax: 812 355 4082

To Maarouf

Contents

List of Illustrations

All pictures are from the author's collection, unless otherwise
stated

Foreword

When I started to think about writing this autobiography, I realised that I was in a similar situation to the late Duchess of Windsor when she decided to write hers, *The Heart Has Its Reasons*, in the early 1950s. Her husband, the former King Edward VIII, told her that her task would be difficult because she was "undocumented," having never kept significant written records of her life.[1] I was in much the same boat, having never kept a diary to record anything more than business and social appointments and those have long ago been lost or destroyed. As I began to dig out as many such old records, souvenirs and photographs as I could locate, I realised that I had more to work from than I had originally thought. However, much of that which is related here relies on memory—I am said by many to have an excellent one—sometimes jogged by family, friends and former colleagues and assisted by limited availability of written records, souvenirs and photographs; the use of the Internet to do some research and to verify facts, figures and dates has been indispensable.

In particular, my thanks are due to a number of people who have read either all of various drafts or sections covering places or subjects with which they are familiar and provided valuable comments, suggestions and assistance, or provided photographs. These include Jila Alikhani, George Christophorou, Peter Clark, Alexander

---

[1] Duchess of Windsor, *The Heart Has Its Reasons*, 1958, Companion Book Club, London

Cooley, Curt Dalton (Dayton History), Josephine Haining (HSBC Bank Plc, Group Archives), Maarouf Joudi, Acis Montanios, Leslie McLoughlin, Duncan Revie, Ayoub-Farid Saab, Fadi Saab, Nigel Spinks, Anne Spruin (TD Bank Group Archives), Brenda and Peter Stibbons, Keith Sutton, Mark Taylor, Joyce Willett and Malcolm Williams.

Throughout the book, there are frequent transliterations of Arabic and Greek words, names and places; in the case of Arabic, I have generally used commonly accepted English spellings aided, of course, by my knowledge of the language obtained at MECAS. My knowledge of Greek is very limited. In this case, relating mainly to places in Cyprus, I have used what I consider to be traditional English spellings rather than those dictated by ISO 843, which, since 1997 have generally been adopted. For example, I use "Larnaca," rather than "Larnaka" and "Ayios" rather than "Agios."

References to that body of water between Iran and the Arabian Peninsula are to the Arabian Gulf or sometimes simply Gulf. I was taught at school that it was called the Persian Gulf, but before going to Bahrain in 1969, I was told to ensure that all mail was addressed to Bahrain, Arabian Gulf as otherwise it was unlikely to be delivered.

In writing this book, I have covered events over a period of almost seventy years. Much of my life and work has been in or involved with the Middle East. While I do not intend the book to be a history of the period or the region or a serious commentary on events current at the times concerned, I have included some background history of circumstances prevailing and events occurring in various places where I have lived and worked in order to put my small role and experiences in context.

December 2012

Chapter 1

EARLY LIFE AND SCHOOL DAYS

My father, Joseph, was born in Youghal, County Cork, in what is now the Republic of Ireland, in 1912, less than a month before the prime minister of the United Kingdom Herbert Asquith introduced the Irish Home Rule Bill in the British House of Commons. Although the House of Commons passed that bill in 1913, the House of Lords rejected it. Parliament passed a Home Rule Act (which excluded six of the counties that formed Ulster) in 1914 but suspended its implementation for the duration of World War I.

Subsequent events changed the situation, and eventually, Ireland was partitioned in 1921, and southern Ireland—the Irish Free State—was granted dominion status in 1922. During my father's childhood, Ireland was passing through troubled times. He often related the story of his encounter with one of the Irish revolutionary heroes Michael Collins. On August 21, 1922, Collins visited Mallow in County Cork to inspect soldiers stationed there. He spotted my father, then aged about ten years, watching the proceedings from his home opposite the barracks. He went over to him, tussled his hair, and asked his name.

The next day, Irish Republican Army (IRA) fighters who were opposed to the terms of the controversial agreement with the British government that Collins had signed in December 1921, which led to the establishment of the Irish Free State, killed him in a gun battle while he was on his way from Mallow to Cork.

My father was the second of three children born to Daniel and Anne Hickey; his older brother, Gerard, had been born three years before and his sister, Mary, was born in 1918. My grandfather died from tuberculosis in 1918, just before Mary was born, when my father was about six years old. My father was sent to stay with his maternal grandmother and two maiden aunts in Mallow, about thirty miles

The author's paternal grandparents, Daniel and Anne Hickey, c 1908

(48 km) from Youghal, during his father's illness and he was to continue to live with them throughout his remaining childhood. His first job was with MacLysaght's Nurseries, near Mallow, where he gained a good grounding in horticulture. In later life, this enabled him to give advice to others on how to prune roses or cultivate geraniums, but I do not recall him putting his advice into practice himself; my mother had the green fingers in the family, and I have usually followed my father's example of limiting my involvement in gardening to the giving of advice. In the 1930s, like so many Irishmen before and since, my father moved to London; in 1936, through a man originally from Mallow who was a manager at Harrods, he found employment with this famous shop in Knightsbridge and chanced to take lodgings in Brentford.

The wedding of the author's maternal grandparents, Ben and Florence Mabel Leggett (née Harrison), 1916

Meanwhile my mother, Beryl, an only child, had been born in Norwich, Norfolk, in 1920. Both of her parents, Ben and Mabel Leggett, had been born in north Norfolk; my grandfather in Aylmerton, and my grandmother in East Runton. She moved with her parents to Chiswick, not far from Brentford, in the 1930s and after leaving school became an apprentice hairdresser.

One evening, sometime in 1939, both my father and mother happened to be in the same pub in Twickenham; my father, on seeing my mother, declared to the friend who was with him that she was the girl he intended to marry. After the outbreak of World War II, my father, like so many Irishmen, enlisted in the British Army; my mother joined the WAAFs, where she continued as a hairdresser at an RAF camp in Gloucestershire. In the meantime, my mother's parents moved from Chiswick to Mundesley in Norfolk.

My father's expressed intention was realised when my parents eventually married at the Church of the Sacred Heart in North Walsham, Norfolk, on October 22, 1940. Immediately after the wedding, my father left from Norwich railway station to Liverpool and then embarked on a troop ship bound for Mombasa, where he was attached to the King's African Rifles in the intelligence corps. He subsequently took part in the liberation of Abyssinia (as Ethiopia was then called) from the Italians and was present for the restoration of the Emperor Haile Selassie on May 5, 1941, being involved in the security arrangements for the emperor. In recognition of his work, the emperor presented him with a gold ring embossed with the Lion of Judah, the imperial symbol, which I now wear.

In 1942, my father developed a problem with his left ear that later turned out to be mastoiditis. He was shipped back from Abyssinia to Nairobi in Kenya and then to a hospital in Glasgow where he underwent what was to be the first of several operations in the course of his life which left him totally deaf in that ear. Subsequently, he was invalided out of the army. After my mother became pregnant, they settled in the quiet north Norfolk village of West Runton, where my father established an estate agency. Later he discontinued this business and joined a firm of builders and contractors in Cromer in a temporary job as an estimator. He remained with them until his retirement at the age of sixty-five in 1977, a temporary job that lasted over thirty years.

I was born on November 8, 1943, when World War II was in its fourth year. The year had begun with the Casablanca Conference in January, at which the president of the United States Franklin D Roosevelt and British prime minister Winston Churchill met to discuss the future conduct of the war. In November, Roosevelt, Churchill and USSR leader Joseph Stalin met in Tehran to discuss war strategy and agreed on plans for the invasion of Europe, which was to start in the following year. In December, Dwight Eisenhower was appointed supreme Allied commander in Europe to lead that invasion. An event that year, which was to influence my future life, the independence of Lebanon from France, took place on November 22.

My birth took place at a house called Innisfree in West Runton, the first of several homes in which the family lived in the north Norfolk area during my childhood. As was common at the time, I was born at home, with the district nurse in attendance.

We later moved to nearby Cromer where my father bought a house at 17 Prince of Wales Road. This was a three-story end-of-terrace property very close to the town centre. My first recollections of early life there include travelling by bus from Cromer to visit my maternal grandmother in West Runton, a journey of about two miles. The memory probably dates from the early postwar years, as I clearly remember that the buses were still painted in wartime grey rather than red, which later became commonplace for the Eastern Counties Omnibus Company's vehicles. On these journeys, which often involved an overnight stay, I usually carried a small suitcase with me containing the necessities for my visit. Visits to stay with my grandmother continued for much of my childhood, and as I grew older, I was allowed to participate in her Saturday evening card sessions; these were regular gatherings with a few of her friends to play such games as Newmarket and Rummy with stakes of a few pennies on the outcome. I kept a jam jar at her house in which my winnings accumulated until I was allowed to spend them. On every visit to my grandparents, I could also expect to receive money from my grandfather and his mother, my great-grandmother, who lived with them—sixpence from each to begin with, later increasing to one shilling from each (five pence today). This supplemented my pocket money considerably.

Another early memory is of the coldest winter on record in 1946-1947. Very low temperatures combined with heavy snowfall, which blocked roads and railways. The weather disrupted delivery of many items, including coal to power stations, which resulted in electricity cuts. Rationing of many items was still in force and was to remain for some items until 1954. Life was still difficult in these early postwar years, and this development lowered public morale even more. When the thaw came in late March, widespread flooding resulted, adding further to the misery of those affected.

I do not remember suffering from the continuing rationing of many items during my childhood, but I do recall the availability of a rather unpleasant form of concentrated orange juice supplied by the government for children only, which I was required to drink "because it was good for me." The availability of only a limited amount of rationed petrol for private motoring soon after the end of the war was of little significance, as my father did not own a car in those days.

Throughout my childhood many summer days were spent on the beaches of north Norfolk, often in the company of family friends. Notwithstanding what I now consider to be unacceptably low temperatures, I and my friends played happily in the sand and the sea.

One of these friends, Lesley Park (née Kirby) now has the dubious distinction of being my oldest friend; we were neighbours when she was born, just a month after me, and we have kept in touch ever since.

The author (left) and Lesley Kirby
(now Park), Cromer beach, 1944

As my mother and father had married in England early in the war, when travel was difficult, if not impossible, none of my father's family from Ireland had been able to attend nor had any of them met my mother. In the summer of 1947, my parents decided that a visit to Ireland to introduce my mother and me to our relatives should take place. While my memories of this trip, at the age of about four years, are limited, I can recall one or two events, and others are fresher in my memory as my father often related them in later years.

We travelled by train from Cromer to London Liverpool Street station and then from Euston to Holyhead to catch the night boat to Dún Laoghaire, just south of Dublin. We first visited my uncle Gerard and aunt Christine and their children—my cousins Frank and Mary—in Dublin. Then we again travelled on by train to Mallow, County Cork, where we stayed with my father's two maiden aunts and their brother, his uncle, by whom he had been brought up following the death of my grandfather. My great-grandmother, who had ruled the household during my father's childhood, had died by then.

My great-aunts kept a small general shop that was attached to the house in which they all lived. In the shop, they sold cigarettes and tobacco, sweets, newspapers and similar items; I was thoroughly spoilt by all of them who vied to supply me with sweet treats from the shop. The house had a feature, which I had never encountered before, a private chapel, which was used for prayer twice a day.

Ever since my parents met, my father had told my mother about the scenic beauty of Ireland and in particular, Killarney and its surrounding lakes, about forty miles (65 km) from Mallow. During our visit, we went to Killarney where we stayed at the Great Southern Hotel. This large hotel, now renamed the Malton, had been built by the Great Southern and Western Railway Company in 1854, when the first railway line to the town was opened and was among the first of the Victorian era railway hotels owned by railway companies and built around that time, wherever railway lines were laid in Britain and Ireland. While staying at the hotel, I became ill and was left in the care of the hotel porter while my parents visited the scenic attractions in the national park. This included taking the obligatory ride in a jaunting car, a horse-drawn carriage famous in the Killarney valley for over two hundred years. It was only after this visit that my father confessed to my mother that in spite of his always singing the praises of the area and having lived so close to it during his childhood, he had never before visited it.

In 1947, with wartime rationing still in place in England, many things were difficult or impossible to obtain but could be found in Ireland. The managing director of the firm for which my father worked had asked him to purchase material for a suit, and this was duly done. It was placed in the bottom of a suitcase, and above it were packed items of mine. When we reached the customs on returning to Holyhead, in the days before red, green and blue channels, the customs officer asked to open the suitcase. When this was done, he started to remove my things, and my reaction was to rush to him and tell him that he could not take my clothes. My innocent intervention distracted him from further investigation of the contents of the suitcase, and the material was eventually made into a new suit for the managing director.

In May 1949, I was admitted to the local hospital in Cromer with an

The author (centre) with parents, Joe and Beryl and sister, Brenda, 1949

undiagnosed illness. I was told that I was seriously ill and at one time not expected to live. Eventually my appendix was removed, and I recovered; I now have an abnormally large scar on my abdomen as evidence of the operation, which invites enquiry every time a doctor sees it. What was wrong remains a mystery to me and, I have always suspected, to the doctor who treated me. At the time, the children's ward in the hospital was closed for renovations, so I was accommodated in the men's ward, where, when I recovered enough, both the nursing staff and patients spoilt me. I particularly remember the ward sister, Sister Doughty, who was known to make a special trip on her bicycle to a nearby shop to buy ice cream for me.

About a month after my illness, my sister Brenda was born, also in West Runton at the home of our grandparents. Again, as was common in those days, my mother was attended by the district nurse for the delivery. The six-year difference in our ages did not contribute to an easy relationship during our childhood. We were always arguing and quarrelling, but the passage of time seems to have narrowed the gap and we never seem to disagree now. Age must have mellowed both of us!

Another early memory is what may well have been my first visit to the cinema to see the 1950 Walt Disney production of *Treasure Island*, starring Bobby Driscoll as Jim Hawkins and Robert Newton as Long John Silver. I was taken, as a special treat, by an elderly lady lodger who was occupying the front bedroom at 17 Prince of Wales Road at the time. Walt Disney Productions was to play another part in my life some twenty years later.

It must have been around this time that I started to spend some of my Saturday mornings at Norman Troller's roller skating rink in Cromer. It was one of the few places in the town where children could gather on Saturday morning to pass a few hours with their friends. Sadly, the rink has long since disappeared, and the site is now a car park for a supermarket.

My father contracted poliomyelitis in 1951, a disease, which, after the availability of a vaccine later in the 1950s, has all but been eradicated in many countries, including England. He was hospitalised in an isolation ward in the West Norwich Hospital from where, he was later to recount, he had a good view of one of the Norwich cemeteries. There was great concern that my sister and I could have been infected by him, which lasted for several weeks until the possible incubation period expired. Luckily we did not contract the disease, and my father recovered, the only after-effect, which remained with him for the rest of his life, being a slight weakness in his left arm.

Shortly after this illness, the family moved across Prince of Wales Road to a flat in a building called Clevedon House, owned by the firm for which my father worked. This was an interim move, pending locating a country cottage to buy in the area. In 1952, the country cottage was identified at 2 Goose Lane, Alby, about six miles (10 km) from Cromer. It was the centre one in a row of three. My father bought this cottage together with an adjoining one, which was rented to a very elderly couple. His intention was that when the aged occupants died, he would combine the two properties and that this would make a very comfortable home. In the meantime, we had to live in the centre cottage, consisting of a sitting room and kitchen downstairs and two bedrooms upstairs. The lavatory was a chemical one at the end of the garden, and we took our weekly bath in a portable tin one in the kitchen, filled with water heated in a gas boiler. This was quite common at the time, when a large proportion of homes in Britain lacked bathrooms and indoor lavatories.

Throughout my childhood, there was a constant presence of American servicemen in north Norfolk and other parts of Britain. There was a large US Air Force base at Sculthorpe, about twenty-five miles (40 km) from Cromer, which had been an RAF airfield during World War II and was then used by the Americans from the time of the Berlin Airlift in 1949 until 1962. Since there were insufficient married quarters on the base, many families lived in rented accommodation in the area, including Cromer and Sheringham. At times, many became our neighbours and friends, some of whom I have maintained contact with since those days. Often these servicemen would bring their American cars with them when posted to England, albeit they were usually large and very unsuited to the country lanes of Norfolk.

I can recall being fascinated and envious of these examples of American wealth and sophistication at a time when car production in England was still recovering from the war years, and car ownership was far from common. Indeed, the first family car that my father bought was a prewar Standard 8, manufactured in 1936, which he acquired in the mid-1950s; I think that it cost £30.00! It was later replaced with a postwar car, a 1948 Morris Eight in about 1958 and that in 1960, by a 1953 Vauxhall Velox, the car in which I eventually learned to drive, of which more later.

It may have been the presence of so many American servicemen that caused me to develop a desire for all things American, although this urge has receded significantly, as I have aged and as I have become more and more disillusioned with the foreign policy of the United States, especially in the Middle East. I recall an incident when I was around nine years old when I saw a plastic model of an American army truck with an anti-aircraft gun mounted on it, in Rex Brown's toy shop near our home in Cromer. I pestered my father for days until I persuaded him to buy it for me; I believe that the cost was two shillings and six pence—12.5p today. My mother did not approve.

The winter of 1953 was a very severe one. In January of that year, widespread flooding affected the southeast coast of England and much of the Netherlands, caused by the coincidence of exceptionally high tides and a strong north wind, causing a tidal surge during the night of January 31-February 1. My father was one of the many volunteers who turned out that night to fill sandbags in an attempt to stem the flow of seawater and render assistance. Norfolk coastal areas suffered severely. Flood defences were broken by the force of the storm, and floodwaters swept up to two miles inland, inundating low-lying areas of the Norfolk coast. Cromer pier suffered severe damage that made it unsafe to use for some time. In all, 307 people were killed, and 24,000 homes were damaged along the Norfolk, Suffolk, Essex and Kent coasts.

The author's parents, Beryl and Joe Hickey, Coronation Day, June 2, 1953

On June 2, 1953, the coronation of Queen

Elizabeth II took place. It was often said to be a once-in-a-lifetime experience to be able to see a monarch crowned in England, and, indeed, such an event has not yet occurred again in my lifetime. As I finalise this book, Her Majesty and her subjects are celebrating her Diamond Jubilee. This is an event that has occurred only once before in English history.

At the time of the coronation, television was beginning to play a part in people's lives, although at the time only in black and white on twelve- or fourteen-inch screens and with only one channel, the BBC. The family was invited to visit American friends, who had previously been based at Sculthorpe and lived in Sheringham, and who then lived near Lincoln, for a few days at the time of the coronation and to watch the event on their television. Sales of televisions prior to the coronation were as spectacular as the event itself, and this can be said to have marked the start of the age of television in Britain; it was not long afterwards that my family acquired its first. The fourteen-inch screen Ferguson set was obtained from Radio Rentals. This company had originally been established in 1932 to provide radio sets on a monthly rental basis. Many people found this more affordable, and the system also provided the security that if the set broke down, a replacement would be provided at no extra cost. It was also possible to upgrade to a better model if such became available. The system was extended to include television sets after World War II. Among the popular programmes for children at the time we got our first television were *Andy Pandy, Bill and Ben, the Flower Pot Men, Muffin the Mule* and *Crackerjack*, a programme originally hosted by Eamonn Andrews, which ran from 1955 to 1984. Children's programmes were broadcast from five to six each afternoon, after which transmission ceased for one hour, during which time mothers were supposed to put their children to bed before the evening programmes began. Like thousands of others of my peers, I sat with my eyes glued to the small screen for the hour and resisted all attempts to get me to bed afterwards.

It is interesting to compare the television coverage of the 1953 coronation with that of the Diamond Jubilee Pageant in 2012. A major difference, of course, was the quality of the picture and the fact that the jubilee coverage was in colour rather than black-and-white.

In 1953, the commentary to the television coverage was provided by Richard Dimbleby, a veteran journalist who covered many state events in his career and whose hushed tones, sometimes described as pompous, became his trademark. Dimbleby paid meticulous attention to accuracy, carrying out most of the research himself.[2] This cannot be said of the several, much more casual journalists who covered the Diamond Jubilee pageant in 2012. The presenters complained that they had not been sufficiently briefed, and during the coverage, I noticed a number of errors of fact in their commentary. Actor and writer Stephen Fry said of the Thames pageant on Twitter that the BBC's jubilee coverage was "mind-numbingly tedious." The BBC received over four thousand five hundred complaints about their coverage of the event. Richard Dimbleby must have turned in his grave.

Among my activities in 1953 was membership of the West Runton Wolf Cub pack. As part of the coronation celebrations, the Queen had given permission for a jamboree camp to be held in the grounds of her Norfolk home at Sandringham between May 23 and June 4. The West Runton Wolf Cub's contribution was a demonstration on road safety, in which I participated by propelling a pedal car around a course which included the usual road markings and signage during a weekend which was to prove to be the hottest of the year. I recall that the course was marked out on an area of quite long grass, and considerable effort was required to move the pedal car on this surface in the warm conditions prevailing.

In the summer of 1957, our neighbours in Goose Lane having shown an inconsiderate lack of willingness to depart this world and so allow my father to convert the two cottages into one, my father decided to sell the cottages in Alby. We then moved to Sheringham, which had always been my mother's preferred town in the area. The last move before I finished school and went out on my own was to North Walsham in 1960. My father had always wanted to run a pub, and at this time, an opportunity arose to do so by acquiring the lease of the Cock Inn in North Walsham. This he did, although he continued his full-time job with the building contractor while my mother

---

[2]   http://en.wikipedia.org/wiki/Richard_Dimbleby, accessed 12 Dec 2012

looked after the pub during the day. As was usual at that time, a brewery owned the pub; in this case, the now-defunct Norwich firm Steward and Patterson and the rules required that the tenant bought all supplies from the owning brewery. During the previous summer holidays, I had worked part-time at the Village Inn, a pub in West Runton, and now I was able to practice what I had learned there in the family business. The pub was closed some years ago, and the building now houses a coffee shop. On the wall is a picture of my father on the night the pub closed, pulling the last pint of beer.

I started my education at the primary school in Cromer in 1947 at the age of just three. The only things that I can recall about my time there are that all pupils were given free milk during the morning break, and after lunch, all the children in my class would be required to have a rest and sleep on camp beds. In 1950, my parents decided to move me to Saint Joseph's, a private Catholic school in Sheringham, which meant that I had to travel the five miles between Cromer and Sheringham by bus every day. Our home in Cromer was near to the bus station, and there was a stop just outside the school in Sheringham. I made the journey alone, even at the age of only seven. After we moved to Alby in 1952, my daily journey was longer and involved a change of bus in Cromer. I would travel as far as Cromer with my father, on his way to work there, but went on to Sheringham unaccompanied. Today the authorities would probably accuse my parents of neglect for allowing a child such freedom.

Saint Joseph's was quite a small school, having around sixty pupils, both boys and girls, aged between five and eleven. Three ladies "of a certain age" taught at the school. They spent considerable time drumming into us the catechism, a summary of Catholic doctrine, organised in a question-and-answer format, which we were supposed to memorise and recite. For years afterwards, I lived in

The author, St Joseph's School photograph, 1953

fear of spending eternity in hell should I ever set foot in a Protestant church.

At an early age, I had shown an interest in the theatre and performing in general. In 1954, I entered, through Saint Joseph's School, the Cromer and North Norfolk Festival of Music and Drama and was awarded a Certificate of Merit for my recitation of "Tony the Turtle" by E.V. Rieu. The following year I came second in the eleven years and under group for my rendition of "Ducks" by F. W. Harvey. My thespian aspirations continued to develop at Saint Joseph's School during my appearance in the eponymous role in "Wiggles the Wizard." I have long since forgotten the plot, but I have recently seen it listed on Amazon's website as *Wiggles the Wizard: The Adventures of a Boy Who Became a Fairy Godfather*.[3] Other stage appearances during the years at Saint Joseph's included an annual participation in the nativity play at the end of each Christmas term, usually as a shepherd or one of the three kings.

The author (extreme right) in *Wiggles the Wizard*, 1952

School reports from Saint Joseph's covering all of my time there have survived, each of them signed by the headmistress, as we were permitted to call her before political correctness took over, Rosemary Snowden. They consistently describe me as "a good worker who tries

---

3   http://www.amazon.co.uk/s/ref=nb_sb_noss/278-9301618-1465252?url=search-alias%3Dstripbooks&field-keywords=wiggles+the+wizard&x=0&y=0
     Retrieved 18 Jan 2012

hard," "a very reliable chap," and "practical and reliable." The regular negative comment was for singing, usually described as "weak" and occasionally "fair." My ability to sing has never improved!

The year 1955 was the one in which the game of Scrabble was first on sale and the United States sent its first "advisers" to South Vietnam. A fifteen-year-old African American girl refused to give up her seat on a bus to a white woman in Alabama after the driver told her to do so, leading to the outlawing of racial segregation on trains and buses in the United States later in the year.

West Germany became a sovereign nation and joined NATO, and independent commercial television began broadcasting in the United Kingdom. Among events that were to have an impact on my later life, the EOKA movement started its campaign for independence from British rule in Cyprus and Disneyland opened in Anaheim, California.

In addition, in early 1955, I was at the age and stage in my education when it was time to take the Eleven-plus exam. This exam was created in the mid-1940s; it established a system of education that had three strands—academic, technical and functional.[4] At that time, testing was considered an effective way to discover to which strand a child was most suited. The results of the exam would be used to match a child's secondary school to their abilities and future career needs. The system came to be characterised by fierce competition for places at the prestigious grammar schools, where, after taking the General Certificate of Education (GCE) O level exams, at about age sixteen, education could continue in the sixth form to age eighteen or thereabouts and prepare students for university entrance after the GCE A level exams. If one did not secure a place at a grammar school, one was destined to continue learning at a secondary modern school from where one would leave at about age fifteen. The Eleven-plus took on a particular significance. Rather than allocating according to need or ability, it became seen as a question of passing or failing, and this led to the exam becoming widely resented. The Eleven-plus

---

[4]   http://en.wikipedia.org/wiki/Eleven_plus_exam, accessed 12 Dec 2012

examination consisted of three papers—arithmetic, including a mental arithmetic test; writing, including an essay question on a general subject; and general problem solving, a test of general knowledge, assessing the ability to apply logic to simple problems.

So in January 1955 I and all of the other students of my age at Saint Joseph's took the dreaded exam. When the results came out, much to my dismay, I was in a marginal category, which required me to take a supplemental exam, which I sat in May and passed. And so I was destined to transfer to the Paston School in North Walsham, a grammar school, the catchment area of which included Sheringham, in the following September, much to the relief of my parents.

I mentioned earlier the significant number of American servicemen who lived in north Norfolk during my childhood. Some of their children attended Saint Joseph's, and one of them, Jane Bagnato (now Jane Meagher), took the Eleven-plus exam at the same time as me. Shortly after we took the exam in 1955, her father was posted back to the United States; at that time, she and I and other English and American students at the school decided to form the E-A (England-America) Club, with a view to maintaining links with each other after the American students returned to their country. In her first letter to the English members, from Kokomo, Indiana, Jane wrote, "Have you chucked Miss Priss herself out yet?"—a reference to a member who must have fallen out of favour with Jane, although I have absolutely no recollection why the unfortunate girl suffered this fate! She went on to instruct us "not to show this letter to Miss Snowdon," the headmistress. Jane was always a somewhat bossy child, as the tone of this letter indicates! As far as I know, Jane and I are the only members of the group who still keep in touch, nearly sixty years after the events. In that time I have visited her in the United States several times, and in 2003 we met up in Sheringham and visited the old school building, no longer a school but otherwise little changed, and adjacent church.

Another American family who became friends during the 1950s were the Corbins—Bob, Marie, and their five children. Bob was an air force captain, flying in-flight refuelling tankers from Sculthorpe, and in August 1958, he and his six crew members were all killed when their plane crashed over Belgium. When my parents told me the news, I was devastated. It was probably the first time in my life that any close friend or family member had died so unexpectedly and suddenly. The air force arranged for the family to return to their home in Flint, Michigan, within a few days of the accident, and there was a somewhat tearful parting before they left. However, I have always kept in touch with them, especially Marie, now approaching ninety, and the elder daughter, Lynn. I visited them several times while I was living in Toronto in the 1960s and during later visits to the United States after I moved to the Middle East. All of the family have made successes of their lives, in spite of the tragedy of losing a husband and father so early in life.

In September 1955, I started attending the Paston School in North Walsham. Prior to the start of the first term, my parents took me to the official supplier of school uniforms, men's outfitters Marjoram Bros. They described themselves as "Purveyors of Men's Wear of Distinction" and at the time had been in business in the marketplace in North Walsham since 1901. Here I was equipped with a navy blue blazer with the school crest on the breast pocket, grey shorts, two light grey shirts, and the school tie. Alas, the shop no longer exists. It closed on March 31, 1988, eighty-seven years after its opening.[5] It seems that it could not survive the school becoming a sixth form college and the resulting demise of uniforms.

Sir William Paston had founded the school in 1606. In the words of the first verse (of six) of the school song:

> Anno Domini sixteen-six,
> As the tale was told to me,
> Is a solemn date for us to fix
> Deep in our memory.
> Sir William Paston, he up and said,
> "The Norfolk lads, I am sore afraid,

---

[5] http://www.northwalshamarchive.co.uk/archive_item.aspx?entry_id=322
Retrieved 24 Jan 2012

Have overmuch liberty.
Come hither, Reverend Michael Tylles,
And into their heads we'll hammer
Godly learning to guide their wills,
Arithmetic, writing and grammar."

Famous students who attended Paston during the almost three hundred and fifty years prior to my arrival included Horatio Nelson, Henry Rider Haggard, and Stephen Fry. In his autobiography, *Moab Is My Washpot,* covering his childhood and adolescent years, Stephen Fry describes how he hated attending the Paston School and how he used to play truant.

> Paston School lived up to all my prejudices, as things always will to the prejudiced. I did not take to the place one bit. I can remember barely anything about it, except that it was there that I started to smoke and there that I learned to play pinball: not within the school grounds, but within the town of North Walsham. For within a very short space of time I started to cut the school dead. I would get on the Cawston bus and dismount at either Aylsham or North Walsham and then head straight for a cafe and spend the day pinballing, listening to records by Slade, the Sweet, Wizard, Suzi Quatro and smoking interminable Carlton Premiums, Number Sixes and Embassy Regals.[6]

I cannot recall playing truant at any time, and I did not start to smoke while there, but nor can I say that my seven years at Paston were the happiest days of my life! Each year there was an intake of about sixty boys divided into two streams, forms 1A and 1B. I started in 1B and stayed in the B stream throughout the five years up to taking the GCE O level exams in 1960. The theory was that the A stream students were brighter than those in the B stream were. The only difference in the curriculum was that those in the A stream had to study Latin while those in the B stream did not. The teaching staff must have followed Sir William Paston's instructions set out in

---

[6]   Fry Stephen, Moab is my Washpot, 1997, Hutchinson, London

the school song as I went on to obtain eight passes in the GCE O level exams in 1960—English language, English literature, history, geography, French, mathematics, general paper, and most usefully, woodwork.

All new students were placed in one of four houses, each named after a famous old boy. I joined Nelson House, named after the famous Admiral, Horatio (1758-1805), the colours of which were yellow and black. The other houses were Tenison, named after Thomas, an Archbishop of Canterbury (1636-1715); Hoste, named after an eighteenth century naval captain, William (1780-1828) and Wharton, named after the seventeenth-century historian and antiquarian, Henry (1664-1695), one of whose claims to fame was that he was born with two tongues. We new boys quickly learned to recognise the school prefects, whose rank was denoted by a yellow band on their blazer sleeves, and the head boy, who had two yellow bands on his.

At the time that I started at Paston, the family was living in Alby, about six miles (10 km) from North Walsham; transport to and from the school was provided by the education authority, using hired buses, which served several villages en route from Aldborough to North Walsham. Later, when we moved to Sheringham, I travelled by train every day. British Railways (as it was called in those pre-Dr. Beeching years) provided a special train for Paston students and the girls who attended the high school in North Walsham, which ran from Sheringham via Cromer and other intermediate stops to North Walsham. This was so that the public would not be inconvenienced by the presence of so many boisterous teenagers on the usual trains. Boys and girls were segregated, of course, on the train as we were at school. However, in the afternoon, if we were able to get out of school a few minutes early and run the short distance to the station, it was possible to catch the Norfolkman, a through train from London's Liverpool Street station to Sheringham, whose heyday was in the 1950s, rather than wait for the school train. Thus, we could inflict ourselves on the normal train travellers. On the Norfolkman, there was no segregation of the sexes.

For my final two years at Paston, when the family lived in North Walsham, the school was a few minutes' walk from the Cock Inn, and I was even able to go home for lunch, thus avoiding the uniformly terrible school dinners. Though some do, however, wax lyrical about the school canteen's spotted dick and custard, I do not belong to that crowd. Spotted dick was again on the menu when I visited Kenya in 1972.

As with the reports from Saint Joseph's School, those from Paston have also survived the last fifty years. My position in the form reached the heights of first among thirty-one in form 3B in the Christmas term of 1957 while the spring term of 1956 witnessed the low point of twenty-second out of a class of thirty-two in form 1B. The former earned me a prize, and I was given the opportunity to choose a book.

I selected the then newly published biography by Cyril Jolly of the recently deceased Henry Blogg, one time coxswain of the Cromer lifeboat, whose bravery had earned him several medals. I had met Blogg in Cromer when, during my early childhood days on the beach, he was often seen renting deck chairs and windbreaks to visitors. A member of one of the fishing families in the town, he was a quiet, humble man who was seldom prepared to speak about his long, heroic voluntary service with the Cromer lifeboat. George Harrap and Company Ltd. originally published this book, and later it went out of print. Recently my brother-in-law's company, Poppyland Publishing, acquired the right to reissue it from the author's widow.

In ten out of twelve reports for the first four years at Paston, I was in the top ten in the class; after that, in the fifth and sixth forms, we were not ranked. Comments were far from universally complimentary—lots of "could do better" and what I now recognise as a somewhat prescient remark "he is too selective in his efforts, I feel." However, in other terms, a form master described me as "a very conscientious boy" and on another occasion said, "It is a pleasure to have him in the form."

At Paston, there was one period of religious instruction each week. Catholic pupils—I was one of three in my year—were exempt from attending these classes lest we be led astray by the teaching of Protestant doctrine. Instead, we visited the house of the Catholic priest in North Walsham, who made sure that we were taught correctly. The first thing that he did was to make each of us recite the Lord's Prayer. After we had all done so we were relieved to learn from him that we had passed the test; no Church of England variations to the Catholic wording had infiltrated our renderings. These lessons did little to dispel the fear of eternal damnation that had developed at Saint Joseph's School.

When reaching the third form, all students, unless they could justify exemption as conscientious objectors (of whom there were none during my time at the school), were required to join the Combined Cadet Force (CCF). Training occupied every Friday afternoon.

The headmaster, Kenneth Marshall, a former lieutenant colonel during World War II, considered the CCF to be an important part of the curriculum. It had three sections—army, navy and air force, although everyone had to start in the army section and only a few transferred to one of the other sections after the first year.

For those with an aptitude for music, there was the Corps of Drums, but as had been noted in my Saint Joseph's School reports and confirmed in those at Paston, music was not one of my strong points. I was destined to remain in the army section for the duration of my time at Paston, where I eventually was promoted to the rank of corporal. I did express an interest in joining the navy section having from time to time thought about the possibility of a career in that branch of the armed services, but nothing came of this request. Uniforms appropriate to our section were provided, and these had to be worn when travelling to and from school on Fridays and during the morning lessons on that day. The uniform had to be pressed for every parade, the webbing belt had to be coated with blanco, the brass buckles polished and the boots made to shine until you could see your face in them.

The CCF had an armoury, and sometimes we would draw World War II vintage Lee-Enfield .303 rifles from the store—located in the schoolyard and controlled by the school's maintenance man—and practice presenting arms and other useful activities. Each section would participate in a field day once a year, in the summer term, and there was the opportunity, never availed of by me, to attend a camp during the summer holidays.

In the last year at the school, I was one of the few who had a driving licence, having passed the test at the first attempt a few months after my seventeenth birthday. Thus, the headmaster selected me to drive the CCF's Land Rover from time to time, including acting as his chauffeur on field day.

During the summer of 1963, while I was working at Barclay's Bank in Sheringham, a lively correspondence started in the local newspaper, the *Eastern Daily Press*, on the subject of the merits of the Paston School Combined Cadet Force. A person signing him or herself Parent started it, suggesting, "Trafalgar was won on the playing fields of Paston and not on its barrack square." I joined in under the pseudonym Old Pastonian. I firmly said, "In my opinion, I had wasted three hundred and fifty hours during the five years that I was in the cadet force; time which could have been far better employed in academic studies." There followed a contribution from Mother of a Young Pastonian who opined, "The afternoon wasted in the CCF would be far more beneficially spent in the classroom. That's where discipline should be taught and not only taught but enforced." The correspondence ended with a contribution from an identified writer who concluded his letter with, "I say, in respect of the Paston School, long live the CCF."

In spite of this wish, the Paston School CCF did not survive for long after the retirement of the wartime lieutenant colonel headmaster in 1976. In a supplement to his *A History of the Paston School*, Charles Forder notes that the CCF storehouse was "disused 1979,"[7] by which

---

[7]   Forder, Charles, A History of the Paston School, 2nd Edition 1975 and Supplement thereto, 1981.

time the force must have been disbanded; otherwise from where would the members have drawn their rifles? The school became a coeducational sixth form college in 1984—there were certainly no CCF activities then.

During most summer holidays, the school would usually organise a trip to somewhere in Europe. Participation was restricted to students in the fifth and sixth forms, and in 1959, the destination was to be Lugano in Switzerland and a small village in the western Austrian province of Vorarlberg called Tschagguns.

I had always had an insatiable desire to travel abroad but up to this time had not had the opportunity. I was able to persuade my parents to allow me to go on this trip, which, I recall, cost about £30.00 for the two weeks. The school advised us to take about £8.00 pocket money for extras and souvenirs. I took £10.

We travelled by train from North Walsham to London, Liverpool Street station, and then by underground to Victoria station and on to Folkestone. We crossed the channel by ferry to Calais and continued the journey by overnight train to Basel in Switzerland. At Basel railway station, the travel agent had arranged for us to have breakfast at the station buffet, the most memorable feature of which was the abundance of Swiss cherry jam available with the continental breakfast. In those days, the "full English," accompanied by tea, was the breakfast that we were used to; the continental breakfast consisting mostly of rolls with butter and jam, accompanied by coffee, was something new.

We continued our journey by train across Switzerland, passing through the Saint Gotthard Tunnel, to arrive in Lugano in the Italian-speaking Canton Ticino after a journey that had lasted over twenty-four hours. During our six days in Lugano, we were accommodated in a youth hostel. We went on excursions around the area by bus and by boat, including visits to Monte Generoso by funicular railway and to Monte Lema by chairlift, both being new experiences for all of us.

At the end of the first week of the holiday, we travelled by train from Lugano via Zurich to Tschagguns in Austria. This is a small village in the Montafon valley at an altitude of about seven hundred meters (2,275 ft), where we were again accommodated in a hostel. Excursions from here included one to Vaduz in Liechtenstein, where banking secrecy was and largely remains sacrosanct, and, yet again, ascents of mountains by chairlift. We returned by train via Zurich to Calais and then retraced the outward journey back to North Walsham.

The following year, 1960, we had a family holiday, touring Scotland in the recently acquired Vauxhall Velox. This was quite an expedition in those days. We drove from Sheringham via York to Edinburgh, where we attended a performance of the Edinburgh Military Tattoo, the first time in my life that I had attended such a spectacular show. Then we went on to Aberdeen, Tomintoul (the highest village in the Highlands) and Inverness. We continued along the shore of Loch Ness, without sighting the monster, and to the Isle of Skye. Here, proving what a small world it was and still is, we chanced to meet friends from Cromer. We then went on to Glasgow, where my father visited the hospital in which he had been treated after returning from East Africa during the war and found that the sister who had nursed him then was still working there and remembered him. We returned to Norfolk down the east coast via Redcar and Scarborough. My taste for travel was gradually being nurtured to reach maturity some years later as will be recounted.

In November 1960, I reached my seventeenth birthday. Well before of this date, I had applied for a provisional driving licence, which was issued in advance, but valid from my birthday and was required in order for me to take driving lessons in preparation for the government test. While holding this type of licence, I was allowed to drive only when accompanied by a driver holding a full licence. Both my grandfather and my father fulfilled this function in the family car many times in between the lessons that I took at a driving school. After about four months of practice, I took the driving test and passed at the first attempt, unlike several of my contemporaries, who had to try more than once.

On April 23, 1961, I answered the phone and was surprised that the caller was my cousin Mary from Dublin. Unfortunately, it was bad news—her father, my father's brother Gerard, had died suddenly after a heart attack that afternoon. It was quickly decided that my father and I would travel to Dublin for the funeral, and the next day we set out by train via London to Holyhead for the night ferry to Dún Laoghaire, arriving in the early morning of April 25. On arrival, we were met by my father's sister, my aunt Mary O'Malley, and her husband, Pearse, who took us to breakfast at the Royal Marine Hotel near the ferry terminal before we went on to meet other family members. The funeral was held the next day, and afterwards, at Mary's suggestion, my father and I accompanied her and Pearse in their car back to their home in Belfast, which we had not visited before.

That night, April 26, as we were motoring north parallel to the railway, the IRA blew up a bridge on the main Dublin-Belfast line on the border between Dundalk, in the Republic and Newry in Northern Ireland. This was just one of the many incidents during the IRA Border Campaign between 1956 and 1962, and it completely disrupted rail traffic on the route. This was unfortunate for us as after our short stay in Belfast, we had to return to Dublin by train and from there retrace our route back to Norfolk. The duration of the train journey to Dublin took considerably longer than usual because of the destruction of the bridge, which necessitated the use of a connecting bus across the border from Newry to Dundalk.

This was the first time that I had met my aunt, who had lived in Belfast since her marriage in 1947. My father had moved to England when he was in his early twenties and seldom expressed any strong opinions about the problems in Northern Ireland or the history of the country. My aunt was different. A fervent supporter of everything Irish and eventual unification of the Republic with the North, she was active in Belfast politics in the 1950s, serving as an Irish Labour Party member of the city council for several years. She went on to establish the Lyric Players' Theatre, initially in an annex to her house in Belfast and later in a purpose-built theatre. The Lyric Players' repertoire was broad, but its pioneer work in performing the plays of Irish poet and playwright (and Irish nationalist) William B. Yeats earned the company a deserved reputation. I have always regretted that I did not get to know my aunt better. Distance separated us, and meetings were rare. We both had a love of and participated in the theatre, but her involvement was at a much higher level than mine was.

In continuing satisfaction of my desire to travel abroad, in 1961, I answered an advertisement in the local newspaper placed by someone seeking others to share a motoring tour in Europe. Eventually a group of four was assembled including the advertiser, who had an almost new Hillman Minx car in which we were to make the trip. In those days, taking a car on a long journey on "the Continent" was something of an expedition. Much planning went into the trip. The Automobile Association (AA) was consulted, and from them, detailed route descriptions and maps were obtained, very helpful in the days before satellite navigation systems were even thought of. We planned a journey through France to the Riviera, along the French and Italian coast to Rome and then back via Florence, Venice and Lausanne. This was considered quite a journey in two weeks when motorways were rare. To keep costs within our limited budget, we decided to camp and only resorted to a hotel for one night.

In 1962, when I was in my last year at Paston, the United Kingdom was debating the pros and cons of joining what was then called the Common Market, now the European Union. There was extensive correspondence in the local newspaper, the *Eastern Daily Press*, between April and July of that year, in which I participated. I firmly believed that Britain should join, and in one letter even went so far as to say that I looked forward to the day "when a United States of Europe would be formed and Britain would be part of a political union with the Continent." Not many people agreed with those sentiments then; many still disagree!

One correspondent, who had been a contemporary at Paston, wrote that he was "filled with horror that a British person should so willingly and anxiously give up his national sovereignty" and went on to prophesy: "If we join we shall be signing our own death warrant as an independent nation." There was much debate in the correspondence and more generally in the country at the time, about desirability of joining the Common Market versus further developing ties with the Commonwealth.

Well, fifty years later, Britain is a member of the European Union, although not the Euro zone, but the Commonwealth has survived with Queen Elizabeth II at its head, although many would argue that it has little real significance. It is, however, the last English-speaking worldwide institution not dominated by the Americans.[8] The organisation includes countries with divergent economies, systems of government and policies. There are no defence or trade agreements to unite them. Undoubtedly, as prophesied, membership of the European Union has led to a loss of sovereignty, although the member states are far from united on many issues. There have been significant gains as well, not least of which are over sixty-five years of peace in Europe, an achievement recognised in 2012 when the Nobel Committee awarded the Peace Prize to the European Union. There are still many euro-sceptics in the United Kingdom, but I do not regret the views that I expressed in 1962, in spite of the present turmoil within the Euro zone, which must eventually lead to greater integration and further loss of sovereignty if the single currency is to survive.

During my seven years at Paston, there was only one occasion when I was able to tread the boards. Usually the school produced a Gilbert and Sullivan operetta each year; given my lack of talent when it came to singing, which had been identified in every end of term report at Saint Joseph's and Paston, there was no chance of my participating in these performances, although watching them turned me into a lifelong fan of the genre.

However, in the summer of 1961, when I was in the lower sixth form, there was a departure from the usual practice when it was decided to produce *1066 and All That*. This was a musical written in 1938 and based on a book of the same name originally published in 1930. It is a parody of the style of history teaching in English schools at

---

[8]   Marr, Andrew, A History of Modern Britain, 2007, Macmillan, London

that time. It purported to contain "all the history you can remember including 103 Good Things, five Bad Kings and two Genuine Dates" and to cover the history of England from Roman times through *1066 and All That* up to the end of World War I, at which time "America was thus clearly Top Nation, and history came to a . . ."[9]

The script included many amusing and memorable lines, including, "Henry VII was very good at answering the Irish Question, and made a Law called Poyning's Law by which the Irish could have a Parliament of their own, but the English were to pass all the Acts in it. This was obviously a very Good Thing" and "Gladstone spent his declining years trying to guess the answer to the Irish Question; unfortunately, whenever he was getting warm, the Irish secretly changed the Question."[10] I never did discover what my aunt Mary might have thought about these remarks. I did not participate in any of the scenes requiring me to sing! I appeared as a pompous subaltern in a sketch about life in the Indian army during the heyday of the Raj. My efforts even got a favourable mention in my report for that term.

In October 1961, while still at Paston, I was again on stage in North Walsham in the North Walsham Dramatic Society's production of *The Happiest Days of Your Life*. This play, first performed in 1948 at the Apollo Theatre in London, is set at the end of World War II. The pupils and teachers of a South

The author (second from right) in *Happiest Days of Your Life*, 1961

[9] http://en.wikipedia.org/wiki/1066_and_All_That, accessed 1 December 2012

[10] Sellar W.C. and Yeatman R.J., 1066 And All That, 1930, Methuen & Co Ltd, London

Coast girls' school are relocated to alternative accommodation, as their own school has been a casualty of wartime bombing. Thanks to a bureaucratic mix-up, they wind up sharing the quarters of a boys' school in Hampshire. The harried headmaster and headmistress, together with both sets of teachers, try to keep visiting parents from discovering the dilemma as the whole thing turns into a battle of the sexes. These problems are forgotten, however, when news is received that a third school is to join them and all unite to repel boarders. The director was my English teacher at Paston, and the cast included two other masters from the school and one other student from my year. I played Rev Peck, a vicar, who was a parent of one of the students. Again, the audience was relieved that no singing of hymns was required of me.

And so, in June 1962, I took the GCE A level exams and obtained passes in history and geography. As part of the geography course work during the final year before these exams, it was necessary to undertake a research project and submit a report that contributed to the final grade. I chose as my subject "The Effects of the Closure of the Midland and Great Northern Railway on North Norfolk." This M&GN line, sometimes known as the "Muddle and Go Nowhere" and after its closure as the "Missed and Greatly Needed," meandered across rural Norfolk from Peterborough to Great Yarmouth with several branch lines wandering hither and thither.

Created in 1893 by a merger of the Eastern and Midland Railway with Midland Railway and the Great Northern Railway, in the early 1960s, it became one of many lines that suffered the effects of the Beeching Axe, so called after the chairman of British Railways (as it was then known), Dr. Richard Beeching. Beeching, formerly an accountant at ICI, published his report "The Re-shaping of British Railways," which led to wholesale line closures throughout the country, including the M&GN in Norfolk.

A copy of my report has not survived, but I seem to recall that at the time most people in the area viewed the closure as a disastrous loss of a valuable means of communication. Many of the lines closed under Beeching are now being reinstated or under consideration for reinstatement in this new golden age of the railway, but not the M&GN. Parts of its route are now roads, including a North Walsham bypass, although the privately owned North Norfolk Railway operates steam and vintage diesel trains on a restored section of the line from Sheringham via Weybourne to Holt.

In July 1962, my school days came to an end, and as I had decided against applying to go on to university, it was time to take up gainful employment. In preparation for this major step, my father took me to buy my first suit. We went to Norwich and visited a branch of the men's outfitter John Collier—"the window to watch," if one believed their advertising slogan. The manager of the Norwich branch was an old friend of my parents; my father had first met him on Norwich railway station in 1940 when they were both to embark on the same wartime journey to East Africa. A grey pin-striped suit, considered suitable for my first incursion into the city of London, was selected, and my father parted with the £7.10s (£7.50 today) that it cost.

In 1984, the Paston School merged with North Walsham High School for Girls to become the Paston Sixth Form College.

Chapter 2

First Jobs

Nineteen sixty-two was the year in which I was to launch myself on the unsuspecting job market. It was also the year that saw the release of the first album on which the Beatles performed. The year when the *Sunday Times* became the first UK newspaper to publish a colour supplement and *Lawrence of Arabia* won the Best Picture award at the Oscars.

Norwich City, my local team, won the Association Football League Cup. Telstar, the world's first communications satellite was launched and relayed the first live transatlantic television broadcast. *Dr. No*, the first James Bond film was released and the world came to the brink of nuclear war over the Cuban missile crisis. In December, a big freeze started in Britain. There were no frost-free nights between December 22 1962 and March 5, 1963.

Events which were to have an effect on my future life included the first use of the term *personal computer* in the media, the outbreak of civil war in Yemen, the Anglo-French agreement to build the Concorde supersonic airliner and Tanganyika (later to merge with Zanzibar to become Tanzania) gaining independence from Britain and becoming a republic within the Commonwealth.

In early 1962, as the time to take GCE A level exams drew closer, I had to decide what I wanted to do after that. From time to time, I thought about applying to universities, possibly to read geography and at others about joining the Royal Navy or becoming a chartered accountant. I also applied to join the foreign office, and after an interview and test, they offered me employment that would have led to a career in the diplomatic service. I often wonder how my life would have developed had I accepted that offer.

In the end, I decided to pursue the idea of a career in international banking, in part as a means to fuel my insatiable desire to travel and with the hope that I would be able to do so at an employer's expense. I applied to a number of British overseas banks, and in due course, the Bank of West Africa offered me employment.

This bank, which had been established in 1893 as the Bank of British West Africa, had a head office in London and, at the time, branches mainly in Britain's former colonies in West Africa, including Nigeria, Gambia, Sierra Leone and Ghana plus Cameroon and a presence in Tangier. This Moroccan city had, from 1923 to 1957 (with some disruption during World War II), been part of an international zone administered by France, Spain and Great Britain, which were joined by Italy, Portugal, the Netherlands and Belgium in 1928. The international zone had been a haven during World War II for the world's rich and famous, and when peace came, many continued to transfer their wealth into the city, making it a precursor of later offshore banking centres. The bank was later to become part of Standard Chartered Bank.

I joined the London office of the bank in September 1962, when I was almost nineteen, as a foreign staff trainee. At that time, the bank would not send an employee overseas until he (never "she" as at that time it was inconceivable that a woman would have been employed on the foreign staff) had reached the age of maturity, twenty-one in those days, and could thus enter into a binding contract of employment.

I lived initially in lodgings in Golders Green in northwest London, commuting daily to the City on the Northern line of the London underground. After a couple of months, I answered an advertisement in the *Evening Standard* for a person to share a flat and ended up moving to Norfolk Square in Paddington, from where there was a shorter commute on the Circle Line.

My net salary at Bank of West Africa, including a "London weighting" was around £50.00 per month. My share of the flat rent was £10.00, and a season ticket to and from work on the underground cost about £4.00 per month. This left around £36.00 for other activities, including food and drink.

I had two flatmates in Norfolk Square; one, Bill, was gay, and the other, Doug, very much heterosexual. I was still undecided. One weekend, Bill suggested that Doug and his girlfriend and I should accompany him to the Pink Elephant, one of the first cabaret clubs in London catering to a gay clientele. Two Americans ran the club, which was near Leicester Square. The mirror of the bar back was tinted pink so that everyone looked wonderful! In an upstairs room, they presented live drag shows, the recorded overture for which was from the album of Gypsy. This contributed to the American atmosphere.[11] To somewhat naive nineteen-year-old who was new to London and had never visited Soho before, it seemed very glamorous and risqué.

Remember, this was 1962, five years before the 1967 Sexual Offences Act legalised homosexual acts between consenting males over the age of twenty-one. I had no idea that such places as the Pink Elephant Club existed let alone how to go about gaining admission. The new law, when passed in 1967, did not change general public attitude and, if anything, led to a greater crackdown by the police on gay men and the venues they frequented. It was only when European Union antidiscrimination laws came into force much later that gay venues were able to cater to their clients in the same way that similar establishments in Amsterdam, San Francisco, and Sydney had done for many years.

This was still the time when "city gents" wore a traditional bowler hat and carried a rolled umbrella and a briefcase, the latter probably containing their lunch! Indeed, the messengers from some financial

---

[11]   http://www.kemglen.talktalk.net/stradivarius/OurHistory1967.htm

institutions still wore top hats when doing their rounds. The unpredictable English weather did cause me to succumb and buy an umbrella, but I cannot claim to have ever worn a bowler hat. I also acquired a briefcase but did not carry my lunch in it, as this meal was usually taken at a "greasy spoon" cafe in Lower Thames Street, close to the bank. Here lunch typically cost about one shilling and six pence (7.5p today), and this cost was covered by "luncheon vouchers" provided by my employer, as was usual in the City, as a tax-free perk.

Most of my time in the Bank of West Africa London branch was spent in the Foreign Exchange Department. In this department, two dealers would buy and sell "cable"—United States dollars against sterling or vice versa—the name originating from the transatlantic cable laid in 1858, which enabled the transmission of messages between the New York and London markets. The selling bank in London would settle the dollar side of such transactions by sending a cable to its New York correspondent, instructing the payment of the dollars from its account to the New York account of the bank to which it had sold them. This was before the days of SWIFT payments—that organisation was established only in 1973—and even the telex was a rarity. To keep the cost of cables down, for which the charge was per word, we used code words to provide the payment details. Thus, a single code word such as *Geronimo* might mean "pay Chemical Bank New York for account of Midland Bank London." The code word would be followed by the currency and amount.

At this time, the sterling area still existed. Formally established at the outbreak of World War II in 1939, at a time when London was the world's leading financial centre and sterling was the main currency for the conduct of international trade, the sterling area included most of the British Empire, with the major exception of Canada. It was a block of countries among which there was no exchange control. Those countries with their own currencies pegged them to sterling, and the members used sterling to settle commercial transactions and maintained the bulk of their foreign currency reserves in sterling in London.

In 1962, the United States was still on the gold standard, meaning that the treasury would redeem dollars for gold at a fixed rate of US$35 per ounce. The Bretton Woods Agreement in 1946 had established a system of fixed exchange rates, which enabled other countries to sell their gold to the US government at this rate, and this was the basis of the establishment of the rates for other currencies against the US dollar and each other; there was little room to speculate. In 1962, the sterling/dollar rate, which at the end of World War II had been US$4.03, was fixed at US$2.80 to one pound; Britain devalued the pound in 1967 to US$2.40.

The 1967 devaluation marked the beginning of the end of the sterling area. Not all members followed Britain's example of devaluing their currencies, and in June 1972, Britain imposed exchange control on most member countries that remained in place until the complete removal of all exchange control by the Thatcher government in 1979.

The Bretton Woods system of fixed exchange rates lasted until 1971 when the United States announced its withdrawal from the gold standard and we entered the beginning of the age of market-driven exchange rates. Initially, rates were allowed to fluctuate within a band 2.25 percent either side of the official rate, but this lasted only until 1976 when rates were allowed to fluctuate freely.

At Bank of West Africa in 1962, and generally at the time, foreign exchange trading was usually restricted to covering customers' requirements rather than speculative; indeed, exchange control still existed in Britain, and this limited transactions in any case. The volume of transactions was a small fraction of that seen today when most foreign exchange trading is undertaken for speculative rather than commercial purposes. The department was also responsible for maintaining the bank's liquidity, in both sterling and other currencies. This involved placing surplus funds with other banks or borrowing in the interbank market, depending on the bank's day-to-day situation.

Most of the deals were done over the telephone, via direct lines to brokers, who matched buyers and sellers of foreign exchange and takers or placers of interbank deposits, initially anonymously until the exchange or interest rate was agreed. When a deal was agreed, my job in the department included recording details of the foreign exchange and money market transactions, preparing confirmations to the counterparties and accounting vouchers and the necessary cables to be sent to paying and/or receiving banks and on a monthly basis checking and agreeing the commission payable to the brokers. As is the case still, deals were usually settled with spot value—two currency business days after the dealing date. Another of my jobs was to process foreign currency cheques deposited by customers of the London branch. This involved preparing schedules listing the cheques and despatching then to the bank's correspondent in the appropriate country. There they would be cleared through the local system and credited to the bank's account. Only after advice of such credit was received would the customer's account in London be credited, often a time-consuming procedure.

I did not adapt easily to living in London and after six months decided to apply to Barclays Bank for a job back in Norfolk. My application was successful, and the first branch to which I was posted was in Sheringham, only about nine miles (15 km) from North Walsham. Thus, I returned to live with my parents who at the time were still running the Cock Inn.

At Barclays Bank, I was the junior clerk in the branch, which had a staff of about ten people. My duties included maintaining the handwritten ledger recording transactions in customers' deposit accounts, periodically balancing this ledger with the general ledger and manually calculating and posting the interest. At the time, although current accounts had been mechanised, using an NCR Class 32 accounting machine, deposit accounts had not.

Another of my jobs was to deal with the local cheque clearing. Junior clerks from each bank would meet at 10:00 a.m. every working day, the location rotating among the banks in the town. These meetings were to exchange cheques drawn on each other, agree the net amounts owed, and issue or receive vouchers for the amounts due, which would then be cleared by the recipient banks through the main clearinghouse in London. This system had the advantage of clearing locally drawn cheques quickly; any unpaid items were returned on the next working day rather than taking three or four days through the main clearing.

After completion of six months' probation at Barclays, the bank confirmed me on the permanent staff and presented me with a book entitled *Money Is Our Business* published by the bank and distributed to all new staff. In the introduction, I was told that I was "a part of a very great enterprise—the largest British bank and the centre of the world's largest branching network." As I write, the bank has suffered severe reputational damage following disclosure that it was involved, with others, in manipulating interest rates; for this, a fine of £290 million has been imposed by US regulators. I wonder what the new staff are told these days.

Very soon after starting work at the Bank of West Africa, I was encouraged to study for the exams of the Institute of Bankers. The bank allowed time off to attend afternoon lectures at the City of London College on Moorgate, a short walk from the office. After joining Barclays Bank in Sheringham, I continued part-time studies at City College Norwich, eventually completing part 1 of the institute's diploma and one subject of part 2.

If anyone asked you where you were and what you were doing on the day when Aldous Huxley or C. S. Lewis died, you would probably be hard-pressed to provide an answer. However, ask anyone the same question about the death of John Kennedy and most people of my generation will remember precisely where they were and what they were doing on Friday, November 22, 1963, when the news broke. I was with my father in a pub in Stalham, Norfolk. We heard the news on the radio, televisions in pubs being very rare at that time. It was early evening and the pub was not very busy; the news flash stunned everyone for a while, and it was followed by speculation about whom, why and how; questions that even today are the subject of much debate and, many argue, have never been satisfactorily answered. Huxley and Lewis died on the same day.

As I have said before, I have always had an insatiable desire to travel. I had joined Barclays Bank because I hoped that in time there would be an opportunity to transfer to their subsidiary, Barclays Bank (Dominion, Colonial and Overseas) as it was then rather pretentiously called (later it was called Barclays Bank International Limited, since merged with the parent bank to become part of Barclays Bank Plc). Before that had a chance to happen, I kept noticing advertisements in the national press placed by Canadian banks that, at the time, were actively seeking junior staff from England who were interested in immigrating to Canada and working in banking there. Successful applicants would have their fare to Canada paid by the recruiting bank and, of course, a job waiting for them. This seemed, once more, to be an opportunity to travel at someone else's expense, so I applied to both Bank of Nova Scotia and Toronto Dominion Bank (now TD Bank Group).

I attended interviews with both banks in London, and in due course, Toronto Dominion Bank offered me employment in Toronto, subject to my satisfying Canadian immigration requirements. I therefore applied to the High Commission of Canada in the United Kingdom in London for approval to immigrate to Canada. This was a comparatively easy procedure then, especially since I had the job offer, and approval was forthcoming quite quickly.

Thus, on March 19, 1964, I travelled to Southampton to board the Cunard liner RMS *Carinthia* bound for Halifax, Nova Scotia. There were two other Toronto Dominion Bank recruits on the same sailing; we met on the boat train from Waterloo to Southampton and shared a cabin on the ship.

Chapter 3

CANADA

In Canada in 1964, Richard Burton appeared in Hamlet at the O'Keefe Centre in Toronto, and the Toronto Maple Leafs won the Stanley Cup (the premier ice hockey trophy in North America) for the third year in a row. Canadians were issued with Social Insurance cards for the first time and the Beatles performed in Toronto. The Queen and Prince Philip made a state visit, and the House of Commons passed a bill creating the new Canadian flag, after a filibuster by Conservative leader John Diefenbaker to try to prevent it.

Elsewhere in the world, Radio Caroline began broadcasting from a ship just outside British territorial waters and thus became the first pirate radio station, and there were two related events, which had an impact on my later life. African nationalist rebels overthrew the mainly Arab government of Zanzibar in January, and in April, Tanganyika and Zanzibar merged to form Tanzania, a country in which I was destined to spend quite a lot of time in the first decade of the twenty-first century.

After a very rough transatlantic crossing, the *Carinthia*, carrying three new immigrants destined for banking careers in the New World, arrived in Halifax on March 26, 1964. We completed customs and immigration procedures and obtained the required Landed Immigrant status stamp in our passports and on a separate identity card. We then boarded the train for Montreal and there changed to another train to Toronto, where we arrived on Friday, March 27, the start of the Easter weekend—eight days after leaving London.

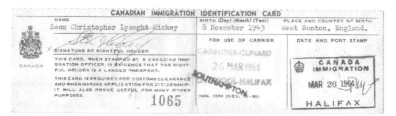

Canadian Landed Immigrant Card

The bank had made reservations for us at the Lord Simcoe Hotel, a twenty-story edifice on the corner of King Street and University Avenue in downtown Toronto. I recall that the en suite bathroom, itself something of a novelty for us, had a shower over the bath, a feature that was almost unknown in Britain at the time; my previous experience of showers had been the communal ones in the gymnasium changing rooms at the Paston School. The Lord Simcoe Hotel closed in 1979, was demolished in 1981 and replaced by the Sun Life Centre in 1984.

Lord Simcoe Hotel, Toronto, c 1964

During the Easter weekend, we had the opportunity to get our bearings in central Toronto, and I had my first (but not the last) brush with the law in Canada. On Easter Sunday, I was on Yonge Street, the main north-south artery of the city, and decided to cross to the other side. Seeing that the road was clear of traffic, I walked across, only to be accosted by a police officer; it seemed that I had crossed when the light for pedestrians was red rather than green and was guilty of jaywalking. On his hearing that I had just arrived in the country, he let me off with the warning not to do it again!

On the same day, I could not help but notice blinds were closed on all of the windows of Eaton's department store situated on the corner of Yonge and Queen streets, a major intersection in the city centre. Later enquiries proved what a conservative place Toronto was in 1964. I discovered that the blinds were closed to prevent passersby from window-shopping; this, of course, at a time when shops did not open for business on the Sabbath. How times have changed!

Not all was bad at Eaton's however. On one occasion, I bought set of three casseroles there as a wedding gift for friends in England. Eaton's shipped the gift, and on arrival, one of the items was broken. I reported this to the store, and they immediately shipped a completely new set. This time it arrived intact, and the recipients are still using it, nearly fifty years later.

The hotel was a short walk from the head office of the bank, which was located on the corner of King and Bay streets, and to which we reported after the Easter holiday weekend. After meeting various people in the head office, we were each told the branch to which we had been posted. Mine was a branch at Queen and John streets, a few blocks west of the downtown area and in the Jewish part of Toronto. It was not far from Spadina Avenue, the heart of the garment business. At the time, this part of Queen Street West was a somewhat aging

Toronto Dominion Bank, Queen and John branch, 1964

commercial area, noted for its "greasy spoon" restaurants, one of which had a delivery service and provided lunch for many of the branch staff. The bank was located in part of a building belonging to the United Church of Canada that accommodated the United Church Publishing House and the Ryerson Press, major customers of the branch. I was to be a teller at the branch, one of four (or five on busy days) out of a total staff of about twelve people. My duties included receiving and paying cash and accepting cheque deposits from both personal and business customers. Neither computers nor ATMs were in use at the time, although the branch's customer accounts were mechanised.

To avoid creating an overdraft, tellers checked each voucher against the balance shown on the ledger card and, after paying out the cash, attached the voucher to the card in case there were more transactions later. At the end of the day, the ledger cards and all vouchers were sent to a central location to be posted overnight; the next morning the ledger cards and vouchers were returned to the branch for checking.

Although the bank was continuing to accommodate us at the Lord Simcoe Hotel, we were expected to arrange our own accommodation within a reasonable time. We decided to look for a furnished apartment to rent, which we would share. Within a few days of starting work, a suitable place was located at 35 Balliol Street, just off Yonge Street, between Saint Claire and Eglinton avenues. It was close to the Davisville subway station from which it was about a fifteen-minute ride followed by a three-minute walk to my branch. In 1964, Balliol Street was tree-lined

35 Baliol Street, Toronto, 1964

with single- or two-story houses, and many of the latter had been converted into two flats. Ours was the ground floor of number 35, and above us lived a friendly Canadian couple; the husband was also a banker, working for Canadian Imperial Bank of Commerce.

Today all of the houses in this street and neighbouring ones have been demolished and replaced with high-rise apartment buildings. Through our upstairs neighbours, I met other people, many of them working in banking, and I established friendships, some of which have lasted until today.

I gradually began to adapt to my new life in Canada and learn the differences in habits and language; a "lift" became an "elevator," the "pavement" was the "sidewalk." A "flat" was called an "apartment" if it was in a purpose-built building, although the word *flat* could still be used to describe part of a converted house. I quickly decided that a car was a necessity but first had to obtain an Ontario driving licence. Although I had held a British licence since soon after my seventeenth birthday, I had to take both a written and practical test in Toronto but managed to pass first time. I then purchased a 1958 Austin Cambridge for about C$300 and, much to my surprise, obtained finance for the purchase, although I had only been in the country for about a month. In later years I moved up to Studebaker Lark and finally to a much-loved Chrysler Valiant convertible.

The author's Chrysler Valiant, 1968

Obtaining finance to buy my first car was an important lesson; in Canada, one's credit rating was critical, and to establish a good one, it was necessary to borrow money and to repay it on time. After a while I acquired store credit cards from Eaton's and Simpsons, the two major Canadian department stores at the time, this being before the days of Visa and MasterCard and their virtually universal acceptance worldwide.

Shortly after I arrived in Toronto, I was able, by prior arrangement, to take the Institute of Bankers exams for which I had been studying in England. These I passed, and I was then able to get exemption from some of the courses required by the Canadian Bankers' Association for their qualification. I continued my studies via courses at Queen's University in Kingston, Ontario, and by 1967 had successfully completed all courses required and became a fellow of the Canadian Bankers Association.

Queen's University

The Canadian Bankers' Association

Queen's University, in accordance with the authority given by The Canadian Bankers' Association does hereby certify that

Sean Christopher Lysaght Hickey

having duly passed the Examinations for the Certificate of the Association, has thereby become a Fellow of The Canadian Bankers' Association.

Given under the Seal of Queen's University

Dated, the 17th day of July, 1967

Fellow of the Canadian Bankers' Association Certificate, 1967

In mid-1965, I was transferred from Queen and John branch to a suburban branch, Lake Shore Boulevard and Third Street in New Toronto, and promoted to be the accountant there. This job in a branch of Toronto Dominion Bank was a sort of office manager, responsible for all administration and reporting to the branch manager. Lake Shore Boulevard was once the main western entrance to Toronto, although by 1965 most vehicles used the Queen Elizabeth Way and the Gardiner Expressway to get to the city centre; the areas of New Toronto and adjacent Mimico were originally dormitory towns for people working in the city. The road was also home to a number of motels used by out-of-town visitors. The customer base of the branch included the

Toronto Dominion Bank, Lakeshore and 3rd Street, New Toronto, 1965

small local businesses and retail outlets as well as individuals who lived in the area, including an internationally famous jazz pianist. By this time, one of the other two recruits who had travelled with me from England had been transferred to Vancouver at his request; the other had left the bank to join the Metropolitan Toronto Police. At about the same time as my transfer, I moved to a new flat in Howland Avenue, shared with an English friend who was on a one-year exchange visit from Barclays Bank in the UK to Canadian Imperial Bank of Commerce in Canada. Again, this was a house converted into two flats in an old residential area with tree-lined streets in midtown Toronto.

I commuted to work by car every day, and on November 9, 1965, as I was driving home to Howland Avenue, Toronto, along with much of eastern Canada and the northeast United States including New York City, was hit by a major power cut which was to last until the next morning. The cause was the failure of a power relay near Niagara Falls on the US-Canada border, and it created both panic and chaos in the evening rush hour. Inevitably, the journey home took much longer than usual as no traffic lights were working, and streetcars powered by electricity were stopped in the position they had reached when the lights went out, further disrupting the traffic flow.

Driving to and from work every day meant listening to the car radio, not just for entertainment but also for traffic news. I became a regular listener to CFRB, a radio station established in 1927 that in the 1960s was, and still is, the oldest broadcaster in the city still using its original call letters and AM frequency, 1010. On the way to work, Wally Crowter, who was the presenter on the station's morning show until his retirement in 1966, entertained listeners.

Another favourite programme on CFRB was *Calling All Britons*. This was a weekly show hosted by Ray Sonin every Saturday afternoon from 1965 until he died in 1991, aimed at Canadians of British origin and including news from "home," something generally lacking in the somewhat insular, parochial Toronto press at the time.

From Lake Shore and Third Street, I was moved to a branch in the Yorkdale Shopping Centre in late 1966, also as the accountant. Yorkdale is situated on Dufferin Street, just south of Highway 401 (now the MacDonald-Cartier Freeway), a major provincial highway running from Windsor to the Quebec border, which, at the time, was also effectively the northern Toronto bypass. Then it had a modest two lanes in each direction; now, in places, it has nine. When Yorkdale opened in 1964, it was the largest shopping centre in the world and is still the largest in Toronto. By this time, I was living in Triller Avenue on the nineteenth floor of an apartment building, with fantastic views over Lake Ontario's Humber Bay and western Toronto, so I had a longer commute to work every day. In early 1968, I was transferred again from Yorkdale to Yonge and Belmont Street branch located in midtown Toronto as assistant manager. The branch was close to the fashionable upmarket residential district of Rosedale, an area favoured by the wealthy Jewish community of Toronto, in a building occupied mainly by an American life insurance company that was an important customer of the branch. In the late 1990s, the office building was converted into condominium apartments, and the branch no longer exists. I now lived in the western suburbs of the city, on Queensway in Etobicoke, so once again I had quite a long drive to and from work.

In 1968, Toronto Dominion Bank, along with Bank of Nova Scotia, Royal Bank of Canada, Canadian Imperial Bank of Commerce and Banque Canadienne Nationale, jointly launched the first credit card in the country—Chargex. The banks issued the card under a licence agreement with Bank of America, which had started issuing its BankAmericard in California in 1958. A similar licence had been granted to Barclays Bank in the United Kingdom, which had started issuing the Barclaycard in 1966.

The cards issued by all of these banks could be used at accepting merchants in any of the three countries. The Chargex card used the same three coloured stripes as BankAmericard and Barclaycard—blue, white and gold—that are still the colours used in the logo on cards issued by banks worldwide under the Visa brand since 1975. The introduction of credit cards to Canada marked a significant shift in the consumer habits of a country whose citizens were traditionally savers. This financial product changed spending habits dramatically by putting instant credit into millions of consumers' hands and allowing them to repay just 10 percent of the outstanding balance each month, provided the cardholder was prepared to pay an effective interest rate of about 18 percent per annum on the unpaid amount. This was at a time when the typical commercial lending rate was around 6 percent, and personal loans were charged about 9 percent. The banks heavily promoted the launch of the card in television and radio advertisements with the slogan "Will that be Cash or Chargex?" and there was a mass mailing of unsolicited cards to customers thought to be eligible for the $300 credit limit initially offered.

When merchants accepted the Chargex card in payment for goods and services the transactions in those days were paper-based. A three part form was completed, one copy for the card-holder, one for the merchant to retain and the third for processing the payment. To obtain credit in their bank account, merchants would place the third copy of all the vouchers in a special envelope, after listing and totalling them on its outside, and deliver them to the branch where they maintained an account. The branch would credit the account with the total and send the envelope to the card centre for further processing.

One of the most popular sports in Canada was, and still is, ice hockey; and many people in Toronto avidly followed the progress of their local team, the Toronto Maple Leafs, during the National Hockey League season. During the time that I lived in Toronto, the Maple Leafs won the sport's premier trophy, the Stanley Cup, twice, in 1964 and 1967. I have never been a particular fan of any sport or team, but it was difficult to avoid the enthusiasm among friends; on one occasion, I was persuaded to follow the team to an away match against the Detroit Red Wings. We travelled to Detroit by bus, a journey of about two hundred forty miles (384 km), taking some five hours. On arrival in Detroit, we had dinner, accompanied by an unusually large (for me) quantity of beer, and then went to the match, where more beer was consumed. Afterwards, we set out on the return journey to Toronto, during which I was extremely ill!

In the 1960s, it was common to see advertisements in the Toronto newspapers placed by people planning to drive to the west coast, inviting others to share the driving and expenses. In September 1965, a friend and I answered such an advertisement and eventually set out with the advertiser for a trip to Vancouver. At first everything went according to plan; we progressed through northern Ontario and eventually arrived in Winnipeg, Manitoba. From there we set out across the Canadian prairies and reached Brandon, Manitoba. Here the car developed an overheating problem, and we went to a garage to get it fixed. The problem seemed to be quite serious, and it was apparent that repairs would take time and be expensive. As our time was limited, my friend and I therefore decided that we would continue the journey to Vancouver by train and so informed the owner of the car. He tried to insist that we should share in the repair cost and expenses for the whole journey to Vancouver, and an argument ensued which became quite noisy and alarmed the garage owner so much that he called the police. The Royal Canadian Mounted Police arrived, in a car rather than on horseback, and, while sympathising with us, decided that it would be better if we left town. They drove us to the Canadian Pacific Railway station and made sure that we bought tickets and boarded the train to Vancouver. In this, my second encounter with the police in Canada, we had been run out of town by the Mounties but had not had to pay anything to the car owner beyond our share of the cost of the petrol from Toronto to Brandon!

After about a week of staying in Vancouver, from where we also visited Victoria on Vancouver Island and Seattle, it was time to return to Toronto. We had always planned that we would fly back and so booked what was to be my first flight, which was on a Canadian Pacific Airlines DC8. This experience whetted my appetite for air travel. Since then I have made literally thousands of commercial flights, on business and for pleasure, in aircraft as diverse as the McDonnell Douglas DC-3 and Concorde, although, with increased security and controls, much of the pleasure has been taken from these journeys in recent years.

The Canadian winters gave me an opportunity to take up skiing. The proximity of such a large body of water as Lake Ontario modifies the climate in Toronto itself, and the city is often said to be in the "banana belt" because its winters can be relatively mild. However, just a few miles north of the lake, winter temperatures are usually much lower and snowfall more than sufficient to provide ski facilities, on slopes very suited to beginners, within easy driving distance from the city. I started skiing, at a resort called *Old Smokey* in the Beaver Valley, in the winter of 1965-1966 and continued each year that I lived in Toronto, although I never became particularly proficient.

The author on skis for the first time, 1965

The following year, in June 1966, after I had been in Canada for two years, I decided that it was time to visit England to see family and friends. In those days international airfares were not the free for all that we see today. International Air Transport Association (IATA) regulations and bilateral agreements between countries controlled the price and all airlines serving the same route, usually the national flag carriers of the two countries, charged the same price. Only British Overseas Airways Corporation (now British Airways) and Trans-Canada Air Lines (now Air Canada), both of them state-owned at the time, operated direct scheduled flights between Toronto and

London. One way to reduce the cost of air travel, particularly between Canada and Britain, was to use a charter flight; but to be eligible, one had to be a member of a club that would charter the plane for the benefit of its members. One such club that organised regular charter flights from Toronto to London was the Maple Leaf Cricket Club. The club was a bona fide sports club that had been established in 1954. I had absolutely no interest in the game and never actually visited the club, but by paying five dollars a year and becoming a social member, I was eligible to travel on its chartered flights to London, and this is how I made my first trip back to Britain.

Later that year, in October 1966, I decided to visit my old school friend Jane Boling (née Bagnato, now Meagher) from Saint Joseph's School days. She was at that time living in the small town of Collegeville, Indiana, which gets its name from Saint Joseph's College, almost the only reason for the existence of the town. Her husband, Gerry, was teaching there. Even today, the town has a population of only 927 people, of whom 654 live in college dormitories.[12] Its only claim to fame seems to be that on July 14, 1936, the town experienced a temperature of 116°F (47°C), the highest ever recorded in Indiana. To reach Collegeville, I took an overnight train from Toronto to Chicago, and from there it was about a two-hour journey on a Greyhound bus to Collegeville. The return journey was also by bus to Chicago, from where I indulged my newfound passion for flying by returning to Toronto with Trans-Canada Air Lines in a Vickers Viscount. While I was staying in Collegeville, Jane and Gerry invited some of their friends to their home to meet me. This proved to be something of a revelation, revealing how parochial many Americans are. In this small Midwestern town, some (though not my friends) had difficulty recalling where Toronto was and certainly had a limited knowledge of international affairs.

In March 1967, I again travelled to the United States, this time to Omaha, Nebraska, to visit other American friends, Dan and Ruth Dolan and their family, whom I had known from the time that they were based at Sculthorpe and living in Sheringham in the mid-1950s.

---

[12]   http://www.city-data.com/city/Collegeville-Indiana.html, accessed 18 Jan 2012

The journey was entirely by air, Trans-Canada Air Lines to Chicago and then on United Airlines from there to Omaha, returning via the same route. Dan was at the time a colonel, based at Offutt Air Force Base, just outside Omaha, where he was flying in-flight refuelling tanker aircraft. The US Air Force had had a presence there since 1918. The base, named after Jarvis Offutt, the first native of Omaha to become a casualty in World War I, was the headquarters for Strategic Air Command and associated command and control centres for use in the event that the cold war turned hot. Offutt's other claim to fame is that the B-29 Superfortress bombers, *Enola Gay* and *Bockscar*, that dropped the only atomic bombs ever used, were built there during the last years of World War II.[13]

In 1967, Canada celebrated one hundred years as a nation. The main event was Expo '67—the World Fair. Originally, the Paris-based Bureau International des Expositions had planned to hold the 1967 World Fair in Moscow to celebrate the fiftieth anniversary of the Russian Revolution, but when the Soviet Union decided to cancel the event, they offered it to Canada, first to Toronto, which refused, and then to Montreal, which accepted with enthusiasm.

The exhibition, located on two islands in the Saint Lawrence River, lasted from April to October 1967 and attracted over fifty million visitors. Among the prominent visitors to Expo '67 was Emperor Haile Selassie of Ethiopia. As will be recalled from chapter 1, my father was present at his restoration in Addis Ababa in 1941 and involved in his personal security arrangements then. Another prominent visitor, French president Charles De Gaulle, caused an international incident on the day before his visit to the fair when he addressed a crowd at the Montreal City Hall and ended with the words "Vive Montréal . . . Vive le Québec . . . Vive le Québec Libre!" This call for a separate, "free" francophone Quebec was made at a time when there was still a significant movement in the province agitating, sometimes violently, for independence from the predominantly anglophone rest of Canada. Canadian prime minister Lester Pearson's response to this undiplomatic outburst

---

[13]   http://freerepublic.com/focus/f-bloggers/2692243/posts, accessed 24 Jan 2012

was "Canadians do not need to be liberated; Canada will remain united and will reject any effort to destroy her unity." His view has prevailed, and talk of Quebec seceding from Canada is rarely heard these days. That having been said, the whole country has become officially bilingual, both English and French being used by all provincial and the federal governments.

With a group of friends, I planned a three-day visit to Expo '67. A Quebec provincial organisation called Logexpo had been set up to organise and book accommodation for visitors to the fair in an attempt to prevent exploitation of tourists. Although much criticised, Logexpo did a reasonable job, including sourcing our accommodation at the newly built Canadiana 67 Motel on Dorchester Boulevard East, five minutes from the expo entrance. A double room was C$22 per day with an extra charge of C$4 per day for each additional person. During our visit, we managed to include the Canadian, British, French, United States and Soviet Union pavilions, among the major ones and, because some of our party originated from Trinidad and Guyana, the pavilions of Trinidad, Tobago and Grenada and Guyana and Barbados.

In October 1967, I made another trip to England, again on a flight chartered by the Maple Leaf Cricket Club. While there, I travelled with my parents and sister to Ireland where we were able to see a number of my father's family in Dublin and visit the places where he was born and brought up, Youghal and Mallow in County Cork. I also visited New York in October 1967, accompanied by a friend from Toronto. Since this was the first visit to this city for both of us, we naturally saw all the usual sights, including the Statue of Liberty, the Empire State Building and Rockefeller Centre and took the Circle Line cruise round Manhattan. Early 1968 saw me in the United States again; this time I flew from Toronto to Tampa in Florida where I met up with friends who had driven there from Canada. We spent about ten days in the state, along with many other Canadians who went there each year to escape the Canadian winter for a while. From Miami we were able to take a short cruise to Nassau in the Bahamas. We then drove back to Toronto, a distance of about one thousand five hundred miles (2,400 km), sharing the driving and stopping only for petrol and food, in about thirty hours.

Washington, DC was the next place that I visited in the United States, travelling there by road in August 1968 to visit my old school friend from Saint Joseph's days, Jane Boling. By then she and her husband had forsaken the small Indiana town of Collegeville for the nation's capital.

In November, I went to Flint in Michigan to see the Corbins, another family that I had known when I was a teenager in the 1950s, and they were stationed at Sculthorpe in Norfolk. It will be recalled that Bob Corbin was killed when his plane crashed in 1958 and that his widow and children had returned to their home in Flint. After my father died in 2000, I found among his papers a letter that I had written to my parents following this 1968 visit to the Corbins. In it I mentioned that each of the three boys in the family participated in the Big Brother organisation. Through this group, each of them had a "big brother," who was usually an older and wealthier man with sufficient time to devote to mentoring their "little brother." Often, as in the case of the Corbin boys, but not always, the "little brothers" had no father.

In June 1968, I got the chance to vote in federal parliamentary elections. At that time in Canada, British subjects with landed immigrant status could vote after living in Canada for only one year. This was the one and only time that I have ever voted in any election. I had left England before I was twenty-one, the minimum voting age then, and since my departure I have never lived in England or qualified for the overseas vote after it was introduced and nor have I lived in any other country which offered a foreigner such a privilege. Indeed, a number of the countries in which I have lived did and still do regard the idea of elections as an anathema! At the time of the election campaign, the leader of the Liberal Party was the comparatively youthful Pierre Trudeau, then aged forty-eight, and Trudeaumania was sweeping the country.

Trudeau was appointed justice minister in the Lester Pearson cabinet in 1967 and was responsible for the landmark Criminal Law Amendment Act, an omnibus bill whose provisions included, among other things, the decriminalization of homosexual acts between consenting adults. Trudeau famously defended the decriminalization of homosexual acts by telling reporters "there's no place for the state in the bedrooms of the nation; what's done in private between adults doesn't concern the Criminal Code." This act preceded the Stonewall riots in New York City by one year and became law shortly after the Sexual Offences Bill, which covered similar issues, received royal assent in the United Kingdom. In April 1968, at the age of only forty-eight, following the retirement of Lester Pearson, Trudeau became leader of the Liberal Party and so prime minister. He was widely perceived as a symbol of generational change and had the support of much of the younger generation in Canada. His party won the election the following June with a substantial majority, to which I contributed my own vote of support.

I decided to visit England again for Christmas 1968, not only to be with my family for the holiday, but also to have an opportunity to attend interviews with British overseas banks in London, to which I had applied for jobs. At this time it was possible to buy an interline air ticket, which allowed travel on multiple airlines via several cities if the total mileage flown did not exceed the maximum permitted for the end-to-end route. Following my desire to travel on as many airlines as possible, I flew from Toronto to New York on Trans-Canada Air Lines and on to London on Qantas, the Australian flag carrier. On the return journey, the London-New York sector was with El Al, the Israeli airline, just a few days after one of their planes had been attacked by members of the Popular Front for the Liberation of Palestine at Athens airport on December 26, 1968, and a retaliatory raid by Israel a few days later had destroyed fourteen civilian aircraft at Beirut airport. Security was tight!

In March 1969, it was time to leave Canada and set out for the Middle East, which was to be the region that dominated much of my remaining life and career. I had begun to put down roots in Toronto, and I realised that unless I took the plunge soon, I might well never leave. And so on March 16, I travelled by overnight train from Toronto to New York from where I sailed to Southampton on the SS *France*. I arrived in New York on St Patrick's Day and was able to watch the city's annual parade before embarking on the ship.

Yvonne De Gaulle, wife of the French president Charles de Gaulle, who caused such controversy in Montreal in 1967, had launched this ship in 1962. The SS *France* had actually spent two weeks docked in Montreal during Expo '67, acting as a secondary French pavilion. She was the longest passenger ship ever built until the *Queen Mary 2* was launched in 2004. I had decided to travel this way rather than fly to London because I had a significant amount of baggage to take, and I knew that I would have limited time in England to deal with it. Travelling by sea meant that my baggage went with me. Although winter, the crossing was reasonable—not nearly as rough as my journey to Halifax in 1964. I arrived in Southampton on March 21 and reported to my next employer, British Bank of the Middle East on the twenty-fourth.

Chapter 4

THE MIDDLE EAST PROBLEM

Before starting to describe my life, work and experiences in the Middle East, I think that it is appropriate to devote a chapter to the "Middle East Problem." It is not my intention that this should be an authoritative dissertation on the subject; many other writers, better qualified than me, have written many volumes on the region, its history, politics and problems over the years. However, it is impossible to talk about my time in the Middle East without mentioning the subject, which directly touched my life on several occasions and has influenced the lives of all of the residents of the region for too long.

The Origins of Israel-Palestine Conflict

The root of the problem is the Israeli-Palestinian conflict, which has its origins in the late nineteenth century, which continues to this day and is mainly due to conflicting claims to the same territory. The idea of establishing a Jewish homeland in Palestine emerged while the region was still part of the Ottoman Empire, mainly because of the persecution of Jews in Europe in the nineteenth century, which led to the creation of the Zionist movement in 1897. This organisation had the declared aim "to establish a home for the Jewish people in Palestine secured under public law." Immigration to Palestine was encouraged by the Zionist Organisation (World Zionist Organisation from 1960), and the Jewish National Fund financed the purchase of land in the region by Jewish immigrants. Concurrently with these developments, Arab nationalism was beginning to emerge, and among the Palestinian Arab population, this manifested itself in opposition to the increasing Jewish immigration. The area was part of the Ottoman Empire for almost four hundred years up to the end of World War I, inhabited mainly by Arab Muslims with small Christian and Jewish communities.

In 1870, the estimated population of Palestine included only 7,000 Jews among 367,000 Arabs.[14] From the late nineteenth century, as Jewish immigration increased, so did Arab opposition to it. By 1914, the Jewish population of Palestine was estimated to be around 40,000 compared to about 525,000 Arabs. In the Ottoman Empire, at around the same time, there was a total Jewish population of some 250,000, of which Istanbul was home to about 48,000, Smyrna (now Izmir) had a Jewish population of around 10,000 and Alexandria 25,000.

During World War I, the Ottoman Empire was allied with Germany and therefore at war with Britain and France. During the war, conflicting undertakings given by the British and French governments to Arabs, Jews, and to each other added fuel to the smouldering fire. Between June 1915 and January 1916, there was an exchange of correspondence between the British high commissioner in Egypt, Sir Henry McMahon, and the Sharif of Mecca, Hussein bin Ali. In the correspondence, Britain committed to the establishment of an Arab state in the area now comprising much of Iraq, Syria, the West Bank, Israel and Jordan if the Arabs, led by the Sharif, would revolt against the Ottoman Empire. In 1916, the secret Sykes-Picot Agreement between Britain and France, negotiated by Sir Mark Sykes and Francois Picot and to which Russia agreed, set out plans for dividing the Arab parts of the Ottoman Empire into British and French areas of interest after the war. Britain was to get control of the area comprising the present-day Israel, Jordan, the West Bank and southern Iraq and France the present-day Syria and Lebanon plus

---

[14]   http://www.adespicabletruce.org.uk/page62.html, accessed 12 Dec 2012

parts of southeast Turkey and northern Iraq. Constantinople (now Istanbul) and Armenia were allocated to Russia. The agreement undoubtedly conflicted with the undertakings given to the Sharif. Then to compound the problem, on November 2, 1917, the British Foreign Secretary Arthur Balfour wrote to Baron Rothschild, the leader of the Jewish community in Britain stating that

> His Majesty's government view with favour the establishment in Palestine of a national home for the Jewish people, and will use their best endeavours to facilitate the achievement of this object, it being clearly understood that nothing shall be done which may prejudice the civil and religious rights of existing non-Jewish communities in Palestine, or the rights and political status enjoyed by Jews in any other country.

The infamous Balfour Declaration created a conflict with both the Hussein-McMahon correspondence and the Sykes-Picot Agreement. The Zionist movement was delighted, seeing the declaration as a major milestone in the progress towards establishing a Jewish state in Palestine, although their enthusiasm was not shared by all Jews—many of whom did not agree with the Zionist aim of establishing a Jewish homeland.[15] The first Arab reaction to the Sykes-Picot Agreement and the Balfour Declaration was disbelief.

The declaration was widely criticized throughout the Arab world and especially in Palestine, as contrary to the spirit of British pledges contained in the Hussein-McMahon correspondence. The Arabs had fulfilled their part of the bargain with Britain by fighting long and courageously against the Turks with the encouragement and leadership of Col. T. E. Lawrence (Lawrence of Arabia), a British army officer. Sharif Hussein demanded immediate clarification from Britain, and the British renewed their pledge of self-determination. The wording of the declaration itself, although painstakingly devised, was interpreted differently by different people, according to their interests.

---

[15]   http://www.rense.com/general69/makf.htm, accessed 4 Feb 2012

Although the carefully worded Balfour Declaration was not a formal and binding commitment and did not even promise that there would ever be a Jewish homeland, let alone a state, it was a strong card in the Zionists' hands. Indeed, Palestine did not exist as a political entity at the time of the declaration; it was not even an administrative division of the Ottoman Empire. What later became part of the British Mandate for Palestine was in Ottoman times divided between the Vilayet of Beirut and the Sanjak of Jerusalem. The British government seemed to be prepared to give away an undefined area of land, that did not belong to it, to a people who were a minority in that land, without consulting the wishes of the inhabitants. Indeed, the British government wanted to keep the Balfour Declaration secret from the Palestinian Arabs, the "existing non-Jewish communities" in Palestine that were over 90 percent of the population and owned the majority of the land! Ultimately, the two undertakings of the declaration were incompatible. Although numerous compromise plans were proposed over the years, Arab interests could never accept that establishment in Palestine of a national home for the Jews could be accomplished with preservation of the rights of existing non-Jewish communities, i.e., the Arabs.

At the end of World War I, Britain occupied most of the area that today comprises Iraq, the West Bank, Jordan, Israel, Syria and Lebanon. The Ottoman Empire was virtually destroyed. Russia was more concerned with domestic issues following the revolution and civil war, and France's influence in the region was limited. The British military successes in the area made her the dominant power. In the end, Britain and France got virtually everything they had planned for under the terms of the Sykes-Picot Agreement.

In 1923, the Treaty of Lausanne formally acknowledged League of Nations mandates which granted France control of Syria and Lebanon and Britain control of Iraq, Palestine and Transjordan. Sharif Hussein bin Ali was rewarded for his leadership of the Arab Revolt with short-lived international recognition of the Hejaz as an independent kingdom; it became part of Saudi Arabia in 1932. However, his sons Faisal and Abdulla went on to become kings of Iraq and Transjordan (later Jordan) respectively.

The Sharif and other Arab nationalists believed that they had been robbed when the British did not fully deliver on their pledges of independence. They believed that the western powers, especially the British, had acted with arrogance, drawing borders and creating nations with little or no regard for demographics or for the wishes of the local inhabitants. In this they were right, and the problems caused by the ways in which the British drew boundaries during the days of Empire and, sometimes, in preparation for the postcolonial period have been a cause of subsequent problems in many locations, not just the Middle East. The fate of Palestine, under the British Mandate, especially provoked Arab frustration and anger. The treaty, which fostered an instability that continues to be a source of conflict today, generated much controversy at the time and has continued to do so ever since.

The British Mandate for Palestine continued through the interwar years and during World War II. Britain divided the region into two administrative areas: Palestine, over which the British imposed direct rule, and Transjordan, under the rule of the Hashemites, as was envisaged in the McMahon-Hussein correspondence. The Balfour Declaration was incorporated into the preamble to the League of Nations Mandate, but later the area east of the Jordan River, Transjordan as it was then called, was exempted from the Jewish homeland provisions of the mandate and in 1946 became the independent Hashemite Kingdom of Jordan, under King Abdulla bin Hussein, son of the Sharif.

Problems first emerged in 1920 when there were four days of Arab-Jewish violence, following a formal public reading of the Balfour Declaration by a British official in Palestine in February, which sparked large demonstrations in Palestinian cities. In April, riots broke out in Jerusalem during Easter Week, and Palestinian Arabs attacked recent Jewish immigrants.

As British officials prepared to govern Palestine, Palestinians had already given warning that they would not accept a British-sponsored settler colony on their land. However, Jewish immigration continued at an increasing rate throughout the 1920s and 1930s during which period Jewish communities developed numerically and economically at a much faster rate than Arab areas. The 1922 census showed a Jewish population of 83,790 compared to 589,177 Muslim Arabs and 71,464 Christian Arabs. By the time of the 1931 census, the last ever conducted, the numbers had increased to 174,606, 759,700 and 88,907 respectively.[16] In 1936, the Arab Revolt against British rule broke out, involving strikes and attacks on British property.

The British government appointed the Peel Commission to consider the future of Palestine; in its findings, released in July 1937, it recommended partition of the area west of the Jordan River into separate Arab and Jewish states. This may well be the origin of the two-state solution. Today even that looks increasingly unlikely. The publication of the Peel Commission report increased activity against the Mandate and Zionism by the Arabs, which led to the Jewish community establishing its own paramilitary organisation, Haganah. The Arab Revolt did not stop Jewish immigration, and in 1939, the British government issued a White Paper, which stated in part:

> His Majesty's Government believe that the framers of the Mandate in which the Balfour Declaration was embodied could not have intended that Palestine should be converted into a Jewish State against the will of the Arab population of the country. His Majesty's Government therefore now declare unequivocally that it is not part of their policy that Palestine should become a Jewish State. They would indeed regard it as contrary to their obligations to the Arabs under the Mandate, as well as to the assurances, which have been given to the Arab people in the past, that the Arab population of Palestine should not be made the subjects of a Jewish State against their will.

> The objective of His Majesty's Government is the establishment within 10 years of an independent Palestine State in such treaty relations with the United Kingdom

---

[16]   http://www.mideastweb.org/palpop.htm, accessed 10 June 2012

> as will provide satisfactorily for the commercial and
> strategic requirements of both countries in the future.
> The independent State should be one in which Arabs and
> Jews share government in such a way as to ensure that the
> essential interests of each community are safeguarded.

This sounded more like support for a one-state solution, an idea that is once again being tentatively mentioned in the early twenty-first century.

At the time, the Jewish population had increased to about 450,000, and under the terms of the white paper, further immigration was to be severely restricted, as were transfers of property from Arabs to Jews. This was too little too late. Both Jews and Arabs opposed the provisions of the white paper, and illegal Jewish immigration became commonplace.

After the end of World War II, when the world became fully aware of the horror of the Nazi death camps in which some six million Jews had perished, Zionists became even more demanding, insisting that the British government allow unlimited Jewish immigration into Palestine. Jewish terrorist groups including the Irgun Zvai Leumi (led by future prime minister, Menachem Begin), Haganah and the Stern Gang (led by another future prime minister, Yitzhak Shamir) escalated their campaign to force Britain's hand. A campaign of violence against both the Arab population and the British presence followed, including the bombing of the British military headquarters at the King David Hotel in Jerusalem in July 1946, which killed ninety-two people. Arabs in the region opposed more Jewish immigration, but in Palestine itself, they lacked unified leadership.

In March 1945, Saudi Arabia, Syria, Lebanon, Iraq, Transjordan, Yemen and Egypt organized the League of Arab States (now the Arab League) to pressure Britain whose new labour government (unlike its predecessor) strongly sympathized with Zionism's goal yet hoped to remain friendly with the Arabs. In 1947, the British government asked the United Nations to propose a solution.

On November 29, 1947, the United Nations General Assembly adopted Resolution 181, calling for the partition of Palestine into two areas, one for Arabs and one for Jews, with Jerusalem as an international zone under UN jurisdiction; the vote was thirty-three to thirteen in favour, with the United States and the Soviet Union supporting it and Britain abstaining. The resolution envisaged the ending of the mandate by August 1, 1948, and the establishment of the new independent states by October 1, 1948.[17]

The Jewish Agency accepted the plan, but the Palestinian Arab Higher Committee, with the support of the Arab League, rejected it. Britain, while accepting the plan, refused to enforce it, as it had not been accepted by both sides. After the passing of the UN resolution, hostilities between the Arab and Jewish communities broke out and increased as the date for British withdrawal came closer.

In September 1947, the British government announced unilaterally that the mandate would end on May 14, 1948. In late April 1948, Egypt, Syria, Iraq, Lebanon and Transjordan began preparations for their invasion of the Jewish areas of Palestine. By May 1948, two hundred and fifty thousand Palestinian Arabs had fled to neighbouring states or had been evicted. In Haifa, the Arab Higher Committee's refusal to allow the Arab population to remain under Jewish control contributed to the departure of most of them from the city. The Jews destroyed most of the Arab villages along the route between Tel Aviv and Jerusalem and, in anticipation of invasion, forced the eviction of Arab communities from strategic areas and from along major routes leading from the borders.

Following the final British withdrawal, the state of Israel was declared on May 14, 1948, in accordance with the UN partition plan. Five Arab countries—Egypt, Syria, Jordan, Lebanon and Iraq—immediately declared war on the new country.

---

[17]   http://www.yale.edu/lawweb/avalon/un/res181.htm, accessed 4 Feb 2012

The Arab-Israeli Wars

In May 1948, the Arab states invaded Israel from Lebanon, Syria, Transjordan and Egypt and, initially, were successful. However, the Israelis soon recovered. The UN appointed a mediator, the Swede, Count Folke Bernadotte, whose efforts resulted in a month-long truce that went into effect on June 11, providing both sides with an opportunity to recover and regroup. After the expiry of the truce period, the Israelis took the initiative and went on the offensive. By then they had merged all the various militias into the Israel Defence Forces and had an army of about fifty thousand; their organisation and equipment were improving all the time. Arab supply routes were long and weak, and as the war dragged on, they had problems replenishing their supplies.

On July 15, a second truce was negotiated. In September, members of the Israeli Stern Gang, the leadership of which included future prime minister, Yitzhak Shamir, assassinated Count Folke Bernadotte. By early October, the second truce had broken down. On January 7, 1949, at the request of Egypt, the UN arranged an armistice. Rhodes was the venue for peace talks, leading to Israel signing armistice agreements with Egypt, Lebanon, Transjordan and Syria although no actual peace agreements were signed at the time. Later, Egypt became the first Arab country to sign a peace treaty with Israel in 1979, and Jordan followed in 1994. Technically, Syria and Lebanon are still at war with Israel, as neither country has signed a formal peace treaty with the country; however, Lebanon did not participate in the subsequent Arab-Israel wars in 1956, 1967 and 1973. The armistices established Israel's new borders, giving the new state more than had been envisaged in the UN partition plan. Jordanian forces remained in occupation of the West Bank and East Jerusalem, exactly where the British had stationed them before the war. Jordan later annexed the areas it occupied while Egypt kept the Gaza Strip as an occupied zone.

According to United Nations figures, 726,000 Palestinians had fled or were evicted by the Israelis between 1947 and 1949, mainly to Jordan, Syria and Lebanon.[18] Most of the Palestinian refugees ended up in large refugee camps in poor, overcrowded conditions and, generally, were denied citizenship and civil rights by the Arab countries that hosted them. Today many of these refugees who are still living, and their descendants, still occupy such camps in Lebanon, Syria and Gaza, although those who went to Jordan have largely been assimilated into the general population and have been granted citizenship.

In December 1949, the UN, in response to a British proposal, established the United Nations Relief and Works Agency (UNRWA) to provide aid to the Palestinian refugees. The agency still operates and is the only UN agency dedicated to a single group of refugees. Following the armistice, Jewish immigration to Israel increased dramatically, including almost all of the Jewish population from Arab countries as well as Holocaust survivors from Europe. The Law of Return, which granted to all Jews and those of Jewish ancestry and their spouses, the right to settle in Israel and gain citizenship came into effect in 1950; in the first ten years of the country's existence, the population increased from about eight hundred thousand to over two million.

The 1948-1949 Arab-Israeli war was the first of four major conflicts. In 1956, following three years of clashes along Israel's borders with the Arab countries, Israeli forces launched an attack on Egypt on October 29. This had been preceded by a secret agreement with France and Britain to coordinate military action. The plan would allow the latter to regain control of the Suez Canal that had been nationalised by Egypt in July 1956, following the United States' decision to withdraw financial support for the construction of the Aswan High Dam and, they hoped, weaken Egyptian president Gamal Abdel Nasser's hold on power.

As agreed, following the Israeli attack on Egypt, Britain and France demanded that both sides withdraw from the Canal Zone and allow them to station troops there. As expected, Egypt refused, and this

---

[18]   http://www.mideastweb.org/refugees1.htm, accessed 4 Feb 2012

was followed by joint British and French air strikes, which included bombing an air base near Cairo and were aimed to destroy the Egyptian air force. Egyptian president Nasser responded by sinking all forty ships then in transit through the Suez Canal, which closed it to shipping for several months, this delaying oil deliveries to Europe and leading to the reimposition of petrol rationing in Britain. Meanwhile, Israel occupied all of the Sinai area, and on November 5, British and French forces landed in the Canal Zone, occupying Port Said.

The actions of Israel, Britain and France were strongly condemned in the United Nations, and two days later, a call for a cease-fire was accepted. A United Nations force was established to supervise the separation of Israeli and Egyptian forces in Sinai, and eventually, Israel withdrew from the area. Britain and France were forced, by international pressure, to withdraw from the Canal Zone. The Soviet Union stepped into the breach to finance the completion of the Aswan High Dam, and Nasser survived as Egyptian president and was a significant influence in the region until his death, from a heart attack, on September 28, 1970. Many in the Arab world are still convinced that he did not die from natural causes.

The next major conflict, the Six-Day War, began in May 1967 when Egypt, Syria and Jordan began building up their forces along their borders with Israel. Egypt cut off Israeli access to the Red Sea by closing the Straits of Tiran at the mouth of the Gulf of Aqaba to Israeli shipping and demanded the withdrawal of the UN force in Sinai. On June 5, Israel launched air strikes and within twenty-four hours had virtually destroyed the Egyptian, Jordanian and Syrian air forces. Over the next few days, Israel gained control of Sinai and Gaza from Egypt, the Golan Heights from Syria and the West Bank and East Jerusalem from Jordan. On June 11, all parties accepted a UN call for a cease-fire. Israel effectively annexed East Jerusalem immediately and formally annexed the Golan Heights in 1981, although neither moves have been recognised internationally. Following this conflict, on November 22, 1967, the United Nations Security Council adopted Resolution 242 which said in part:

Affirms that the fulfilment of Charter principles requires the establishment of a just and lasting peace in the Middle East which should include the application of both the following principles:

- Withdrawal of Israeli armed forces from territories occupied in the recent conflict;
- Termination of all claims or states of belligerency and respect for and acknowledgement of the sovereignty, territorial integrity and political independence of every State in the area and their right to live in peace within secure and recognized boundaries free from threats or acts of force;

Affirms further the necessity

- For guaranteeing freedom of navigation through international waterways in the area;
- For achieving a just settlement of the refugee problem;
- For guaranteeing the territorial inviolability and political independence of every State in the area, through measures including the establishment of demilitarized zones.

All parties accepted this "land for peace" plan, although perhaps each put its own interpretation on the text. It has been the basis of all subsequent negotiations, none of which has succeeded in producing the "just and lasting peace" envisaged by Resolution 242.

The fourth and, so far, last major conflict was in 1973. On October 6, Yom Kippur, the holiest day in the Jewish calendar, that in this year fell during the Muslim holy month of Ramadan, Egypt and Syria mounted surprise, coordinated attacks on Israel. During the first three days, the Syrians made substantial gains in the Golan Heights and Egyptian forces crossed the Suez Canal into occupied Sinai. However, Israel quickly recovered, and their forces moved from the Golan Heights farther into Syria, reaching a point forty kilometres from Damascus while on the Egyptian front, having crossed the Suez Canal, they were only one hundred kilometres from Cairo. A first attempt at a cease-fire on October 22 was not successful, but on October 25, one was imposed.

In September 1978, following secret negotiations, Egyptian president Anwar Sadat and Israeli prime minister Menachem Begin signed the Camp David Accords, intended to be frameworks for a peace treaty between the two countries and for a settlement of the Israeli-Palestinian problem. This did lead to the conclusion of a peace treaty between Israel and Egypt the following year but contributed little to the solution to the main problem in the region. An outcome of the Madrid Conference in 1991 was a peace treaty between Israel and Jordan, concluded in October 1994, making Jordan the second Arab country after Egypt to make peace with Israel. The treaty normalised relations between the two countries and resolved territorial disputes.

Talks between Syria and Israel, sometimes direct and sometimes through intermediaries, have occurred from time to time over the years since 1973. In US-sponsored talks in 1999, Israeli prime minister Ehud Barak offered to return virtually all of the Golan Heights to Syria, save for a small strip of land on the eastern side of Lake Galilee. Unusually, Syria showed flexibility, but Barak then got cold feet, and the talks ended.[19] It is interesting to speculate about the effects on Lebanon, had the talks led to a peace treaty between Syria and Israel—this I shall do later in this book.

The Palestinian-Israeli Conflict

Meanwhile, in May 1964, at an Arab League summit in Cairo, the Palestine Liberation Organisation (PLO), initially led by Ahmed Al Shukairy, was founded, with the goal of liberating Palestine through armed struggle. After Yasser Arafat replaced Shukairy as PLO chairman, Shukairy lived in Shemlan, the Lebanese village in

---

[19]   Blanford, Nicholas, Warriors of God, 2011, Random House, New York

which MECAS, the Arabic language school that I was to attend, was located. The original PLO charter claimed Palestine as the area defined at the time of the British Mandate and called for a right of return of refugees and self-determination for Palestinians. Egypt and Jordan were in favour of a Palestinian state on land they considered occupied by Israel, but in their view, this excluded lands under Jordanian and Egyptian military occupation, at the time amounting to 53 percent of the territory allocated to Arabs under the 1948 UN Partition Plan. As a result, the charter excluded any claim to territorial sovereignty over the West Bank and the Gaza Strip. There was no mention of statehood in the original charter; however, ten years later, in 1974, by which time Yasser Arafat was the leader of the organisation, the PLO called for an independent state in the territory of the British Mandate for Palestine.[20]

Over the years, the PLO has included various factions, the political leanings of which have been left wing, advocating varying degrees of militancy. Among the groups that have been included under the PLO umbrella from time to time are:

- Fatah—the largest faction, advocating left-wing nationalism
- Popular Front for the Liberation of Palestine (PFLP)—second largest, radically far-left militant and communist
- Democratic Front for the Liberation of Palestine (DFLP)—third largest, communist
- Palestinian People's Party (PPP)—social democratic, non-militant
- Palestine Liberation Front (PLF)—a minor left-wing faction
- Arab Liberation Front (ALF)—a minor faction, aligned to the Iraqi Ba'ath Party
- As-Sa'iqa—Syrian-controlled Ba'athist faction
- Palestine Democratic Union (FIDA)—a minor left-wing faction, non-militant

---

[20] http://www.un.int/wcm/content/site/palestine/cache/offonce/pid/12354;jsess ionid=704B7796CCBC72ACC579828A2197F8B9, accessed 31 Jan 2012

- Palestinian Popular Struggle Front (PPSF)—minor left-wing faction
- Palestinian Arab Front (PAF)—a minor faction[21]

Over one hundred countries have recognised the PLO as "the sole legitimate representative of the Palestinian people," and in 1974, it was granted observer status at the UN. The resounding victory of Israel over the Arab states in the 1967 war led to changes in the structure of the PLO and a more radical policy of guerrilla warfare against Israel. With the support of Jordan during 1969 and 1970, there were many attacks on Israeli targets, leading to Israel raiding PLO bases in Jordan. In September 1970, King Hussein of Jordan decided to end the Palestinian activity in his country, which was becoming a threat to his rule. The violence in Black September led to the expulsion of the PLO and its guerrillas from Jordan, and they found a new haven in Lebanon. Here they based their activities in the fertile environment of the many refugee camps and in areas of southern Lebanon where Palestinians had already established themselves since 1968.

Throughout the 1970s and 1980s, the PLO undertook a number of attacks, the most notorious of which included the following:

- The 1970 Avivim school bus massacre by the PFLP, which resulted in the death of nine Israeli children and three adults and crippled nineteen.
- The 1970 Dawson's Field hijackings in which four aircraft, belonging to TWA, Swissair, BOAC (now British Airways) and Pan American Airways were hijacked by the PFLP. The Pan American Boeing 747 was flown to Cairo and blown up there; the other three were flown to a disused RAF airstrip in Jordan, Dawson's Field, and eventually blown up there. This event precipitated Black September in Jordan.
- The 1972 Lod Airport massacre when, on behalf of the PFLP, Japanese Red Army members entered the waiting area of Lod Airport in Tel Aviv and fired indiscriminately at airport

---

[21]   http://en.wikipedia.org/wiki/Palestine_Liberation_Organization

staff and visitors, killing twenty-four people and injuring seventy-eight.

- In 1972, the Munich massacre of Israeli Olympic athletes by Black September.
- In 1974, the Ma'alot massacre by the DFLP, in which a school in Israel was seized, and a total of twenty-six students and adults were killed and over seventy were wounded.
- The 1978 Coastal Road massacre killing thirty-seven Israelis and wounding seventy-six, carried out by Fatah.
- In October 1985, the hijacking of the cruise ship *Achille Lauro* to Syria and holding its passengers and crew hostage by the PLF, demanding the release of fifty Palestinians in Israeli prisons. One passenger, Leon Klinghoffer, a Jewish American, who was celebrating his thirty-sixth wedding anniversary with his wife, was shot in the forehead and chest while sitting in his wheelchair.
- In December 1985, intending to hijack El Al jets and blow them up over Tel Aviv, Palestinian gunmen opened fire with rifles and grenades at the international airports in Rome and Vienna, killing eighteen civilians and wounding 138. Six of the seven terrorists were either killed or captured. Responsibility was claimed by the Abu Nidal Organisation.

Events such as these, together with cross-border attacks on Israel from Lebanon by the PLO, led to retaliatory attacks against individuals believed to be members of Palestinian groups and on targets in south Lebanon.

An incident in December 1987, when an Israeli army tank transporter ran into a group of Palestinians from Jabalya refugee camp in the Gaza Strip, killing four and injuring seven, marked the start of the First Intifada (an Arabic word, literally meaning "shaking off" but usually translated as "uprising" or "resistance").[22] Violence, riots, general strikes and civil disobedience campaigns by Palestinians spread across the West Bank and Gaza Strip, largely because of

---

[22] http://www.palestinefacts.org/pf_1967to1991_intifada_1987.php, accessed 31 Jan 2012

the frustrations felt by the Palestinian population following Israel's capture of these areas in the 1967 war. Since then, Israeli settlements in the occupied areas had increased (and have continued to do so ever since), a factor that has made any negotiating process even more difficult than before. Israeli forces responded with tear gas, plastic bullets and live ammunition. Soon after the outbreak of the First Intifada, Hamas (Islamic Resistance Movement) was founded and quickly began to carry out attacks on Israeli targets, initially military but in time civilian as well.

In August 1988, Jordan separated the West Bank from Jordan legally and administratively, abandoning its claim to the area in favour of the PLO. This was followed in November by a unilateral declaration of the establishment of a Palestinian state by the Palestine National Council meeting in Algiers. The following month, Yasser Arafat, now having assumed the title of president of Palestine, said that the PLO would support a solution to the conflict based on UN resolutions 242 and 338. Thus, he effectively, but not specifically, recognised Israel's right to exist within its pre-1967 borders, provided that the Palestinians would be able to establish their own country in the West Bank and Gaza.

Under the sponsorship of the United States and the Soviet Union, a conference convened in Madrid in October 1991, marking the first coordinated attempt by the international community to start a peace process involving not just Israel and the Palestinians, but all other Arab states as well. This was the first time since the Rhodes conference in 1949 that ended the first Arab-Israel war that all the parties had sat down together. Due to Israeli objections, the PLO was required to be part of a joint Jordanian-Palestinian delegation, but in spite of these objections, throughout the conference the Palestinians in the team were in regular contact with the PLO, at that time headquartered in Tunis.

The Madrid Conference led to secret negotiations between Israel and the PLO in Oslo, culminating with the first face-to-face agreement between the two parties, the Declaration of Principles on Interim Self-Government Arrangements. These Oslo Accords, as they became known, announced in August 1993, were intended to be a framework for future negotiations and relations between the Israeli government and Palestinians, within which all outstanding "final status issues" would be addressed and resolved. This effectively ended the First Intifada. Prior to the signing of the accords, the PLO recognised the right of Israel to exist in peace and security, and Israel in turn recognised the PLO as the representative of the Palestinian people. This achievement led to the award of the Nobel Peace Prize to Yasser Arafat, Shimon Peres and Yitzhak Rabin in 1994. Considering the lack of progress since the Madrid Conference, one may be forgiven for thinking that the Nobel Committee was somewhat premature in granting this award.

Following on from the Oslo Accords, on September 24, 1995, Israel and the PLO signed an Interim Agreement on the West Bank and the Gaza Strip, sometimes called Oslo II, at the Egyptian Sinai resort of Taba. A few days later, on September 28, PLO chairman Yasser Arafat and Israeli prime minister Yitzhak Rabin signed the formal agreement in Washington, DC in the presence of US president Bill Clinton. The most significant provision of the interim agreement was the establishment of a Palestinian Interim Self-Government Authority, an elected body known as the Palestinian Legislative Council, which would consist of eighty-two members elected from the West Bank and Gaza Strip. It set out the powers and responsibilities of the council and the matters that the Israeli government would transfer to the council's jurisdiction. A clause on cooperation said, in part, that both sides

> shall accordingly abstain from incitement, including hostile propaganda, against each other and that their respective educational systems contribute to the peace between the Israeli and Palestinian peoples and to peace in the entire region, and will refrain from the introduction of any motifs that could adversely affect the process of reconciliation.

Both parties largely ignored these very desirable sentiments. The Interim Agreement of 1995 became the basis for subsequent negotiations and agreements, including the Hebron Protocol of 1997, the Wye River Memorandum of 1998 and the road map for peace of 2002.

In January 1997, Yasser Arafat and Benjamin Netanyahu agreed to the terms of the Hebron Protocol, which included an Israeli withdrawal from 80 percent of Hebron within ten days; Israeli withdrawal from rural areas of the West Bank in two stages and final withdrawal from all areas of the West Bank apart from settlements and military locations by mid-1998. The agreement also envisaged the commencement of final status negotiations, which were to be completed by May 1999.

The Wye River Memorandum of October 1998 was the next step in attempts to move forward with the interim agreement. A summit between Yasser Arafat and Benjamin Netanyahu was hosted by US president Bill Clinton at the Wye River Conference Centre in Maryland. The agreement included further transfers of areas of the West Bank to full Palestinian control, action by the Palestinian Authority to combat terrorist organisations and illegal weapons, security cooperation, various economic issues including the opening of Gaza port and the resumption of permanent status negotiations. Although some small transfers of areas to the Palestinians were made, little more was achieved from this agreement.

Continuing his efforts to find a solution to the Palestinian-Israeli conflict, US president Bill Clinton convened the Camp David Summit in July 2000, between Israeli prime minister Ehud Barak and Palestinian Authority chairman Yasser Arafat. It was aimed at reaching a final status agreement based on the provision in the Oslo Accords of 1993 that agreement should be reached on all outstanding issues between the Palestinians and Israeli sides—the so-called final status settlement—within five years of the implementation of Palestinian autonomy. The summit ended on July 25, without reaching an agreement, but with a statement in which Arafat and Barak agreed on the following principles to guide future negotiations:

- The two sides agreed that the aim of their negotiations was to put an end to decades of conflict and achieve a just and lasting peace.
- The two sides committed themselves to continue their efforts to conclude an agreement on all permanent status issues as soon as possible.
- Both sides agreed that negotiations based on UN Security Council resolutions 242 and 338 were the only way to achieve such an agreement, and they undertook to create an environment for negotiations free from pressure, intimidation and threats of violence.
- The two sides understood the importance of avoiding unilateral actions that prejudged the outcome of negotiations and that their differences would be resolved only by good faith negotiations.
- Both sides agreed that the United States remained a vital partner in the search for peace and would continue to consult closely with President Clinton and Secretary Albright in the period ahead.

On September 28, 2000, right-wing Israeli opposition leader, Ariel Sharon, made a provocative visit to the Temple Mount in Jerusalem that had been administered by the Muslim community as a *waqf* (a religious endowment in Islamic law, denoting a building or plot of land for Muslim religious or charitable purposes) since the time of the Crusades. The day after the visit, violent confrontations erupted between Muslims and the Israeli Police, marking the start of the Second Intifada.

The outbreak of the Second Intifada, the failure of the Camp David Summit, upcoming elections in Israel and the imminent end of his second term prompted US president Bill Clinton to offer his parameters for a Permanent Status Agreement in late 2000. The Clinton Parameters, which were presented to both sides on December 23, 2000, were a non-negotiable take-it-or-leave-it plan that could be accepted or rejected with no possibility of changes. The parameters included the following:

- Palestinian sovereignty over Arab areas of East Jerusalem, the entire Gaza Strip, plus a contiguous Palestinian area of about 96 percent of the West Bank involving land swaps to compensate for areas annexed by Israel, which included 80 percent of the Israeli settlers.
- Palestinian waiver of the right of return to areas that had become part of Israel and Israeli recognition of the need to address the refugee problem in conjunction with an international commission. The new Palestinian state was to accept all refugees who wanted to settle in it with the remainder being assimilated in their host countries or assisted to immigrate to third countries. Only a very limited number would be allowed to settle in Israel.
- Security arrangements, including an international force in the Jordan Valley for three years, Israel being allowed to establish radar installations in the West Bank and limitations on the strength of Palestinian armed forces.
- The ending of the conflict by the passing of a UN Security Council resolution declaring that previous resolutions 242 and 338 had been implemented.

Both sides chose to accept the Clinton Parameters, but with "reservations" which effectively killed the idea. The main reservations of both sides related to the core problems of the right of return and Jerusalem.

The Second Intifada continued; there were civilian strikes and riots, attacks on Israeli settlers, suicide bombings and military conflicts between the Israel Defence Forces and the Palestinian forces. Israelis considered the Second Intifada to be planned terrorism whereas the Palestinians thought of it as part of their struggle to establish their own state. Israel enforced strict curfews in some areas and set up checkpoints to control the movement of Palestinians.

After almost two years, in March 2002, the UN Security Council adopted Resolution 1397, demanding an end to violence. The resolution was significant in that it mentioned "a vision of a region where two states, Israel and Palestine, live side by side within secure and recognised borders." It was the first UN resolution to mention the two-state solution, although the Peel Commission report conceived the idea in 1937, and the 1947 partition plan included it.

In March 2002, an Arab League Summit in Beirut made an unprecedented proposal, which originated from Saudi Arabia, for a comprehensive peace treaty between Israel and all Arab states, including normalisation of relations, in exchange for an Israeli withdrawal from the territory occupied in the 1967 war and a just settlement of the refugee issue. Although the offer was endorsed unanimously, there were a number of absences among Arab heads of state, including King Hussein of Jordan and Egyptian president Hosni Mubarak. Israel prevented Yasser Arafat from attending by informing him that if he left the West Bank, he would not be allowed to return; he participated in the conference via a video link. Attempts to arrange a cease-fire to give the proposal a chance to succeed failed; the Second Intifada continued until November 2006, when a truce was implemented between Israel and the Palestinian Authority. The offer was repeated at a 2007 Arab League Summit but to no avail; Israel has still failed to respond officially.

In April 2002, the Quartet on the Middle East was established, consisting of the United Nations, the European Union, the United States and Russia. It was intended to be a forum to follow up and encourage peace initiatives. In April 2003, at a meeting in Egypt, the Quartet announced a road map for peace, which gained the support of Arab leaders. The plan had originally been announced by US president George W. Bush who optimistically described it as "the framework for progress towards lasting peace and security in the Middle East." Notwithstanding the view of the Quartet's special envoy, former British prime minister Tony Blair, that solving the Arab-Israeli problem could be easier than solving the Northern Ireland situation (something he had achieved when prime minister), little has been accomplished by Mr. Blair or this group.

In an attempt to reduce Palestinian attacks on targets within Israel, in June 2002, the Israeli government began construction of a 760 kilometres (475 miles) long security fence to separate the country from the West Bank. The line of the barrier follows the 1949 armistice line in part, but much of it is within Palestinian territory, causing the United Nations to describe it as "an unlawful act of annexation." Likewise, the International Court of Justice has opined that the barrier is illegal under international law.

In March 2003, in part the result of the Quartet's initiative and in an Israeli and United States attempt to sideline Yasser Arafat, Mahmoud Abbas was appointed as the first Palestinian prime minister. Following the death of Yasser Arafat in November 2004 (widely believed in the Arab world to have been caused by poisoning by the Israeli intelligence organisation, Mossad),[23] Abbas became head of the PLO and, in January 2005, was elected as president of the Palestinian National Authority.

Israel unilaterally withdrew from the Gaza Strip in August and September 2005, removing all settlements and military equipment in the process. Although there is now no Israeli presence or jurisdiction in Gaza, Israel still controls airspace, borders and ports, making the inhabitants virtual prisoners in the Strip. Since the withdrawal, Palestinian militant groups have used Gaza as a base to launch rocket attacks against Israel.

In January 2006, Hamas, the Islamic group, secured an unexpected victory in elections for the Palestinian parliament. They won seventy-four seats, compared with Fatah's forty-five, in the 132-seat assembly in an election that saw a turnout of about 74 percent of the eligible voters. There were no credible allegations of vote rigging or other irregularities. The head of the European Parliament's monitoring team, Edward McMillan-Scott, described the polls as "extremely professional, in line with international standards, free, transparent and without violence." His colleague, Italian Communist MEP Luisa Morgantini said there was "a very professional attitude,

---

[23]   http://www.aljazeerah.info/News/2009/July/21%20n/Israeli%20Mossad%20
         poisoned%20Arafat%20through%20his%20medications,%20says%20
         Bassam%20Abu%20Sharif.htm, accessed 31 Jan 2012

competence and respect for the rules."[24] Notwithstanding these views, the United States, the European Union, Israel and some other countries announced that they would not deal with the democratically elected Palestinian government controlled by Hamas unless the party renounced violence. Aid was significantly curtailed, and economic sanctions imposed. Following the elections, in January 2007, after Saudi sponsored negotiations, Hamas and Fatah formed a national unity government with Hamas as leader and Ismail Haniya as prime minister. The marriage did not last long. In June 2007, Hamas took control of Gaza and removed all Fatah members from government positions there. As a result, the Palestinian territories now consist of two areas, the West Bank, controlled by Fatah, and Gaza, controlled by Hamas.

After the Hamas takeover of Gaza, Israel and Egypt imposed a total land, sea and air blockade of the area while, at the same time, terminating the international sanctions against the Fatah-controlled West Bank. Israel claimed that the blockade was necessary to limit Palestinian rocket attacks on its cities from the Gaza Strip and to prevent Hamas from obtaining other weapons. At the time, Egypt maintained that it could not fully open its side of the border since doing so would represent Egyptian recognition of the Hamas control of Gaza, undermine the legitimacy of the Palestinian National Authority and formalise the split between Gaza and the West Bank. The blockade against Gaza, intended to weaken Hamas, has caused severe shortages of virtually everything, great hardship for the inhabitants and contributed to very high unemployment. Even UNRWA has difficulty in importing goods for its humanitarian work. There has been some easing of the blockade since mid-2010, but the UN has concluded, in February 2011, that there has been little improvement in people's livelihoods because of the easing.[25] After the 2011 revolution in Egypt, the new leadership opened the Rafah crossing to the Gaza Strip on May 28, but only for women,

---

[24] http://domino.un.org/UNISPAL.NSF/db942872b9eae454852560f6005a76fb /236f02cf539aa9418525710600587785, accessed 31 Jan 2012

[25] http://www.ochaopt.org/documents/ocha_opt_special_easing_the_ blockade_2011_03_english.pdf, accessed 31 Jan 2012

children and men aged over forty. Men aged between eighteen and forty require a permit to cross. Trade is prohibited, and Palestinians leaving Gaza are required to carry ID cards issued by Israel.

Meanwhile, in November 2007, US secretary of state Condoleezza Rice organised the Annapolis Conference to which over forty countries and organisations were invited. The conference was held during a month that included the thirtieth anniversary of Anwar Sadat's historic visit to Israel in 1977 to sign a peace agreement and the sixtieth anniversary of the United Nations approval of the Partition Plan in 1947. This plan had proposed dividing Palestine into two states, one Arab and one Jewish, with Jerusalem to be designated an international city under UN control. The objective of the conference was to produce a substantive document on resolving the Israeli-Palestinian conflict along the lines of President George W. Bush's road map for peace, with the eventual establishment of a Palestinian state. It only produced a joint statement, signed by Mahmoud Abbas and Ehud Olmert, which said, in part:

> we agreed to immediately launch good faith, bilateral negotiations in order to conclude a peace treaty resolving all outstanding issues, including core issues, without exception, and that, the final peace settlement will establish Palestine as a homeland for the Palestinian people just as Israel is the homeland for the Jewish people.

Yet more fine-sounding words, which led to nothing. A year later, Israel launched Operation Cast Lead invading Gaza again in response to renewed Hamas rocket attacks on Israeli civilian targets. After twenty-two days of fighting during which over one thousand four hundred Palestinians were killed, Israel and Hamas each declared separate unilateral cease-fires. In September 2010, US president Barrack Obama tried to launch direct negotiations between the Palestinian Authority and Israel, but these failed when, in response to political pressure from his extreme right-wing supporters, Israeli prime minister Netanyahu refused to extend a freeze on settlements on the West Bank.

Conclusion

More than ninety years after the Balfour Declaration, more than sixty years after the creation of the state of Israel and after four Arab Israeli wars. After prolonged Palestinian resistance, both violent and peaceful, to what it considers occupation of its land, after innumerable UN resolutions, peace conferences, negotiations and road maps, a solution to the problem seems as elusive as ever. Indeed, at the time of writing, no one is even talking about talks, let alone getting down to serious negotiations. Every year that passes makes a solution more difficult; the core issues are well known—borders, refugees and the "right of return," settlers and the status of Jerusalem—and neither side is ever going to obtain 100 percent of its stated aims. Meanwhile, some five million people of Palestinian origin (the number eligible for UNRWA services) one-third of who live in fifty-eight recognised refugee camps in Jordan, Lebanon, Syria, the Gaza Strip and the West Bank, including East Jerusalem, await a solution.[26]

---

[26]   http://www.unrwa.org/userfiles/2011080123958.pdf, accessed 31 Jan 2012

Chapter 5

BAHRAIN

Nineteen sixty-nine was the year in which the Beatles gave their last public performance, the Boeing 747 made its maiden flight, Neil Armstrong became the first man to set foot on the moon, regular colour television broadcasts began in Britain and the half penny ceased to be legal tender in the United Kingdom. Among events that were to influence my future life, Yasser Arafat was elected as leader of the Palestine Liberation Organisation, the first Concorde test flight was successfully concluded and the Stonewall riots in New York marked the start of the gay rights movement in the United States and throughout the world.

There was a coup d'état in Libya replacing the monarchy with Col. Muammar Gaddafi, the first automatic teller machine was installed in a bank in New York and the first message was sent over ARPANET, the forerunner of the Internet. The section of my school magazine, the *Pastonian*, devoted to the activities of old boys, noted, "S C L Hickey has exchanged the rigours of the Canadian winter for a hot, humid Bahrain summer."

In January 1969, while on a visit to England from Canada, I had arranged interviews with a number of British banks with overseas networks. These included the Hong Kong and Shanghai Banking Corporation (as it was then named, now HSBC Bank in most of its worldwide locations), Chartered Bank (since absorbed into

Standard Chartered Bank) and The British Bank of the Middle East (BBME). BBME was then a wholly owned subsidiary of the Hong Kong and Shanghai Banking Corporation and since then has been renamed HSBC Bank Middle East Limited. In response to my initial application, BBME provided me with a booklet entitled *A Career in Overseas Banking*. The opening paragraph announced that the booklet "outlines the opportunities offered by The British Bank of The Middle East to adventurous young men of character and ability who wish to make their careers abroad in work, important to Britain, which renders outstanding service to the countries in which it is performed, which is full of interest and from which a man may eventually retire knowing that he has made his contribution to the pioneer development of a key region of the world."

Powerful words indeed. I read on to discover that the bank had been established in 1889 as the Imperial Bank of Persia and had gone through several name changes before reaching its present form in 1952. Although the bank had withdrawn from Persia (as Iran was then called) in 1952, by 1969, it had branches, affiliates and associates in places ranging from Casablanca to Bombay and Tehran to Aden, with a large concentration of branches in the Arabian Gulf, where it had often been the first bank to be established in many of the sheikhdoms. The bank established branches in Kuwait in 1942, Bahrain in 1944, Dubai in 1946 and Muscat in 1948.[27]

I attended an interview at the bank's London office and in due course, after my return to Toronto, was offered employment on the foreign staff. We agreed that I would report to the London office for a period of familiarisation and training in mid-March 1969, and this I did. On arrival, I was informed that I would only be able to spend one week in London, following which I would be given two weeks embarkation leave before flying to my first posting—Bahrain. This was a much shorter stay in Britain than I had expected and necessitated dealing with a number of personal and business matters very quickly.

---

[27]   HSBC A Brief History, 2009, HSBC Group Archives, London

It was the bank's practice to pay an outfit allowance of £200 upon first appointment to the foreign staff. This was duly received, and I was advised that the best place to spend it would be at a shop called Alkit Limited, situated in Cambridge Circus, at the junction of Charing Cross Road and Shaftesbury Avenue. This firm had outfitted several generations of men setting out for India and other points east, and one could still purchase a solar topee or a canvas washbasin on a wooden stand, although I resisted the temptation to do so. The bank strongly suggested that my purchases should include a dinner jacket, an item of clothing that I had not hitherto owned. In spite of the recommendation from the bank to all of its overseas staff and the fact that it was the preferred outfitter for many military officers, Alkit went into liquidation in 1989, and the site is now a Pizza Hut restaurant. Was the decline in demand for solar topees responsible for Alkit's demise I wonder?

Before starting my embarkation leave, I was provided with my BOAC (British Overseas Airways Corporation, now British Airways) ticket from London to Bahrain, departing on April 9, 1969. Subsequently, because of a strike at BOAC, my reservation was changed to a Qantas flight leaving later in the day, which meant that my arrival at Muharraq airport in Bahrain was at a somewhat antisocial time in the early hours of Friday, April 10. I was met by two colleagues who transported me to the bank's bachelors' mess situated in Yateem Gardens, then one of the upmarket residential areas of the capital, Manama, favoured by foreigners. Neighbours included other bankers, senior managers of British companies and the Australian trade commissioner.

At that time, there were usually five foreign staff bachelors working in the bank in Bahrain, and they were accommodated in the bachelors' mess, which was run along the same lines as a *chummery* in circumstances reminiscent of the Raj. The building was protected at night by a *chowkidar* (derived from a Hindi word meaning one that inhabits a guardhouse), and our laundry was collected regularly by the *dhobi* (derived from the Hindi word *dhona*, meaning to wash). Married colleagues with children might employ an *ayah*, a word also derived from Hindi to describe a nursemaid or governess.

At the bachelors' mess, we each had our own room with a private bathroom and shared communal living and dining facilities. The bank employed a cook and a houseboy to attend to our needs, and the general running of the household was organised by the mess president, usually the officer who had been living there the longest.

In order to be able to buy alcoholic drinks in Bahrain, all non-Muslims had to obtain a permit, which they could then use at the two importers authorised to supply alcohol. In the case of the BBME mess, the permit was issued in the name of the mess, thus making it unnecessary to obtain new permits for each officer as he arrived. The mess maintained accounts at a *cold store* (grocery shop), and one of the two companies authorised to supply alcoholic drinks, to which all purchases were charged. At the end of each month, the mess president would present each of us with a bill for our share of the communal expenses—mainly food and drinks.

At the time, Bahrain, as well as other sheikhdoms in the Arabian Gulf, was still in a treaty relationship with the United Kingdom, which had originated in 1820 when the joint rulers of Bahrain, sheikhs Salman and Abdulla, signed the general treaty with the East India Company. Later, in 1880 and 1892, the ruler and the British government signed two treaties, the terms of which included the ruler binding himself not to enter into any relationship with a foreign government other than the British, without the latter's consent. A British political agent took up residence in Bahrain in 1902, and the island became the centre for the British administration of all of the territories in the Gulf with which it had treaty relationships. During my time there, Sir Jeffrey Archer became the last chief political resident in the Gulf resident in Bahrain. The political agent was Alexander Stirling and the ruler was His Highness Sheikh Isa bin Salman al Khalifa,

Bab al Bahrain, 1969

who had succeeded his father in 1961 and ruled until his death in 1999. The prime minister was the ruler's brother, Sheikh Khalifa bin Salman Al Khalifa, who, more than forty years later, as I write this chapter, still holds that position in spite of serious anti-government protests in the country.

In accordance with the 1892 treaty with Great Britain, no other country had a diplomatic presence in Bahrain, although there were other types of representation, such as the Australian Trade Commission and the New Zealand Meat Marketing Board. British embassies around the world issued visas to non-British applicants to enter Bahrain; British citizens did not need a visa. The treaty relationship had also resulted in many government positions being filled initially by British subjects. Over time, many of the incumbents and their successors became advisors to Bahrainis appointed in their stead, but as late as 1969, the secretary to the government, the director of medical services, the postmaster, the director of public works and the director of transport were still all British. Indeed, my residence permit was signed (in green ink) by an Englishman, Harry Parrett, director of immigration.

Oil had been discovered in Bahrain in the 1920s, and exports commenced in 1932, before Saudi Arabia and other Gulf states began to discover and exploit their reserves. The country's reserves were small compared to its neighbours; production has never exceeded sixty thousand barrels per day (bpd) and in recent years settled around forty-eight thousand bpd. A refinery was built in 1935, the first in the Gulf, with a capacity of about two hundred fifty thousand bpd, most of which has always been supplied from Saudi Arabia via an undersea pipeline.

In 1969, there were four banks in Bahrain—the Eastern Bank, later merged with the Chartered Bank which, in turn became part of Standard Chartered Bank, which had been established in 1919; BBME, which had opened its first branch in 1944; National Bank of Bahrain, locally incorporated, which had commenced operations in 1957 and Arab Bank (Jordanian). Although more banks, both foreign and local, were to establish domestic operations in Bahrain in the next few years, it was only in the mid-1970s when the Bahrain Monetary Agency set up a system for licencing offshore banking units that the number of banks in the country increased dramatically.

When I arrived in Bahrain, the main branch of BBME was located in Khalifa Road, Manama, one block south from Government Road, which then ran beside the sea along the north coast of the island. All of the land now existing between Government Road and King Faisal Highway had yet to be reclaimed from the sea. The bank's normal opening hours to the public were 8:00 a.m. to 12:30 p.m. Saturday to Thursday, with staff generally working until 2:00 p.m. at which time we returned to the mess for lunch, the main meal of the day, followed by a siesta. Friday was the one-day weekend.

Site of Hilton Hotel Bahrain, yet to be reclaimed from the sea, 1970

Initially I was put in charge of the current accounts department. Through this department passed all vouchers originated in various departments of the branch for posting on the customers' ledger cards prior to cash being paid out or any value given. Any transaction creating an unauthorised overdraft was referred to the branch manager or assistant manager for approval before being released. This was an extremely busy department. As well as myself, there were two Bahraini officers, an Indian senior clerk, two

BBME Manama main branch, 1969

junior clerks, four accounting machine operators and two messengers whose main duty was to ferry the vouchers between departments. How these all ended up in the right place at the end of the day was then, and remains today, a mystery to me. Another job in the department was the personalisation of cheque books; in the days before MICR encoding, this was achieved by first embossing a metal plate with the customer's name and account number and then stamping each cheque in the book, using a manually operated addressograph machine, which created a lot of noise each time a cheque was stamped. In the afternoon, a second shift of four machine operators came on duty. Their job was to post all of the approved vouchers on the customers' statements after which one of the officers, working on a rotation basis, would check the postings and ensure that the balances on the ledger cards posted in the morning agreed with the statements posted in the afternoon. The person whose task this was had no opportunity for a siesta after lunch!

Echoes of the Raj did not end in the bachelors' mess. Both the bank and most of its customers employed Indian clerical staff to prepare correspondence, among other duties. Their English skills seemed to be based on the form of the language used in India from the time that the British first arrived there. Thus, the bank was often admonished to "do the needful" and in one letter was informed, "You will be intimated shortly."

In the course of my work in Bahrain, I first witnessed the practical uses of letters of credit (LC), which were the mainstay of the business of BBME in Bahrain and most of the banks for which I was to work in the region later. Essentially, an LC is an instrument, commonly used in international trade, issued by the bank of an importer, at the importer's request, in favour of an exporter in another country, which guarantees to the exporter that it will be paid for goods shipped upon presentation of certain documents evidencing such shipment. Usually the importer's bank will advise the LC to the exporter through its correspondent bank in the country in which the importer is located and will authorise this bank to pay the exporter to the debit of its account upon presentation to it of credit-conforming documents. Sometimes the correspondent bank will be asked to "confirm" the

LC; this constitutes a guarantee by the correspondent bank that payment will be made to the exporter if the correct documents are presented, even if the importer's bank has insufficient funds or otherwise fails to make payment. BBME's customer base in Bahrain included many of the major merchants in the country, and even in the days before the oil price boom, they were using the LC to cover the purchase of goods that they imported to fulfil the normal daily needs of the population, including foodstuffs, vehicles, building materials and consumer goods.

The author, Manager BBME Ghudabiya branch, 1970

In early 1970, I was transferred from the current accounts department to be manager of a small branch in Gudaibiya, a suburb of the capital, Manama. This branch served mainly the British navy and army units based on the island and their officers and a few local businesses and individuals living or working in the area. I had a staff of only four plus a messenger. This proved to be a much less hectic assignment than the main branch. Usually I had finished the day's work, including checking the posting of the customers' ledger cards and statements, and was home for lunch by 1:00 p.m. Afternoon work was not necessary here.

At this time, the bank used NCR Class 32 accounting machines for maintaining its customer records. Originally established as National Cash Register Company in 1884, by the 1960s NCR Corporation, as it was then called, had a virtual monopoly in the supply of equipment to banks

NCR Class 32 accounting machine, (The NCR Archive at Dayton History)

in the Gulf, having been established in each centre of the region for a long time. The Class 32 machine had first been conceived in 1950 and was used by all branches of BBME in the area as well as many other banks. So dependent was the bank on the company and because the bank was such a large customer, NCR ran a series of courses in Beirut to train BBME officers in the use of its products.

In October 1969, I was selected to attend one such course, scheduled to last a week. Much envied by my colleagues because I was to get the chance to visit the *Paris of the Middle East*, I joined colleagues from other branches in the Gulf at the Alcazar Hotel in Saint George's Bay in Beirut, which was conveniently situated a block from the NCR offices in Phoenicia Street, where the course was to be conducted.

St George's Bay, Beirut, 1969. The Alcazar Hotel is the building on the left

Surprisingly, considering the damage suffered in this area during the civil war in Lebanon, the company is still at the same address. The hotel was also conveniently located for Beirut's red-light district; whether or not any of the officers on the course visited this area, I could not say. BBME maintained its Saint George's Bay branch next door to the hotel. The Alcazar was destroyed during the Battle of the Hotels in the Lebanese civil war (1976-1990). On the site is now the main Beirut branch of HSBC Bank (Middle East) Ltd, as BBME has been renamed. The course covered several NCR products as well as the Class 32 accounting machine, and time was spent showing us how to construct the programme bars that controlled what the machine did and when.

The author (second from right) NCR course Beirut, October 1969

Unfortunately, the last two days of the course had to be cancelled because of the imposition of a curfew in Beirut following the outbreak of hostilities between Palestine Liberation Organisation guerrillas and Lebanese security forces. This was my first experience of the security problems that Lebanon was, and still is, experiencing. During our enforced stay in the hotel, some of us became bored, so we decided to venture out in spite of the curfew. We took a taxi and visited the Jeita Grotto just north of Beirut one of the natural wonders of the country. We returned to the hotel without mishap. The curfew was lifted in time for us all to fly back to the Gulf as scheduled on the Sunday.

Friday was the weekend in Bahrain and most of the region and was often spent at the ruler's beach at Zallaq, about halfway down the west coast of the island, where entrance was restricted to Westerners.

The ruler, His Highness Sheikh Isa bin Salman Al Khalifa, had a beach house there, and it was not uncommon to be invited to tea during the afternoon, especially if one's group included attractive young ladies. Another popular activity on Thursday or Friday was the curry lunch, a regular way to receive and repay hospitality, which was another legacy from the days when the Gulf was ruled from British India.

The ruler's beach, Bahrain, 1969

Among the customers of the bank at the time was the wife of an RAF corporal, based at Muharraq, whose account was very active and accumulated significant balances that, from time to time, she transferred to her account with one of the high street banks in England. Even in the days long before "know your customer" and anti-money laundering regulations, the size and regularity of the transfers caused her bank to make enquiries of the BBME head office in London, through which the Bahrain branch routed the payments. The head office duly wrote to the branch manager asking for his comments. It was generally believed that the customer in question was profiting from assisting members of the ruling family with introductions to expatriate ladies, some of whom, perhaps, had been sighted at the ruler's beach. The manager replied, with his usual dry humour, that the lady was a member of the oldest profession in the world; nothing more was heard on the subject.

A ritual, observed by all of the expatriate staff at BBME and many more from the foreign community, was to call on the ruler on the first day of the Eid holidays, one being at the end of the Muslim fasting month of Ramadan and the other at the culmination of the pilgrimage to Mecca known as the Hajj. We would make our way to the ruler's palace at Rifa'a, about ten kilometres (six miles) from Manama, where we would line up with all the other well-wishers, perhaps for some time, until it was our turn to shake His Highness's hand and wish him, "Eid Mubarak" (Blessed Eid).

Another Muslim observance, which took place not long after my arrival in Bahrain and which I was to experience again in Lebanon, many years later, was the Day of Ashura. This occurs on the tenth day of the Islamic month of Muharram when Shia Muslims commemorate the martyrdom of Hussein bin Ali, grandson of the Prophet Mohammed at the Battle of Karbala in AD 680. Shia Muslims still mourn his death on this day, and the story of the battle and martyrdom is related and sometimes performed. Although banned in some places, self-flagellation, using swords or chains to draw blood, sometimes takes place, as was the case in Bahrain in 1969, where the majority of the population were, and still are, Shia.

One of the first things I was encouraged to do shortly after my arrival was to join the British Club. This club, which still exists, was originally opened in 1935 when it was called the Gymkhana Club. Its facilities included a swimming pool, tennis courts, a mock-Tudor bar and a restaurant; the club was run very much as similar establishments had been operated in imperial India. Membership was limited to British citizens, and a proposer and seconder were required in order to have an application considered. Being an officer at BBME, I was virtually guaranteed acceptance! The British Club was also the venue chosen by the Royal Society of Saint George for its annual banquet and ball held on Saint George's Day. This was a black tie affair with toasts proposed to Her Majesty the Queen and His Highness the Ruler. The menu for the 1970 dinner included roast baron of beef and gooseberry pie and cream. It also notes, "Traditional red roses were presented by British Overseas Airways Corporation." In looking at the club's website as I wrote this chapter, I noticed that they were promoting their special Ramadan Friday lunch buffet; the choices included roast pork and apple sauce.[28] Not, perhaps, the most diplomatic choice to offer in a Muslim country during Ramadan, but surely a sign of the tolerance and cosmopolitan atmosphere that still is Bahrain.

The treaty arrangements with Britain meant that there was a presence of all three branches of the British armed forces on the island. The Royal Air Force was based at Muharraq, which also served as the civil international airport; the Royal Navy at Juffair, where they maintained a shore base and just one ship, a minesweeper, and the British Army, represented at the time by the Fourth Battalion, the Royal Anglian Regiment, at Hamala, in the desert, southwest of Manama. The British expatriate community, which was by far the largest group of Westerners in Bahrain at the time, regularly came into contact socially with the members of the armed services stationed in Bahrain, and BBME provided banking facilities to all three branches and many of their members.

I became involved in two theatre groups—Muharraq Amateur Dramatic Society, centred on RAF Muharraq, and Juffair Players and Singers, based at HMS Juffair, the Royal Navy headquarters. With the former, I was involved in four productions, *Sheer Madness*, a review devised by the group, *Bell, Book and Candle* by John Van Druten, Joe Orton's *Loot* and *Dear Charles* by Alan Melville with jobs ranging from business manager to lighting and

---

[28]   http://www.britishclubbahrain.com/menu.htm, accessed 27 July 2012

even onstage appearances. With the Juffair Players and Singers, I became the resident lighting expert, undertaking two major productions—Gilbert and Sullivan's *Iolanthe* and *South Pacific* by Rodgers and Hammerstein as well as William Douglas-Home's *The Reluctant Debutante* and *A Dead Secret* by Rodney Ackland. All of this added up to involvement in eight productions during the fifteen months that I lived in Bahrain. As if this were not enough, I advised the students of Muharraq school drama club on lighting for their December 1969 pantomime *The Rise and Fall of Dick Dimmington* and lit *Rosencrantz and Guildenstern are Dead* by Tom Stoppard for Manama Players at the British Council.

Another spare-time activity in Bahrain was being treasurer of the Christian Community Cemetery Committee, a voluntary organization made up of representatives of the various Christian churches and congregations on the island under the chairmanship of the British political resident. The churches included Saint Christopher's Cathedral (Anglican), the Sacred Heart Church (Roman Catholic), the National Evangelical Church, the Bahrain Malayalee Church of South India, Saint Mary's Orthodox Church (Greek Orthodox), Saint Peter's Jacobite Syrian Orthodox Church and the Mar Thoma Church. By tradition, it seemed that as the committee's bank account was with BBME then the treasurer should be from the bank. Thus, when a colleague, the incumbent treasurer, left the island, I took over the job.

On July 21, 1969, Neil Armstrong became the first man to set foot on the moon. Bahrain had no television station then, but it was possible, with a large aerial and favourable weather, to pick up transmissions from a station about thirty-five kilometres (22 miles) away in eastern Saudi Arabia, operated by the Arabian American Oil Company (Aramco) to entertain their expatriate employees living in company towns in the Al Khobar and Dammam area. Dhahran TV, named Channel 3 later, was the first TV channel in the Gulf and the second in the Middle East. It had started broadcasting in September 1957 and was sometimes the object of humour for its airing of dated and censored entertainment programming and a bland nightly news broadcast, but on this occasion, it allowed us to witness history being made. A colleague in the bank had a television, and he invited a number of friends and colleagues to watch the historic event at his home, which we duly did, accompanied by copious supplies of gin and tonic.

Just one week before the moon landing, the ruler of Bahrain had officially opened the first satellite earth station in the Middle East, at Ras Abu Jarjur. Marconi built this earth station for Cable and Wireless, a British company that, at the time, operated the telephone system in Bahrain and many other British colonies and former colonies in the world. This was the early days of satellite communications; the first transatlantic television pictures had been transmitted in this way via Telstar only about seven years previously. The first satellite operated by the International Telecommunications Satellite Consortium, Intelsat I, was launched in 1965 and had only 240 telephone circuits. By the time of the opening of the Bahrain earth station, Intelsat III was in use, having a capacity of 1,200 telephone circuits and the capability to carry television transmissions. Concurrently with the

Bahrain earth station, 1970

opening of the earth station was the introduction of international direct dialling from Bahrain, something we take for granted now, but initially only to the United Kingdom.

It is appropriate to comment on communication facilities in the Gulf at this time. Most matters were dealt with by airmail, which was quite efficient between Bahrain and London, and the other major cities with which the bank conducted business, but still two or three weeks could elapse between sending a letter and receiving the reply. If a matter required a quick answer, a cable, usually at "overnight" rates, might be used; and in matters of extreme urgency, one might use the telex, although both of these facilities were considered to be extravagant expenditure. The fax had not yet made its debut, and the Internet and e-mail were still dreams.

Christmas 1969 was the first that I spent in the Gulf. It was traditional that the manager of BBME would host a black tie dinner on Christmas Day to which all the British staff and their spouses were invited. However, on Christmas Eve, the members of the bachelors' mess were invited for drinks at the home of the branch accountant. He decided to serve exclusively martinis, a drink that I had never consumed before. This proved disastrous; I drank far too many martinis and as a result had a severe hangover the next day, which prevented me from attending a lunch to which I had been invited. Although I dragged myself to the manager's dinner, I was still not able to participate and enjoy it. I have never touched a martini since, nor have I ever had another hangover!

In early 1970, a team from Walt Disney Productions arrived in Bahrain to make a film for the series *The Wonderful World of Disney*. Initially to be called *The Boy from Bahrain* and finally renamed *Hamad and the Pirates*, the film eventually aired in two parts on NBC television in the United States in March 1971. I met the director, Richard Lyford, shortly after he arrived in Bahrain and became involved on the fringes of the production, assisting with their financial arrangements and administration, which earned me a place in the credits at the end of the film. The star of the film was Khalifa Shaheen who was assigned to the project by his employer, Bahrain Petroleum Company (BAPCO), where he worked as a newsreel cameraman, to act as guide, contact man and interpreter for the Disney team. Eventually the director cast him as the pirate captain. During the shooting of the film, it was necessary to portray a dhow with abnormally powerful engines escaping from the authorities at speed. Since such a vessel was not available, the Royal Navy was persuaded to lend the company its minesweeper, the only ship it had based in Bahrain. A mock-up of the rear part of a dhow was constructed over the stern of the minesweeper, and the scenes of the escape were thus filmed with that vessel sailing at full speed. The film premiered in Bahrain in the presence of the ruler before it was shown on television in the United States. By then I had left

Bahrain and have never succeeded in obtaining a video or DVD of the production, so I have never actually seen the final product.

In February 1970, I was allowed to take "local leave" and decided to travel to Cyprus. It was my first visit to the island that was to become an important part of my life in later years. In the absence of any direct flights, I travelled via Kuwait and Beirut to Nicosia airport from where arrangements had been made for a car to take me to my hotel, the Dome, in Kyrenia. This gave me my first exposure to the political problems existing on the island, which were to have such a devastating effect a few years later.

At the time of this visit, it was only possible for Greek Cypriots to travel via the direct road from Nicosia to Kyrenia through a Turkish Cypriot area in twice-daily convoys, escorted by United Nations troops. Therefore, as my arrival time did not coincide with the timing of a convoy, my Greek Cypriot driver had to take me through exclusively Greek Cypriot areas, via Morphou and Myrtou to Kyrenia, a journey of about seventy-five kilometres (forty-seven miles), compared with twenty-five kilometres (sixteen miles) via the direct route. In spite of this inconvenience, I enjoyed a pleasant week on the island, managing to visit as far afield as Paphos, Famagusta and Limassol in a car that I hired. At the time, a former colleague from Bahrain was staying with friends in Kyrenia, and we were both invited to dinner by the former manager of the BBME Bahrain branch. He was then living in Nicosia where he represented BBME on the board of Cyprus Popular Bank (now Marfin Laiki Bank), in which BBME had taken a minority shareholding, which has long since been sold.

In June 1970, I was informed that I was to be transferred to the bank's Beirut branch for the balance of my first overseas tour as soon as Lebanese work permit formalities were completed. This took about a month, and in July, I was able to set out, for the second time, to the *Paris of the Middle East*.

The mainstay of air communications in the Gulf in 1970 was Gulf Aviation (now Gulf Air). The airline had been established in Bahrain in 1950 as a small commuter service, operating DC3 and Fokker Friendship aircraft on short intra-Gulf routes. BOAC was a major shareholder until 1970, the year in which Gulf Aviation started services to London using a VC10 aircraft. In 1973, the governments of Abu Dhabi, Bahrain, Oman and Qatar became the equal shareholders, and the name was changed to Gulf Air. Following the establishment of indigenous airlines in Dubai, Abu Dhabi, Oman and Qatar in the 1980s and 1990s, the government of Bahrain became the sole shareholder in Gulf Air. In 1970, Gulf Aviation had acquired its first jet aircraft—a BAC111—and it was on this plane that I began my journey to Beirut.

Gulf Aviation BAC 111 at Muharraq Airport,
Bahrain, 1970 (Peter Langsdale)

Chapter 6

A BRIEF HISTORY OF LEBANON

Just as I found it necessary to devote a chapter to the Middle East problem to put events in my life into context, so, I believe, it is necessary to try to provide the reader with some background to the state of affairs in Lebanon. I first visited the country in 1969, some six months after moving to the Middle East, and it has played a significant part in my life ever since.

Early History

Lebanon's internal problems began long before the creation of the State of Israel and the resulting Palestinian presence in the country, but they were increased greatly by these events after 1948. The country was part of the Ottoman Empire from 1516. During the mid-nineteenth century, conflict between the Druze and Christians led to the landing of French forces to protect the Maronite Christians; after that, Lebanon was granted regional independence within the Ottoman Empire, with Lebanese administration and armed forces.

Until then Lebanon generally referred to the landlocked Maronite heartland of Mount Lebanon and did not even include Beirut. After the end of World War I, a League of Nations mandate granted France control of present-day Syria and Lebanon. In August 1920, France established the state of Greater Lebanon. To Mount Lebanon were added Beirut, the Bekaa Valley, South Lebanon, including Tyre and Sidon, and North Lebanon, including Tripoli, all previously controlled from Damascus but under the French Mandate. France thus incorporated areas in which lived very diverse religious communities into one country with very artificial borders, albeit, still under French control. This somewhat arbitrary amalgamation of different sects has contributed significantly to the problems that Lebanon has experienced ever since. The British were not the only nation to leave problems in the wake of their empire.

In 1926, the first Lebanese constitution was promulgated. Although suspended twice during the remaining French Mandate period and amended at various times since, much of it, including confessionalism, still prevails today. In 1936, in parallel with independence negotiations between France and Syria, the mandatory power negotiated a treaty with Lebanon, granting it "internal independence" with defence and foreign affairs still controlled by France. In the treaty, signed on November 13, France recognised Lebanon as an independent state and guaranteed the borders it had defined in 1920. Earlier, in the Franco-Syrian treaty, signed on September 9, Syria had dropped its demands to annex Lebanon into Greater Syria. The dropping of the demand then, however, does not mean that everyone in Syria and Lebanon has forgotten the idea, even today.

In 1941, Britain supported the Free French Forces led by Gen. Charles de Gaulle in a successful coup to end Vichy control of Syria and Lebanon. Part of the British involvement included a landing by five hundred commandos near the mouth of the Litani River, just a few kilometres from my present home. Their mission was to capture the Qasmieh Bridge over the Litani River on the coastal road from Tyre to Sidon, a mission that succeeded but not without mishaps.[29]

Some sixty-five years later, this bridge was the first target to be bombed by the Israelis when they launched their 2006 war on Lebanon.

---

[29]   Barr, James, A Line in the Sand, 2011, Simon & Schuster UK Ltd, London.

Eventually, after some persuasion by the newly appointed British Envoy Extraordinary and Minister Plenipotentiary to Lebanon, Sir Edward Spears, the Free French Forces officially recognised the full independence of Lebanon. A general election resulted in the appointment of Bishara al Khoury as president and Riad al Solh as prime minister on September 21, 1943. On November 8, the day that I was born, parliament amended the constitution, effectively terminating the French mandate. France immediately declared the changes illegal and proceeded to arrest and imprison the president, prime minister and other ministers. The French action led to civil unrest in which some eighteen people were killed and many injured. Following intervention by British prime minister Winston Churchill and French general Charles de Gaulle, France released the imprisoned politicians on November 22 and declared the end of their mandate. This date is celebrated as the Lebanese Independence Day.

French troops finally left Lebanon in 1946. Earlier, in 1943, prior to the end of the mandate, prominent Christian and Muslim leaders came together to agree the terms of the National Covenant, then and still an unwritten agreement, supplemental to the written constitution, intended to be a new and unique concept of confessional democracy. In a society where allegiance was then, and remains today, more likely to be to a feudal chief or religion rather than to the country, the covenant has caused, over time, conflict rather than promote harmony. The covenant established that the president should be a Maronite Christian, the prime minister a Sunni Muslim, and the speaker of parliament a Shia Muslim. Members of parliament were to be in the ratio of six Christians to five Muslims and public offices distributed proportionally among the recognised religious groups, of which there are now eighteen. The original calculations were based on a 1932 census, which revealed the breakdown of the main confessional groups to be Maronite 351,187 (33.57%), Sunni Muslim 194,305 (18.57%) and Shia Muslim 166,545 (15.92%).[30] There has been no new census taken since 1932, although the ratio between the

---

[30]   The Monthly, Issue 62, September 2007 and http://www.dailystar. com.lb/News/Politics/Aug/30/Its-the-end-of-Lebanon-as-we-know-it. ashx#axzz2DEEEck7H accessed 30 Nov 2012

various sects has, undoubtedly, changed due to differing birth and emigration rates. Under the terms of the Taif Accords in 1989, which ended the civil war, some of the powers of the Maronite president were reduced in favour of the prime minister and the cabinet. The membership of the parliament was increased from 99 to 128, equally divided between Christians and Muslims. Other provisions of the Taif Accords remain largely unimplemented.

United Sates Intervention

In 1958, there was a major internal conflict in Lebanon. Lebanese Muslims and Druze, inspired by the ideas of Egyptian president Gamal Abdel Nasser and by the recent but short-lived union of Egypt and Syria as the United Arab Republic (UAR), campaigned for Lebanon to join the new country. At one stage, the mainly Sunni Muslim area in the north of the country declared its secession from Lebanon and applied to join the UAR[31] and Nasser threatened to use force to integrate Lebanon into the UAR. Naturally, this idea did not appeal to Lebanese Christians. Domestic tensions had been building up for some time and came to a head with the assassination of a Christian journalist, Nasib Matni, on May 8. Following the overthrow of the monarchy in Iraq on July 14, Lebanese president Camille Chamoun requested United States assistance to combat a potential invasion from Syria. The United States obliged, invoking the Eisenhower Doctrine, allowing intervention to resist "international communism," represented in their eyes by Nasser—an early example of the misguided policies of the United States government in the Middle East since World War II.

The first marines, an advanced guard of the eventual fourteen thousand men who were going to arrive, landed on the beaches at Ramlat al Baida in West Beirut on July 15; they were somewhat bemused to be greeted by Beirutis enjoying the late-afternoon sun and sea. The US forces remained until October. During this period,

---

[31]   Hirst, David, Beware of Small States: Lebanon, Battleground of the Middle East, 2010, Faber and Faber

the Americans oversaw the replacement of President Chamoun, who had been trying to extend his term in office in violation of the constitution, by the former commander of the army Fuad Chehab, who had refused to allow the army to be involved in the civil conflict.

Palestinian Influence

The Palestinian presence was a major factor contributing to the start of the 1975-1990 civil war in Lebanon. The influx of Palestinians began in 1948 with the arrival of about one hundred and fifty thousand refugees at the time of the establishment of the State of Israel. More refugees followed, especially because of the 1967 Arab-Israel war, and throughout the 1960s there was a gradual build-up of PLO guerrillas in southern Lebanon. The first clashes between the Lebanese army and the PLO guerrillas took place in southern Lebanon in 1966. Their numbers increased greatly after King Hussein expelled the PLO from Jordan in Black September 1970. One example of the suffering caused to Lebanon by the Palestinian presence occurred in December 1968; on December 26, two PFLP members attacked an El Al aircraft at Athens International Airport, killing an Israeli mechanic. The Israeli Defence Forces responded to the incident during the night of December 27-28 when Israeli commandoes landed on the coast south of Beirut and destroyed fourteen aircraft belonging to Middle East Airlines, Trans Mediterranean Airways and Lebanese International Airways at Beirut airport.

Since the end of World War II, there was increasing tension between the Maronite Christians, who dominated the political scene and sought close ties with the west, and a growing Arab nationalist sentiment that attracted Muslims and secular leftists. After he came to power following the coup d'état in 1952, Egyptian president Nasser actively promoted the idea of Arab nationalism and unity: people throughout the Middle East followed his campaign. It was said that if one wanted to undertake a robbery in Cairo, the best time was either on Thursday evening, when the famous Egyptian singer Umm Kalthoum gave a radio concert or at any time that Nasser was speaking on the radio. At such times, the attention of every Egyptian would be on one performance or the other.

When the Palestinian presence in Lebanon was added to the confessional mix in the country, everything exploded. After the arrival of the Palestinians forced out of Jordan in 1970, they had twenty-three thousand armed men in the country—more troops than the Lebanese army. As a result, the different Lebanese confessional groups began to arm themselves and build up militias. On one side was the Lebanese National Movement (LNM) founded by the Druze leader Kamal Jumblatt, which was a secular left-wing group that was pro-PLO and opposed to what it perceived as excessive Maronite power. On the Christian side, Pierre Gemayel's Phalange party, established after his visit to Nazi Germany in 1936, also built up its own militia as did other groups. The Lebanese army was weak and divided along sectarian lines.

For residents of Lebanon, especially the south, the PLO's presence was the beginning of a nightmare that has still not ended in spite of the fact that the PLO withdrew from Lebanon to Tunisia in August 1982 following an Israeli invasion.

Under the guise of preparing armed resistance to Israel, the PLO insisted on political, policing, and economic control of the refugee camps as well as access to large areas of south Lebanon and the Bekaa Valley that were used for training. This generated increasing friction with the Lebanese population. Clashes over who was in charge between the Palestinians and Lebanese security and military led to armed incidents flaring up all over Lebanon, as the Palestinians were operating from refugee camps in the south, in and around Beirut and in the north.

In April 1969, there were large demonstrations for and against the Palestinian presence in Lebanon during which there were many fatalities. This led to the negotiation of an agreement between the government and the PLO signed in Cairo on November 3, 1969. The terms of the agreement, which were kept a secret at the time, included Lebanese recognition of the right of armed PLO guerrillas to be in Lebanon and to move around freely and effectively and gave them control of refugee camps without any interference from Lebanese forces. Even today, Lebanese security forces never enter the refugee camps.

Civil War and the Arrival of the Syrian Army

On February 26, 1975, the army fired on a demonstration by fishermen in Sidon, killing a Nasserite member of parliament, Maarouf Saad, among others. The fishermen were demonstrating against a plan to establish a large fishing company, in which former president Camille Chamoun was a major shareholder; they feared that it would destroy their livelihood.

Pres. Suleiman Franjieh prevented an investigation into the killings. Left-wing groups, including Saad's supporters together with PLO guerrillas, became involved in fighting with the army in Sidon while in East Beirut the Phalange demonstrated in support of the army. Eventually, on April 12, the fishing project was cancelled. However, on April 13, PLO guerrillas fired on a church in the Christian area of Ain al Rummaneh in Beirut in what was thought to be an attempt to assassinate Phalangist leader Pierre Gemayel, killing four people. Later that day, Phalangist militia retaliated, ambushing a bus carrying Palestinians, killing twenty-seven passengers. This is generally believed to have been the spark that ignited the civil war, which was to continue until 1990.

Over the next year or so, Jumblatt's LNM, trained and funded by the PLO, made substantial gains against the Phalangists and their allies, in the process taking over many army barracks, especially in the south of the country. In the autumn of 1975, the LNM and the Phalangists fought major battles in the Kantari area of Beirut, which came to be known as the Battle of the Hotels. During the battle, control of the main hotels, including the Alcazar, where I had stayed in 1969, Holiday Inn, Phoenicia and Saint George as well as the nearby Murr Tower changed hands from time to time. However, by the end of the year, each side was in much the same position as at the start of the fighting.[32] On December 18, Syrian intervention led to the conclusion of a cease-fire.

During the course of this battle, a colleague at the Toronto Dominion Bank representative office in Beirut, who was staying in the Holiday Inn, was one of the many guests evacuated to the airport in armoured personnel carriers by the Lebanese army during a short cease-fire on October 29. He returned to Toronto, never again to set foot in the Middle East.

During November, the parties agreed another short cease-fire, during which the merchants who had shops in the gold souk were allowed to remove their stocks with the protection of the Lebanese army. The merchants took much of what they salvaged from the area to the Bab Idriss branch of British Bank of the Middle East, where I had worked a few years earlier, for safekeeping; much of it must have disappeared in the following year, during the world's biggest bank robbery.

In January 1976, Lebanese Christian militias overran the Palestinian refugee camps at Karantina and Tel al-Zaatar, killing many non-combatants; and in retaliation, the PLO attacked the Christian town of Damour, a few kilometres south of Beirut, executing everybody who surrendered. Following these incidents, President Franjieh requested Syria to send troops to put an end to the fighting, and over the next few months, an army of thirty thousand occupied all but the extreme south of the country. They were to remain in Lebanon until 2005. Prior to the arrival of the Syrian army, the Phalangists had suffered defeats at the hands of the LNM and PLO forces, including the loss of the Holiday Inn, their last stronghold in West Beirut, and President Franjieh had been forced to take refuge in East Beirut after the presidential palace in Baabda was shelled.

The Syrian intervention brought to an end the gains of the PLO and its allies over the Christians, and both sides reached an agreement on

---

32   http://en.wikipedia.org/wiki/Battle_of_the_Hotels#December_1975, accessed 19 Jan 2012

restoring order in the capital. Syrian president Hafez al-Assad feared that a leftist-PLO victory would undermine Syria's role in the region and bring on the wrath of Israel. However, some would claim that this was Syria's attempt to take over Lebanon, the independence of which at the end of the French mandate in 1943, it had never really recognised and with which formal diplomatic relations had not been established. This had to wait until 2008.[33] In September 1976, Elias Sarkis replaced Suleiman Franjieh when his term as president ended. In October, an Arab League summit in Riyadh legitimised Syria's intervention in Lebanon by creating the Arab Deterrent Force, consisting largely of the Syrian army already in the country, but with the addition of a few troops contributed by Egypt, Saudi Arabia and other Arab countries, with the aim of restoring peace. An uneasy peace followed, but it did not last, as both the Lebanese Christians and the Israelis grew increasingly concerned about the Syrian role in Lebanon.

Following the Syrian intervention, the civil war went through several phases including periods when Christians fought the Syrians; Druze and Shia joined forces against the Christians; the Shia fought the Palestinians; different Christian groups fought each other and Christians fought the Syrians again.

The First Israeli Invasion

In March 1978, in response to the Coastal Road Massacre in which the PLO killed thirty-eight civilians on a bus travelling along Israel's coastal highway, Israel launched Operation Litani invading south Lebanon, in an attempt, largely successful at the time, to remove the PLO from the border area and prevent cross-border attacks. They occupied the area as far north as the Litani River, with the exception of the city of Tyre. In response to the invasion, the UN Security Council passed Resolutions 425 and 426, calling for the withdrawal of Israeli troops from Lebanon and creating the United Nations Interim Force in Lebanon (UNIFIL) to enforce the withdrawal and

---

[33]   http://www.reuters.com/article/2008/08/13/idUSLD532098, accessed 19 Jan 2012

restore peace and sovereignty to the area. Thirty-four years later, UNIFIL is still in southern Lebanon, a force much enlarged since the 2006 war with Israel.

In the first stage of the civil war in 1975-76, the Lebanese army had broken up, and a battalion in the south, two thousand five hundred mainly Christian men led by Maj. Saad Haddad, had become the foundation of the Army of Free Lebanon, later renamed the South Lebanon Army (SLA). Outside the control of the Lebanese government but still paid by them for several years, the SLA initially waged a campaign against the Palestinians in the south and later against the Shia Muslim groups, Amal and Hezbollah.

The SLA was strongly supported by Israel, which provided them with weapons, uniforms, equipment and funding for salaries, at the rate of US$500 per soldier per month,[34] after the Lebanese government ceased paying them. After the Israeli withdrawal in June 1978 and the deployment of UNIFIL, a strip of land along the Lebanese-Israeli border from Naqoura on the coast to Mount Hermon was left as a buffer zone. This area was under the control of the SLA, with a strong presence of Israeli "advisors." UNIFIL could not enter the zone. Following the death of Haddad from cancer in 1984, Antoine Lahad replaced him as commander of the SLA. After the foundation of Hezbollah in the early 1980s, the SLA cooperated with Israel in trying to control its activities. When Israel finally withdrew from virtually all of Lebanon in 2000, the SLA disintegrated, many of its members including Lahad, fearful of reprisals from Hezbollah, fled to Israel with their families. Many were later allowed to immigrate to other countries, especially Canada.

In the meantime, in 1978, the Syrians, who, probably correctly, considered that their intervention in 1976 had saved the Christians, turned their guns on the Christians in East Beirut. Their action was prompted by the assassination, in his northern stronghold of Ehden, of Tony Franjieh (son of former president Suleiman Franjieh), his

---

[34]   http://middleeast.about.com/od/arabisraeliconflict/p/me081026b.htm, accessed 19 Jan 2012

wife and child, plus thirty-two others by Phalangist militia, led by Samir Geagea on June 13, 1978. In 1994, after the end of the civil war, Geagea was tried and convicted on charges of ordering several political assassinations. He was sentenced to death, but this was commuted to life imprisonment; in 2005, he was granted a pardon. He is the only militia leader to have been brought to trial and imprisoned for civil war period crimes.

Between July and September 1978, the Phalangist militia and the Syrian army fought a one-hundred-day battle during which they subjected East Beirut to continuous artillery bombardment. At the end, the Syrians withdrew from East Beirut, and the leader of the Phalangist militia Bashir Gemayel had become the acknowledged leader in the Christian area. In 1980, he became commander of the newly created Lebanese Forces militia.

The Second Israeli Invasion

In the middle of the changing alliances among various Lebanese parties, Israel fought the PLO again. On June 6, 1982, there was an unsuccessful attempt to assassinate the Israeli ambassador in London, Shlomo Argov, by the Abu Nidal Organisation, a group that had broken from the PLO in 1974. In response, Israel launched Operation Peace for Galilee. The operation had several objectives, including the elimination of the PLO threat to Israel's northern border (yet again) and the destruction of the organisation's infrastructure in Lebanon, the removal of the Syrian military presence in the Bekaa Valley and the reduction of Syrian influence in Lebanon, and the creation of a stable Lebanese government. Only the first can be said to have been achieved, but the PLO was soon replaced in the border area by what has proved to be a much more formidable foe—Hezbollah, the Party of God. Israel failed dismally in attempts to reduce Syrian influence or create a stable government in Lebanon.

The Israeli invasion of Lebanon reached to within a few kilometres of central Beirut, which was surrounded by June 13, 1982. Beirut airport and parts of the southern suburbs of the city were occupied.

Although the United States denied giving Israel a green light for the invasion, Pres. Ronald Reagan and Secretary of State Alexander Haig put no pressure on them to withdraw. Their reasoning was that the Israeli presence in Lebanon might unite the country's various groups against both Syrian and Israeli forces and that this would allow the president, Elias Sarkis, to enact legislation to give the Palestinian refugees Lebanese citizenship. This was another unlikely dream of an American administration, which, again, failed to understand the situation in the region.

The invasion eventually led to the evacuation, during August and September, of an estimated fourteen thousand PLO fighters from Lebanon to Jordan, Syria, Iraq, Sudan, North and South Yemen, Greece and Tunisia, although subsequently, many ended up in the West Bank and Gaza. Yasser Arafat himself went to Tunis, which became the new PLO headquarters. The Syrian Army Eighty-fifth Infantry Brigade, which had been in Beirut and the Chouf mountains, withdrew to Syria in disgrace following the Israeli successes. It was disbanded a few days later. The departure of the PLO fighters was monitored and controlled by a multinational force (MNF), comprised of troops from the United States, France and Italy; after this was completed, the MNF withdrew on September 10. After their departure, and in contravention of the agreement reached between all the parties, which had been negotiated by US envoy Philip Habib, Israel moved into West Beirut on September 15 and allowed their Christian Phalangist allies from East Beirut to carry out massacres of many of the remaining Palestinians in the Sabra and Shatila refugee camps. It is estimated that this action, watched by the Israeli forces, led to three thousand further deaths, this time mostly women, children and older people. Lebanese estimates, compiled from International Red Cross sources, police and hospital surveys, calculated that 17,825 Lebanese had died and over 30,000 had been wounded up to this point in the conflict. The Israeli Kahan Commission found that Ariel Sharon, defence minister at the time, bore personal responsibility for failing to prevent the massacre and for failing to act once he learned that a massacre had started and recommended that he be removed as defence minister and that he never hold a position in any future Israeli government.[35] Sharon eventually did resign as Israel's defence minister; however, he remained in Begin's cabinet as a minister without portfolio and subsequently became Israel's eleventh prime minister in 2001. He suffered a stroke in January 2006 and has been in a coma ever since. Poetic Justice?

During this period, Bashir Gemayel was elected as president of Lebanon on August 23, 1982. On September 14, he was assassinated, probably by Syrian agents who did not approve of his policy of cooperation with Israel, when a bomb demolished the Phalangist headquarters in East Beirut. Israel's and the United States' hope that they could force Lebanon to enter into a peace treaty died with Gemayel. On September 23, Bashir Gemayel's brother, Amine, was elected president and took office. On September 26, Israel withdrew from West Beirut after a siege that had lasted seventy days. Shortly thereafter, on September 29, the MNF, whose governments were somewhat embarrassed by the massacre which had taken place after their premature departure in August, returned as a symbol of support for the new government. Thereafter, the Americans tried in vain to broker a peace deal between Lebanon and Israel, but they achieved nothing beyond the Israeli withdrawal from West Beirut. At the same time, fighting was ongoing in the Chouf area between the Druze and Phalangist Christians and in other areas between the Lebanese army and Muslim forces.

The Emergence of Hezbollah

On November 11, 1982, a suicide bomber destroyed the Israeli military headquarters in Tyre, killing seventy-five Israelis. Although few realised it at the time, this was among the first actions of a new force in the Lebanese conflict that was to gain such importance in later years—Hezbollah, the Party of God. Ibrahim al-Sayyed had

---

[35]   Schiff, Ze'ev, Ehud, Ya'ari, *Israel's Lebanon War*, 1984 Simon and Schuster, New York

announced its formation in Baalbek the previous September.[36] The next major attack accredited to the new organisation was a massive suicide truck bomb that destroyed the US embassy in Beirut on April 18, 1983, with the loss of over sixty-three lives. The dead included the CIA's top Middle East analyst and Near East director Robert C. Ames, Station Chief Kenneth Haas and most of the Beirut staff of the CIA.[37] Ames' severed hand, identified by his wedding ring, was found floating a mile offshore.[38] As 1983 wore on, the MNF especially the US Marines, were often involved in fighting with armed elements of PLO, Syrian-supplied Druze, or Lebanese Muslim factions.

American efforts to arrange a deal continued as did the fighting between various Lebanese factions until, on May 17, 1983, an agreement was struck on Israeli withdrawal from Lebanon, provided Syria and the remaining PLO forces did likewise; the agreement included the maintenance of a "security zone" along the Israel-Lebanon border.[39] Syria, however, refused to discuss the withdrawal of its forces, arguing that they had been invited into the country by the Lebanese government and that their army was there with the approval of the Arab League, whereas Israel had invaded the country. The agreement was never implemented and was later revoked by Lebanon in March 1984. During 1983, there was fighting between the Lebanese army and Muslim militia and between the Druze and Christians; most of the latter were displaced from the conflict area and moved to East Beirut. Israel unilaterally withdrew from the Chouf area in August to a new line north of Sidon, leaving their Christian allies and the Druze to continue fighting.

---

[36] http://www.thenational.ae/thenationalconversation/comment/thirty-years-later-hizbollah-is-just-another-corrupt-party#page1, accessed 2 September 2012

[37] http://en.wikipedia.org/wiki/1983_United_States_embassy_bombing#cite_note-facts-3, accessed 19 Jan 2012

[38] Hirst, David, Beware of Small States, 2010 Faber and Faber, New York

[39] http://www.lebanese-forces.org/lebanon/agreements/may17.htm, accessed 19 Jan 2012

Hezbollah again came to prominence on October 23, 1983, when suicide bombers simultaneously attacked the US Marines base and the French headquarters, resulting in 241 US and 58 French fatalities. In response, US warships shelled Muslim areas around Beirut.

In November 1983, Lebanon's feuding leaders met in Geneva to try to achieve national reconciliation. As well as the president Amine Gemayel, the warlords attending included former presidents Suleiman Franjieh and Camille Chamoun and former prime ministers Rashid Karami and Saeb Salam. Walid Jumblatt, leader of the Druze since the assassination of his father (probably by the Syrians) in 1977; Nabih Berri, head of the Shia Muslim Amal militia; Adel Ossarian, one time speaker of parliament and Pierre Gemayel, father of the president and founder of the Phalange party were present. Syrian foreign minister Abdul Halim Khaddam also attended. The conference produced no lasting results.

The Israeli military headquarters in Tyre suffered its second suicide bombing on November 11, 1983, resulting in twenty-eight Israeli fatalities, again attributed to the embryonic Hezbollah organisation. By February 1984, active fighting had broken out between Syrian-backed Druze and Muslim militia forces and the Lebanese Army and the former gained control of West Beirut. The position of the MNF as peacekeepers became untenable and their withdrawal was ordered. By February 26, the last US Marines had been moved out of Lebanon to ships offshore. A second "reconciliation conference" took place in Switzerland, which, like the first, produced no results. During 1984 came the official declaration of the creation of Hezbollah; the organisation denied any involvement in the various incidents that had been attributed to it in the preceding two years, although it had been active in the resistance against Israel since 1982.

A feature of the Lebanese civil war was the abduction of Westerners, an activity generally attributed to Hezbollah, although they have always denied this. Among the victims were:

- American University of Beirut president, David Dodge, abducted July 19, 1982, and freed on July 21, 1983.

- William Buckley, the former CIA bureau chief in Beirut, who was taken hostage on March 16, 1984. Press reports stated that Buckley had been transferred to Iran, where he was tortured and killed. Former American hostages later revealed that Buckley actually died of a heart attack brought on by torture, probably on June 3, 1985. His remains were found in a plastic sack on the side of the road to the Beirut airport in 1991.

- Benjamin Weir, a Presbyterian minister, who had lived in Lebanon since 1958, was kidnapped in May 1984 by three armed men while strolling with his wife. He was released in mid-September 1985.

- Terry Anderson, chief Middle East correspondent for the Associated Press, was the best-known and longest-held hostage. Anderson was seized on March 16, 1985, finally being released on December 4, 1991.

- Alec Collett, a British employee of UNRWA, was kidnapped on March 25, 1985. In a videotape released in April 1986, Collett was shown being hanged by his kidnappers. His body was found in November 2009.

- Thomas Sutherland, former dean of agriculture at the American University of Beirut, was kidnapped near his Beirut home on June 9, 1985. He was released on November 18, 1991, at the same time as Terry Waite, having been held hostage for 2,353 days.

- Terry Waite, the Anglican Church envoy, who disappeared on January 20, 1987, while on a negotiating mission to free the other kidnap victims, spent almost five years in captivity, nearly four years of it in solitary confinement, after he was seized from a go-between's house in Lebanon. Terry Waite's activities came to my attention in Cyprus.

- On May 13, 1989, Jackie Mann, a former RAF pilot who had joined Middle East Airlines after World War II and lived in Beirut for over forty years, was kidnapped by a group demanding the release of Palestinian prisoners it claimed were being held in Britain. Mann was eventually released on September 24, 1991. He had spent time with other UK and Irish hostages, notably journalist John McCarthy, church envoy Terry Waite and author Brian Keenan. After his release, he and his wife, Jackie, moved to Cyprus where they lived in Nicosia. I became acquainted with them during their years there. His wife died in Nicosia in 1992, and Jackie died there in 1996, at the age of eighty-one.

Throughout the early 1980s, there was fierce resistance to the Israeli occupation of southern Lebanon in response to the occupier's iron-fist policy that was led by the Shia organisations Amal and later Hezbollah. In 1985, Israel started to withdraw from most of the country, by June leaving only its self-proclaimed security zone in the south, which, as after the 1978 invasion, was controlled mainly by the South Lebanese Army.

Israel's Operation Peace for Galilee, lasting from June 1982 to June 1985, had a number of consequences, but peace was certainly not one of them. The most significant development was the emergence of Hezbollah, supported by Syria and Iran, as the main force opposing the continuing Israeli occupation of parts of Lebanon. In his book *Pity the Nation*, Robert Fisk describes how he first identified Shia fighters in 1982 when he saw them on the beaches at Khalde, south of Beirut, wearing headbands like those of the Iranian Revolutionary Guards. Neither he nor anyone else at the time realised the significance of this. In 1983, he saw Iranian Revolutionary Guards in Baalbek, where they had established a sizeable presence with the professed objective of exporting the Iranian revolution.[40] It is unlikely that their presence in Lebanon could have occurred without Syrian approval. Hezbollah's early activities, which started in 1982, concentrated on ending the Israeli occupation; over the next four years, there were thirty-six suicide attacks in Lebanon. Hezbollah, although it denied involvement, was accused of perpetrating most of these.

Since 1982, Hezbollah has emerged as a military, political and social force in Lebanon and has proved to be an even more serious threat to Israel than the PLO. The group's manifesto, published in 1985,

---

[40] Fisk, Robert, Pity the Nation, 1990, Andre Deutsche Limited, London

includes among its goals "Israel's final departure from Lebanon as a prelude to its final obliteration." Hezbollah leaders regularly continue to call for the destruction of Israel, which they refer to as a "Zionist entity built on lands wrested from their owners." The 1990 Taif Accords that ended the civil war left Hezbollah as the only armed militia in Lebanon; this justified by its status as a resistance organisation fighting the continuing Israeli occupation of the country. By that time, Hezbollah had completely replaced the PLO guerrillas in southern Lebanon, and its continued harassment of the occupation forces and their ally, the South Lebanese Army, led eventually to Israel's unilateral decision to withdraw from Lebanon on May 24, 2000. Hezbollah claimed the credit for forcing them to do so, and many Lebanese who were not necessarily their supporters or members regarded this as a great victory and the organisation's popularity rose. Since then Hezbollah has argued that the withdrawal was not complete, as required by UN Resolution 425, since Israel remained in two disputed areas, Shebaa Farms and northern Gajjar. Although small and relatively insignificant areas, which some say may be Syrian territory anyway, this continuing Israeli presence has enabled the organisation to argue that it should not be required to surrender its arms, as other militia did after the end of the civil war, as they are required to liberate the remaining occupied areas. More recently, in view of the possibility that Israel might actually withdraw from these areas, the organisation has emphasised its role as a deterrent to future Israeli aggression to justify retaining its weapons.

While the Israeli occupation of the "security zone" continued, so did the civil war. In 1985-1986, the Shia Amal militia engaged in a protracted war against the Palestinian camps in Beirut and southern Lebanon, and in 1987, they took on the Druze militia in Beirut, which led to the return of Syrian troops to the capital. Throughout 1988, fighting continued. In April, the two Shia militias, Amal and Hezbollah, engaged in fighting for the control of Nabatieh, an important town in the south; Amal won. On May 27, the Syrian army entered the southern suburbs of Beirut, following an agreement sponsored by the Iranian and Syrian governments to end fighting there. In early September, the Lebanese army and the Christian Lebanese Forces militia fought in Sin el Fil.

Two Governments

On September 22, 1988, Amine Gemayel's term as president ended, and parliament was unable to agree on a replacement. The outgoing president appointed Gen. Michel Aoun, a Maronite Christian and commander of the army, as interim prime minister while the post of president remained vacant. This resulted in Lebanon having two rival governments. In East Beirut was a military one, led by Gen. Michel Aoun. In West Beirut, the other was led by Sunni Muslim Selim al-Hoss, who had been constitutionally appointed a year earlier after the assassination of his predecessor, Rashid Karami. In this situation, I made my only visit to Lebanon during the civil war period. In November, in spite of the presence of the Syrian army in West Beirut, fighting broke out again between the rival Shia Amal and Hezbollah militias, which continued into the following year.

The year 1989 commenced with confrontations between the Lebanese army, led by General Aoun, and the Christian Lebanese Forces militia during which the Syrians shelled both East and West Beirut. On March 14, Aoun declared his "War of Liberation" against Syrian occupation, an impossible battle to win. It is worth noting that he later became one of Syria's allies in Lebanon. The Syrians and their Lebanese allies besieged East Beirut until September 22 when the Arab League managed to arrange a cease-fire.

The Taif Accords

Following the cease-fire, Lebanese and other Arab leaders met in Taif, Saudi Arabia, under the leadership of Rafic Hariri, a Sunni Muslim from Sidon who, at the time, was living in Saudi Arabia and had close contacts with the Saudi royal family.

The Taif Accords were intended to be the basis for ending the civil war and incorporated provisions to respond to demographic changes since independence, although no census has been undertaken since 1932 to establish real demographic facts. The membership of parliament was increased from 99 to 128, equally split between Christians and Muslims (previously 6:5 in favour of Christians), and some of the powers of the president were transferred to the prime minister and cabinet. There was no change in the allocation of the three senior positions—the president remained a Maronite Christian, the prime minister a Sunni Muslim and the speaker of parliament a Shia Muslim.

The issue of the withdrawal of Syrian forces from Lebanon was not discussed. On October 22, 1989, the Lebanese parliament met in Taif and agreed the constitutional changes. General Aoun rejected them and dissolved the chamber. On November 5, parliament met (despite having been dissolved) at the Quoleyet military base in northern Lebanon and elected René Mouawad as president. Just seventeen days later, on November 22, Lebanon's Independence Day, he was assassinated. Elias Hrawi was elected to replace Mouawad, and shortly thereafter, Gen. Émile Lahoud was nominated to replace Michel Aoun as army commander.

The Taif Accords called for the disarmament of all militias in Lebanon, with the exception of Hezbollah, which was allowed to retain its weapons for its resistance to Israeli occupation. The Syrian army undertook disarmament of other militias in 1991. At the time, Israel's proxy in southern Lebanon, the South Lebanon Army, refused to surrender its weapons. Taif also legitimised continuing Syrian involvement in Lebanon. In 1991, a Treaty of Brotherhood, Coordination and Cooperation was signed between the two countries and the Syrian Lebanese Higher Council, chaired by the two presidents, was established.

Despite Taif and subsequent events, in January 1990, fighting resumed between the Christian Lebanese Forces and army units still loyal to Michel Aoun. Later in the year, following Syrian cooperation with the United States over the Iraqi invasion of Kuwait, the Syrian forces received a green light from the United States to bring the battle with Aoun to an end. On October 13, they launched a devastating air and land attack on the Christian areas, eventually taking control of the presidential palace, where Michel Aoun had his headquarters. Aoun took refuge in the French embassy. This day is marked as the official end of the civil war.

After the Civil War

In August 1991, following a general amnesty for all crimes committed during the civil war and a presidential pardon, Aoun went into exile in France, where he lived until his return to Lebanon in 2005.

The first parliamentary elections since 1972 were held in August and September 1992, following which Nabih Berri, leader of the Shia Amal organisation, became speaker of parliament, a position that he still holds. A cabinet of technocrats was formed, headed by Prime Minister Rafic Hariri, who had been instrumental in convening the meetings in Saudi Arabia that had led to the signing of the Taif Accords. Hariri remained in office until 1998, during which time he was the driving force behind the efforts to rebuild the war-ravaged capital. Although the methods used and the results have come in for some criticism, without his drive (and money), it is unlikely that the work would have progressed so quickly or in such a co-ordinated manner.

During the mid-1990s, all was far from quiet in the southern border area. Hezbollah continued to harass the Israelis and their proxy, the South Lebanon Army. In June 1993, Hezbollah launched rockets against an Israeli village. The following month, attacks by both Hezbollah and the Popular Front for the Liberation of Palestine-General Command killed five Israeli soldiers inside the occupied area of Lebanon. In July, Israel launched a weeklong attack against Lebanon named Operation Accountability with three objectives: to strike directly at Hezbollah, to make it difficult for Hezbollah to use southern Lebanon as a base for striking Israel and to displace refugees in the hopes of pressuring the Lebanese government to intervene against Hezbollah. Israel certainly succeeded in its last objective, as some three hundred thousand refugees fled from the south to Beirut and other areas during the week of bombardment of villages in the area. However, this did not have the desired effect of prompting the Lebanese government to take any action against Hezbollah. Israel also bombed infrastructure targets such as roads, bridges and power stations. Hezbollah's reply was to fire rockets at civilian targets in northern Israel, but their impact was far less than that of Israel on Lebanon. The United States negotiated a cease-fire in the form of an oral agreement, whereby Israel agreed to refrain from attacking civilian targets in Lebanon while Hezbollah pledged to stop firing rockets into northern Israel. However, neither side respected that agreement.

In chapter 12, I will mention people and events during my time in Cyprus associated with the Irangate scandal. This affair had an ironic effect in southern Lebanon during the 1990s, when Hezbollah was harassing the Israeli occupation forces and their Lebanese allies, the South Lebanon Army. In 1995, Hezbollah received deliveries of US-made antitank missiles from Iran that Israel had delivered originally to Iran as part of the arms for hostages deal in the 1980s.[41] Hezbollah put these weapons to very effective use in its attacks on Israeli Merkava tanks in southern Lebanon.

The next major engagement occurred in April 1996, a further attempt by Israel to stop Hezbollah's activities in southern Lebanon. On March 30, in response to the killing of two Lebanese by an Israeli missile, Hezbollah launched missiles into northern Israel; the Israeli Defence Forces then acknowledged that their attack was a mistake. About a week later, a roadside bomb caused the death of a fourteen-year-old Lebanese boy and injury of three others, and Hezbollah responded by firing more missiles into northern Israel on April 9.

On April 11, Israel launched Operation Grapes of Wrath in retaliation for the Hezbollah shelling, which had injured six Israeli civilians. Israeli aircraft and artillery bombarded southern Lebanon as well

---

[41]   Blanford, Nicholas, Warriors of God, 2011, Random House, New York

as targets in the Beirut area and in the Bekaa Valley, including civilian infrastructure, some of which Israel said was being used for military purposes. Once again, somewhere between three hundred thousand and five hundred thousand people were displaced. This was followed by an Israeli blockade of Beirut, Sidon and Tyre ports from April 13 and bombing of power stations the next day. Among the Lebanese civilian casualties were 106 people who had taken refuge at a UNIFIL base in Qana, which was shelled by Israel. Four UN soldiers were seriously injured in this incident. Israel denied deliberately shelling the compound. A United Nations enquiry conducted by Maj. Gen. Franklin van Kappen of the Netherlands concluded, "While the possibility cannot be ruled out completely, it is unlikely that the shelling of the United Nations compound was the result of gross technical and/or procedural errors."[42]

Effective April 27, the United States arranged a cease-fire. The agreement, signed by Lebanon, Israel, the United States, France and Syria banned cross-border attacks on civilian targets as well as using civilian villages to launch attacks, but it specifically allowed Hezbollah to continue its military activities against Israeli forces inside Lebanon. A monitoring committee for the implementation of the Grapes of Wrath Understandings was set up, comprising representatives from the five countries, to monitor and discuss infringements of the understandings by the two sides.

Israeli Withdrawal (Almost)

Harassment of Israeli forces and the South Lebanon Army by Hezbollah continued until May 2000 when, following the collapse of the SLA, Israel unilaterally withdrew from virtually all of the areas it had occupied in southern Lebanon, leaving two small areas in dispute. This together with the failure of the Syria-Israel peace talks a few weeks earlier determined the next period in the history of Lebanon and Hezbollah. Had Syria and Israel signed a treaty in

---

[42]   http://www.undemocracy.com/S-1996-337/page_6/rect_47,1018_949,1260, accessed 19 Jan 2012

2000, the following years might have seen a Lebanon-Israel peace treaty, the end of any justification for Hezbollah to keep its weapons, no 2006 war and peace and prosperity in southern Lebanon.

In November 1998, following the end of Elias Hrawi's term, Gen. Émile Lahoud, former army commander and Syrian protégée, had become president. A new cabinet was formed under Prime Minister Selim al-Hoss, which included only two members from the previous Hariri government. His administration lasted until October 2000, when Rafic Hariri was again appointed prime minister. In September 2004, the UN Security Council passed a resolution calling for the withdrawal of Syrian forces from Lebanon. Syria ignored it and arranged for its allies in the Lebanese parliament to pass a bill extending the term of Émile Lahoud by a further three years.

Following lengthy political deadlock, Hariri, who had opposed the extension of Lahoud's term, resigned as prime minister in October 2004. Omar Karami, always ready to take office when no one else will take on the job, replaced him.

The Assassination of Rafic Hariri and its Aftermath

On February 14, 2005, as he was travelling in a supposedly well-protected convoy from the parliament building to his home in the Qoraitem area of Beirut, Rafic Hariri was assassinated. A massive car bomb was exploded as his car passed the ruins of the Saint George Hotel, and Hariri, along with twenty-two others in the convoy, was killed. Hariri's anti-Syrian position was no secret. After his death, the Druze leader, Walid Jumblatt, claimed that Hariri had been threatened by the Syrian president Bashar al-Assad during an August 2004 meeting in Damascus, at the time that Syria was engineering the three-year extension of Pres. Émile Lahoud's term. Assad is purported to have told Hariri, "If you and [French President] Chirac want me out of Lebanon, I will break Lebanon."

Six months later, in the wake of the assassination, it was widely speculated that Syria was responsible for Hariri's death, and there was a wave of pro and anti-Syrian activity in Lebanon. This activity was accompanied by calls for the withdrawal of Syrian troops, which had been in the country since the early days of the civil war in 1976, in accordance with UN Security Council Resolution 1559 of September 2, 2004. Prime Minister Omar Karami, generally perceived as pro-Syrian, resigned on February 28, was asked to form a new government, failed to do so, and was replaced by Najib Mikati in April.

Throughout March and April, there were huge anti-Syrian demonstrations in the country as Lebanon experienced its Cedar Revolution. These culminated on March 14 with a rally in Martyrs' Square in Beirut that attracted over one million people. Syrian troops completed their withdrawal on April 26, 2005, but the euphoria was short-lived. Although the armed, uniformed forces had left Lebanon, Syrian influence remains and is maintained through various pro-Syrian political groups in the country. Following the withdrawal, in August 2008 the two countries finally reached an agreement for the establishment of diplomatic relations, although it was not until December 2008 that a Syrian ambassador took up residence in Beirut, and in April 2009, his Lebanese counterpart arrived in Damascus.

During May and June 2005, parliamentary elections were held, the result of which was a victory for the March 14 alliance led by Saad Hariri, son of the assassinated Rafic. They won 72 seats in the 128-seat parliament. Fouad Siniora, a close confidant of the Hariri family, became prime minister.

Shortly after the assassination of Rafic Hariri, the UN sent a fact-finding mission to Beirut; it concluded that the Lebanese investigation had been seriously flawed.[43] Under Security Council Resolution 1595 dated April 7, 2005 the UN International Independent Investigation Commission was formed to investigate the assassination of Rafic Hariri. Initially, the investigation was

---

[43] http://unispal.un.org/UNISPAL.NSF/0/79CD8AAA858FDD2D85256FD50 0536047, accessed 27 July 2012

headed by Detlev Mehlis, a German senior public prosecutor from Berlin. Many people commented from time to time about the similarity between the appearance of Mr. Mehlis and me, which led to an incident that will be related later. In its report dated October 19, 2005, the commission said in its conclusions:

> It is the Commission's view that the assassination on 14 February 2005 was carried out by a group with an extensive organization and considerable resources and capabilities. The crime had been prepared over the course of several months. For this purpose, the timing and location of Rafic Hariri's movements had been monitored and the itineraries of his convoy recorded in detail.

> Building on the findings of the Commission and Lebanese investigations to date and on the basis of the material and documentary evidence collected, and the leads pursued until now, there is converging evidence pointing at both Lebanese and Syrian involvement in this terrorist act. It is a well-known fact that Syrian Military Intelligence had a pervasive presence in Lebanon at the least until the withdrawal of the Syrian forces pursuant to resolution 1559. The former senior security officials of Lebanon were their appointees. Given the infiltration of Lebanese institutions and society by the Syrian and Lebanese intelligence services working in tandem, it would be difficult to envisage a scenario whereby such a complex assassination plot could have been carried out without their knowledge.

After the publication of the commission's report, Prime Minister Saad Hariri called for the continuation of the UN investigation and the establishment of an international tribunal to bring the culprits to justice. In June 2006, the security council extended the mandate of the commission to include other assassinations in Lebanon between 2004 and mid-2006. These included Samir Kassar, a journalist on the daily newspaper *An Nahar*, well known for his anti-Syrian views and George Hawi, former head of the Lebanese Communist Party and another critic of Syrian involvement in Lebanon. Gebran Tueni, a Christian member of parliament and anti-Syrian publisher of *An Nahar* and Pierre Gemayel, cabinet minister and yet another opponent of Syrian influence in Lebanon later suffered the same fate.

On July 12, 2006, Hezbollah precipitated a thirty-four-day war with Israel by undertaking a cross-border raid in which it killed three Israeli soldiers and kidnapped two others. The Israeli response was, as usual, totally disproportionate; during the war, some 1,200 Lebanese civilians were killed and hundreds of thousands of inhabitants of southern Lebanon were temporarily displaced. Israeli bombing of roads, bridges and Beirut airport inflicted significant damage on the country's infrastructure. After thirty-four days of fighting, a truce became effective on August 14 and, under the terms of UN Security Council Resolution 1701, which ended the war, in September the Lebanese army began to deploy south of the Litani River and along the border with Israel for the first time since the 1960s. My personal experiences of this conflict are told in chapter 14.

To the Brink of Another Civil War

In November 2006, just before the cabinet was to approve the draft plans for the establishment of the international tribunal, ministers from Hezbollah and Amal resigned from the government. Following these resignations, there were large demonstrations in Beirut calling for the resignation of the government; in January 2007, the Hezbollah-led opposition tried to increase the pressure on the government by calling a general strike. The anti-government group set up a tent city in downtown Beirut, paralysing the area and bringing business to a halt. This remained in place until May 2008.

Eventually, on May 30, 2007, the security council authorised the establishment of the special tribunal for Lebanon to try suspects in the Hariri assassination. Unusually, the tribunal was established under chapter 7 of the UN charter, which permits the security council to impose punitive measures, including economic sanctions and military force to achieve the objectives of the resolution.[44] Some security council members considered this interference in Lebanon's domestic affairs; Qatar and South Africa abstained in the vote. The powers conferred by chapter 7 have so far not been invoked.

In November 2007, yet another constitutional crisis arose. The term of Pres. Émile Lahoud came to an end, and parliament failed to elect a replacement. Prime Minister Fouad Siniora invoked the clause in the constitution that allowed the cabinet to assume the powers of the presidency in the absence of an incumbent. No progress was made to resolve the crisis, resulting in gridlock. In May 2008, clashes occurred between Syrian-backed militia, mainly Hezbollah and Amal, and western supported pro-government groups, including the Future Movement, led by Saad Hariri; the Lebanese Forces, led by Samir Geagea and the Progressive Socialist Party, led by Walid Jumblatt. The government of Prime Minister Fouad Siniora then decided to close Hezbollah's private telecommunications network and dismiss the head of security at Beirut airport, who was a member of Hezbollah. These decisions were to take Lebanon to the brink of another civil war. Hezbollah considered the actions a "declaration of war" and demanded their revocation.

On May 7, a strike, which had been planned for a month, turned violent, and the opposition used this as an excuse to take action. Hezbollah-led militia seized control of parts of West Beirut from militia loyal to the government. They later handed over control to the Lebanese army, which pledged to reverse the government decisions. Street battles continued on May 8-9 during which time the Hezbollah-led forces took total control of West Beirut. On May 10, the fighting spread to Aley and northern Lebanon and there was fierce fighting between Hezbollah and Druze militia in the Chouf area. On the same day, the government backed down and agreed that the army should resolve the issues that had caused the outbreak of fighting. On May 13, the army began to take control to prevent further fighting between the rival groups, and the next day, Lebanon's

---

[44] http://www.un.org/en/documents/charter/chapter7.shtml, accessed 19 Jan 2012

pro-government and opposition factions agreed to revoke the two decisions that sparked the fighting, and the opposition ended its civil disobedience campaign.

The ruler of Qatar, Sheikh Hamad bin Khalifa Al Thani, invited all Lebanese political parties to Doha to seek an agreement to end the ongoing political crisis and avoid another civil war. A conference involving all of Lebanon's political leaders was held in Doha from May 16-21, 2008. Eventually an agreement was reached that included a plan for a consensus presidential candidate Gen. Michel Suleiman to be elected by parliament, the formation of a national unity government comprising thirty ministers and changes to electoral constituency borders. Immediately following the signing of the agreement, the opposition ended the sit-in in downtown Beirut, which had begun in December 2006; and on May 25, 2008, Lebanon's parliament elected Gen. Michel Suleiman as the new president of the country, a post that had been vacant since November 2007. Following the dismantling of the barricades in downtown Beirut and the election of the new president, Lebanese of all political persuasions heaved a collective sigh of relief and a celebratory concert was held in Martyrs' Square; the performers included Haifa Wehbe, Ragheb Alama, and Assi El Helani.

The events of May 2008 marked the first time that Hezbollah had used its weapons against fellow Lebanese in order to achieve its objectives—a significant event. Previously, the theory was that Hezbollah retained its weapons after the civil war in order to defend the country from Israel and end their occupation of parts of southern Lebanon. When it withdrew in 2000, Israel left Hezbollah an excuse to claim that it should continue to retain its weapons because it did not withdraw from two small areas.

New Government—Same Old Problems

In June 2009, parliamentary elections were held, in which the March 14 alliance, led by Saad Hariri, won 71 seats in the 128-seat assembly. Pres. Michel Suleiman asked Hariri to form a government, a task that took almost six months. In its policy statement, the new Hariri government endorsed Hezbollah's right to keep its weapons, an arsenal that, by then, was generally thought to be significantly larger than before the 2006 war with Israel and which since has almost certainly grown even larger. From mid-2010 onwards, Hezbollah started a campaign to discredit the UN tribunal investigating the assassination of Rafic Hariri in anticipation that it would indict members of the organisation. In August, Hezbollah secretary-general, Hassan Nasrallah, accused Israel of perpetrating the assassination and in October, he urged all Lebanese to boycott the ongoing investigation. In one of the stranger incidents at this time, two officials from the investigating team arrived, by prior appointment, at a gynaecologist's clinic in the Hezbollah stronghold of southern Beirut. Their mission was said to be to review patient files. They were chased away by a crowd of women![45]

In January 2011, Hariri's government collapsed when ministers from Hezbollah and its political allies, including Michel Aoun's Free Patriotic Movement, resigned from the cabinet. The president asked a Hezbollah-supported Sunni candidate, Najib Mikati, to form a new government. Much bargaining and horse-trading was conducted over the next five months, and in June, the new cabinet finally emerged. Hezbollah and its allies were allocated sixteen out of the thirty portfolios. Just two weeks later, on June 30, the UN tribunal issued its first four indictments, which were sealed, to the Lebanese prosecutor; within 24 hours, the names were leaked to the press. All four of those indicted were members of Hezbollah.

Conclusion

Lebanese, and foreigners who have lived in or visited the country often look back with nostalgia on the "good old days," generally meaning the period between independence in 1943 and the start of the civil war in 1976. Did Lebanon really have any such days?

---

[45] http://www.naharnet.com/stories/676-men-disguised-as-women-likely-involved-in-attack-on-un-investigators-in-dahiyeh, accessed 4 Feb 2012

Since independence in 1943, the country has at times been described as the Switzerland of the Middle East and Beirut as the Paris of the Middle East. Certainly during the first three decades as an independent country, Lebanon was, for want of a better word, more sophisticated than most other countries in the region, especially the Gulf oil-producing states, which were beginning to build up wealth which was unimaginable a few years earlier. The Lebanese quickly became intermediaries between the newly wealthy rulers and citizens in the Gulf and banks and exporters in Europe and the United States.

Beirut and the nearby mountains became popular destinations for visitors from the oil-producing states, seeking a lifestyle more liberal than that available at home. Many bought property in Lebanon. However, underneath all the glamour and glitz, problems were always simmering. The laisser-faire attitude that prevailed in the country allowed people to do virtually whatever they wanted wherever they wanted, with minimal government intervention. This has still not changed. Social services have always been very limited. The rich grew richer and the poor struggled to live. Some Lebanese families only managed to survive because there was at least one member of the family working outside the country who was able to send money home each month. This situation still prevails, probably more than ever before. It was this divergence in wealth, as much as religion, that contributed to the outbreak of the civil war and, later, to the success of Hezbollah in gaining the support of the Shia population of the country.

The Lebanese like to blame their problems on others. True, other countries have exerted influence in the country in the years since independence. France and Great Britain initially, the United States since 1958, Saudi Arabia, Syria, Iran and Israel, as well as the Palestinians have all played their part in the modern history of the country. Most of the foreign parties that have become involved in Lebanon since its independence have left with their tail between their legs after escalating violence. The PLO theoretically responded to an appeal from Lebanon's Sunni Muslims for help in obtaining equality with the Christians. When the PLO left in 1982, their movement was severely weakened, and even the Sunnis were glad to see it go. Syria intervened at various stages of the war on behalf of the Christians, the Palestinians and the Shia. The eventual departure of their army in April 2005 was welcomed by the vast majority of Lebanese. Israel came in 1982 promising to help the Christians. When it left in 2000, not even the Christians had a good word for them. As for the United States' brief encounters with Lebanon in 1958 and again in 1982-1983, and later interference in the region, the less said, the better. However, all of these nations have had their political allies within Lebanon who have been only too willing to implement their foreign patron's plans and that situation continues today.

Chapter 7

LEBANON FIRST TIME AROUND

In 1970, the Beatles released their last album. Events in that year which were to influence my future life included the first supersonic test flight by Concorde, a coup in the sultanate of Oman that replaced Said bin Taimur with his son Qaboos and Israeli forces fighting Palestinian guerrillas in southern Lebanon. In the same year, Pan American, Trans World Airways and Swissair aircraft were hijacked by the Popular Front for the Liberation of Palestine; Egyptian president Gamal Abdel Nasser died; Hafez al-Assad came to power in Syria and Libya nationalised all foreign banks in the country, including a subsidiary of BBME.

We have seen in chapter 6 how the Middle East problem disrupted my stay in Beirut in 1969, and against this background, I travelled again to Beirut in July 1970, this time to work at BBME's main branch in Bab Idriss in downtown Beirut. It will be recalled that the treaty arrangements between Bahrain and the United Kingdom meant that there was no diplomatic representation in Bahrain other than the British. This meant that I had to fly to Beirut via Kuwait in order that my Lebanese visa could be issued by the embassy there. I stayed overnight with a colleague working at the Kuwait branch of the bank and was able to fly on to Beirut on the second day, after the visa was stamped in my passport. It was during my stay in Kuwait that, in spite of prohibition, my colleague introduced me to the pleasure of drinking gin and tonic, something that continues to this day.

At the time, the Lebanese authorities imposed strict limits on the number of work permits that it would allow to enable foreigners to be employed in the country. The bank had arranged for mine, which was an addition to the usual number that it was permitted, by setting up an exchange scheme whereby, while I was working in Beirut, a Lebanese member of the staff there was sent to the London head office for training. Four other British staff were employed in Lebanon, three at the main office in Beirut and one at the branch in Tripoli, in the north of the country.

As mine was a new position, the first thing that I had to do was find suitable accommodation. In those days, before the civil war, Ras Beirut, the western part of the city that juts out into the Mediterranean

View from the author's apartment,
New Mallas Building, Beirut, 1971

Sea, was an area popular with foreigners living in Beirut. After a brief search, I found what I considered a very suitable bachelor pad in the New Mallas building on Rue de Californie, a building that, since the end of the civil war, has been replaced with a taller and more luxurious edifice. It was a large one-bedroom apartment, with a very big balcony, from which there was a fantastic view to the northwest across the city towards Jounieh and the mountains. It was close to the homes of my three British colleagues and the popular shopping and entertainment area of Hamra and the American University of Beirut campus were close by.

Having found somewhere to live, I next addressed the issue of getting a driving licence and buying a car. The former was an easy process; a Lebanese licence was issued on the strength of my British licence. Buying a car and transferring the ownership was slightly more tortuous but was accomplished with the assistance of the bank's "fixer," and I became the proud owner of a second-hand 1968 Vauxhall Victor. It had a feature that I have never seen in a car before or since, a record player, which could accommodate 45-rpm vinyl discs. I never used it!

Since my posting to Beirut was to a newly created position under the exchange arrangement agreed with the Lebanese authorities, it was, to begin with, unclear as to what I was actually going to do. Gradually various duties were assigned to me, including the job that I had done in the Bahrain main branch, checking the posting of the customer accounts. Early in 1971, the branch moved into new premises at Bab Idriss in downtown Beirut, and among the jobs then assigned to me was control of access to the vaults, including the one that housed the customers' safe deposit lockers.

These vaults were to feature prominently in the early days of the Lebanese civil war. In 1976, to quote the bank's publication, the *History of the British Bank of the Middle East* volume 2, "the robbing of the bank's safety deposit boxes earned it the doubtful honour of an

BBME Bab Edris branch, after the robbery, 1976 (HSBC Holdings Plc)

unsubstantiated entry in the Guinness Book of World Records, under the heading of 'The World's Biggest Bank Robbery.'"[46] Responsibility for the robbery has never been conclusively established. Various theories have been advanced, including the PLO with the assistance of Corsican locksmiths and safecrackers and the Phalange militia. However, the most bizarre theory must be one published in the London *Daily Mail*. The writer, Damian Lewis, theorised that the British SAS perpetrated the robbery, in a mission launched from Cyprus to "seize documents of value

---

[46]   Jones, Geoffrey, The History of the British Bank of the Middle East, Volume 2, 1987, Cambridge University Press

to Her Majesty's Government."[47] The story further claims that as well as the documents, items of value, including stocks of unissued travellers' cheques and the contents of safe deposit boxes, were stolen to make the break-in seem like a genuine robbery and that not all of these were turned over to the British government. Whoever was responsible, there is little doubt that the customers' safe deposit lockers that were looted must have contained items of significant value, the amount of which would have been unknown to the bank and for which the bank had no responsibility. Sometime after the robbery, it was reported that the issuers of the stocks of travellers' cheques that were stolen were approached by an intermediary, offering to return them for a percentage of the face value. I do not know if this offer was accepted, but since there was a risk that these instruments could otherwise be used and be presented for payment at face value, it would not surprise me if a deal had been done.

In 1970, Beirut was considered a plum posting by most of my colleagues in BBME and many envied me. At the time, the city was often described as the Paris of the Middle East. Certainly, the francophone influences were present because of the country's historic connections with France. These stemmed in part from French protection given to the Maronite Christian community during the Ottoman period and in part to the League of Nations mandate over the country and Syria, given to France after the end of World War I and the breakup of the Ottoman Empire. Of course, in 1970 the rest of the Middle East, and the Gulf area in particular, was far less developed than today. Many things, which one now takes for granted in Dubai or Bahrain, were simply not available there but could be found in Lebanon.

Notwithstanding the glamour and sophistication associated with Beirut, underneath the glossy surface, the country was tense. Just a month after I arrived, Suleiman Franjieh was elected as president in a vote that was not without controversy. There was high inflation and

---

[47]   http://www.dailymail.co.uk/home/moslive/article-459185/Soldiers-Fortune. html, accessed 13 Jan 2012

unemployment, causing unrest among the less privileged Lebanese. As explained in chapter 6, the expulsion of Palestinians from Jordan in Black September 1970 led to a large influx of Palestinian fighters to Lebanon and the formation of a PLO offshoot named after the fateful month. The following year, 1971, Georgina Rizk became the first and only Lebanese to win the Miss Universe title, and she was crowned at a ceremony in Miami Beach, Florida. In 1978, she married a Palestinian who was a member of Black September, Ali Hassan Salameh. In 1979, agents of the Israeli Secret Service, Mossad, assassinated him in Beirut while he was on his way to his mother's home to attend a birthday party.[48]

On September 28, 1970, Gamal Abdel Nasser, president of Egypt, died. Viewed throughout the Arab world as a symbol of dignity and freedom, Nasser had had a significant impact on the politics of the entire region since his participation in the Egyptian revolution that overthrew the monarchy in 1952. When news of his death was announced, three days official mourning was proclaimed in Lebanon, and thousands of people poured onto the streets in Beirut and throughout the region. A colleague in the bank was staying with me for a few days en route from London to his next posting in Jeddah. Together, from the balcony of my apartment, we could watch the burning of tyres, a traditional Lebanese pastime when demonstrations occur, on the Avenue de Paris below. In the resulting chaos of the demonstrations, some twelve people died in Beirut during those three days of mourning.

The Lebanese frequently claim that in their country, it is possible to ski in the morning and swim in the afternoon. While the proximity of some ski slopes to the coast makes this physically possible, I have never met anyone who has actually done so. However, with the arrival of winter, I was able to revive my interest in skiing that had started when I lived in Canada. The most famous ski area is at the Cedars of Lebanon situated in the north of the country at an altitude of over 3,000 metres (10,000 ft), but this is at least a three-hour

---

[48]   http://www.sccs.swarthmore.edu/users/08/ajb/tmve/wiki100k/docs/Ali_Hassan_Salameh.html, accessed 20 Jan 2012

drive from Beirut. The nearest slopes to Beirut are at Faraya, a little over a one-hour drive from the city, where skiing is possible at an altitude of about 2,200 metres (7,100 ft).

On one weekend in February 1971, the bank's social club organised a weekend at Faraya, and I set out for the hotel there after work finished at lunchtime on Saturday. I was transporting three colleagues in my car. Once we got above the snow line, we encountered a blizzard, and the road became increasingly difficult to navigate until we reached the point where it was impassable. By this time, it was dark. Along with the occupants of many other cars, we abandoned them and set out by foot to find shelter. In fact it turned out that we were not far from a hotel, although not the one at which we had reservations. Nevertheless, there were rooms available, and we grabbed them as it was obviously going to be impossible to reach our hotel, a farther five kilometres (three miles) up the mountain or to return to Beirut that night. I and many other bank staff remained snowed in at this hotel and others nearby until late on the following Monday, by which time snow ploughs had made their way as far as the hotels at which we had taken refuge. This left the bank somewhat understaffed on Monday morning, and in order to open the vaults and get access to cash, colleagues had to withdraw duplicates of my keys from safe custody at another bank. Unfortunately, when snow ploughs cleared the road, my car, which had been completely buried under the snowdrifts, refused to start; and as a result, we had to return to Beirut by taxi and retrieve the car later in the week.

The engine of the author's car, Faraya, 1971

On May 9, 1971, the Beirut English language newspaper, the *Daily Star*, ran an article about the foreign community in Lebanon, for which I was interviewed. Statistics quoted in the article stated that as of January 1971, there were 536,797 non-Lebanese residents in the country, including 9,608 French, 7,285 British, 255,264 Syrians, 7 from Iceland, 6 from Trinidad and 1 from Vietnam. Of these only 1,237 held work permits, and I was one of only 76 British subjects holding one. The article quoted me as criticising the complete disregard of law and order in Lebanon—"people driving the wrong way up one way streets, overtaking on the wrong side, going through red lights, all that is really annoying." Nothing has changed in 2012!

In Lebanon, I continued my involvement in amateur theatre by joining the American Repertory Theatre (ART). The group included many members working at the American University of Beirut (AUB) and usually performed in one or other of the university's buildings. In January 1971, I was stage manager for their production of *Hadrian the Seventh*, a play based on the autobiographical fantasy of Frederick Rolfe. The review of this play by Anthony Irving in the *Daily Star* on January 22 said in part, "This ART presentation did not reach the level of production required by the play itself, nor did it more regrettably, meet the minimum standards previously set by this theatre group. It is easy to see why the Assembly Hall (at AUB) should have an attraction but the selection of a space with no proper stage, no stage lighting, no curtain, unsuitable seating and appalling acoustics places almost insurmountable obstacles in the way of both producer and director." I agreed: building the set in such a venue had presented insurmountable problems, and compromises had been necessary. In April 1971, I was again stage manager for ART's production of *Toad of Toad Hall* by A. A. Milne, in the more suitable venue of West Hall at AUB, which at least had a proper stage! This time the reviewer in the *Daily Star* was Joyce Said, who wrote on April 2: "*Toad Hall* proves to be smash hit for all." The last production in which I was involved was *The Killing of Sister George* by Frank Marcus at the Baalbek Festival Theatre in Beirut, where I was in charge of set construction.

In December 1970, I attended the Christmas ball at the Middle East Centre for Arab Studies (MECAS) in Shemlan, little knowing at the time that three years later I would be there again, this time as a student. The social columnist of the *Daily Star*, Peggy Johnson, covered this event and many other social gatherings. Although not always on the guest list, she seemed to attend just about every event in the social calendar and reported on them in her distinctive, breathless style. Her daily ramblings on the back page of the newspaper, listing many of those present at gatherings she had attended and describing their attire, were the first item that I read each morning. Unusually, for I seldom win anything, I won a raffle prize, which was a return ticket from Beirut to Athens on Middle East Airlines. I decided to use it in April 1971 when I made my first visit to Greece over the Easter holiday long weekend.

Shortly thereafter, the man who was responsible for establishing BBME's first branch in the Yemen Arab Republic passed through Beirut on his way to London, and we had an opportunity to meet. He told me about the plans to open three branches—in Hodeidah, Taiz and the capital, Sana'a, and I expressed an interest in being involved. He must have mentioned our conversation to the higher authority in London because shortly after his visit to Beirut, the head office informed me that after my end of tour leave, due to run from July to October 1971, I was to go to Hodeidah as the first accountant at the new branch there.

Therefore, in July 1971, just before my Lebanese work permit expired, I left Beirut for three months' home leave. I travelled via Istanbul and Rome to London, spending a few days in each city on the way. The following month I set out on a trip to North America, including stays in New York, Toronto, Flint, Calgary, Vancouver, San Francisco, Los Angeles, Mexico City and Miami where, in most places, I was able to meet up with friends. In Los Angeles, I was entertained by the Disney organisation, members of which I had met in Bahrain in 1970, when they were filming *Hamad and the Pirates*.

Chapter 8

YEMEN ARAB REPUBLIC

The introduction of decimal currency and the lifting of restrictions on gold ownership in the United Kingdom marked the year 1971. The British government also commenced new negotiations to join the European Economic Community (later the European Union), leading to a vote in favour of joining in the House of Commons in October. Among events which influenced my later life, six (later to be seven) Trucial States established the United Arab Emirates following the British decision to withdraw from east of Suez. In this year, the United States pulled out of the Bretton Woods Accord and therefore would no longer convert dollars to gold at a fixed rate and negotiations started between western oil companies and the Organisation of Petroleum Exporting Countries (OPEC) to stabilise oil prices.

The Kingdom of Yemen had become a monarchy after the end of World War I and the breakup of the Ottoman Empire. Some six imams ruled until 1962 when the then monarch Mohammed Al-Badr Ibn Ahmad was deposed in a republican revolution inspired by the philosophy of Egyptian president Gamal Abdel Nasser.

In 1971, the Yemen Arab Republic had only recently emerged from the civil war that had started with the revolution against the royal family in 1962 and dragged on until 1970. During that war, the Republicans received support from Nasser's Egypt, and the Royalists were aided by Saudi Arabia. Egyptian troops were deeply involved, fighting with the Republicans in support of Pres. Abdullah al-Sallal to the point where Egypt began to refer to Yemen as "their Vietnam."[49] Eventually, Nasser had to withdraw his troops in 1967 at the time of the Six Day War against Israel. After this withdrawal, al-Sallal's regime fell, leading to reconciliation between the Republicans and Royalists and the establishment, in 1970, of a new Republican government under Pres. Abdul Rahman al-Iryani. The Yemen Arab Republic, as the country was named, remained under his rule until 1974, and in May 1990, the country was united with the Peoples Democratic Republic of Yemen (also called South Yemen).

In October 1971, at the end of my leave, I set out for the Yemen Arab Republic. Prior to my departure from London, I called on the general manager of the bank, as was customary. He told me the story of a large valuable Persian carpet that had at one time graced the floor of the house of the manager of the Aden branch of BBME. After the bank, along with all others operating in what was then the People's Democratic Republic of Yemen, was nationalised in 1969, the chairman of the bank had written to the authorities in Aden and asked if the carpet could be returned to the bank in London. Much to the amazement of everyone, it was, and in 1971, it was on the floor of the chairman's office!

I travelled out from London via Athens, where I stopped over to meet up with a colleague on leave there at the time, and Beirut, where I arranged the shipment of my personal effects to Yemen. I then went on to Jeddah, one of the very few places from where it was possible to get a flight to Hodeidah. The Saudi Arabian Airlines flight from Jeddah to Hodeidah made an intermediate stop in Jazan in southern Saudi Arabia. It was a small propeller aircraft with no more than twenty passengers on the flight, and the airport at Jazan was small and informal. All the transit passengers left the plane and wandered around on the apron while the plane was refuelled, and I decided to take some photographs. An official spotted this activity. He informed

---

[49]   http://findarticles.com/p/articles/mi_m0IAV/is_1_93/ai_n6123802, accessed 14 Jan 2012

me that it was forbidden and insisted that I remove the film from my camera and hand it over to him. I should have known better.

The arrival in Hodeidah was even more informal. The airport consisted of a relatively short runway with a small building housing administrative offices and check-in facilities; however, matters relating to arrivals were dealt with on the apron under the wing of the aircraft. Customs and immigration officials arrived at the plane in a Land Rover, and various meeters and greeters drove up in their cars, including my colleague, the manager of the Hodeidah branch. Passports were quickly stamped and baggage cleared and loaded in the manager's Mercedes. We then proceeded the short distance to the place that was to be my home for the first three months; the best accommodation Hodeidah could offer, the Al-Ikhwa Hotel, where the cook's pièce de résistances were "fried cow meat" (usually a tough steak) and crème caramel.

After a few months, following the arrival of a shipment of furniture

from London and my personal effects from Beirut, I was able to move into an apartment above the branch in Hodeidah. The manager, his wife and two children also had an apartment there, as did the owner of the building, a Yemeni who had studied law in England and had a

BBME Hodeidah branch, 1971

German wife. I quickly recruited a cook-houseboy, who had previously worked for various British expatriates in Aden when it was a British colony, and domestic life settled down to a reasonably comfortable routine. Local fishermen began to call regularly offering freshly caught seafood. I have never eaten fish but did enjoy the local lobster that the fishermen offered.

One of the problems that we faced in Yemen was ensuring a regular supply of alcoholic drinks. Although there was no objection to the consumption of alcohol by non-Muslims, there was no official source of supply within the country. Sometimes we would obtain a permit from the government to import ourselves, and usually we sourced supplies through the office maintained by our landlord in Aden, which the supplier then sent by airfreight, usually to Taiz. On another occasion, we sought the assistance of the London head office of the bank, which organised a shipment from the UK by a company that for many years had regularly supplied British diplomatic outposts with their requirements. In both cases, we used at least one bottle from the consignment to ensure that our "fixer" could clear the rest without any problems or delays. We also rewarded the "fixer" for his efforts with a bottle or two.

Another source, although unofficial, was well known and very reliable. We would drive to the coastal town of Mocha, about two hundred kilometres (124 miles) south of Hodeidah and park near the town centre. Within minutes, a number of men would invariably approach us and enquire if we wanted to buy whisky. In fact, they could offer virtually anything, including beer, gin, wine and cognac as well as whisky. The inhabitants of Mocha smuggled all of this in from the French colony of Djibouti in the Horn of Africa, just across the Red Sea and sold at very reasonable prices. They could even supply the tonic to go with the gin! Having ascertained our interest, we would be invited to follow the supplier's car out of the town to a location in the desert where the goods would be transferred from

their store, usually a hole in the ground under a decrepit building, to our vehicle, and payment would be effected. We often undertook this excursion on a Friday, the weekly holiday in the Muslim world, and combined it with a picnic on the beach near Mocha.

The author, digging out the Land Rover,
Yemen, 1972

Banking in Yemen was certainly different from anything I had experienced before. When I arrived, I discovered that the branch, which had only been open for a few weeks, was in a building that would have been more suitable as a godown (an Indian term for a warehouse, used in the region). It was mainly one large space with a very high ceiling, making it difficult to cool in the hot, humid weather of the Tihama plain. The bank had installed a number of air conditioners, but their effect was limited, given the large volume of air that required cooling. The other shock was to discover that NCR, on which the bank relied to provide and maintain accounting machines in most of its branches, had not yet established a presence in Yemen; and as a result, all of the accounting records were maintained by hand. Fortunately, within a few weeks of my arrival, NCR opened in the country; and before long, we were able to install the ubiquitous Class 32 accounting machines and mechanise our accounts. The training course that I had attended in Beirut in 1969 finally came in useful.

The day-to-day business of the bank was very different from that experienced previously in Bahrain or Beirut, let alone London, rural Norfolk or Toronto. At the time, and even now, there were many Yemenis working in Saudi Arabia. The bank maintained accounts for several of the mainly Jeddah-based Saudi exchange dealers. They would regularly instruct the bank to pay substantial sums of cash to their agents in Hodeidah. The agents would turn up at the branch with a pickup truck and a large supply of sacks. The cash, in small denomination notes, as there were few large ones, was placed in the sacks and thrown into the back of the pickup. The agent would then travel around the small towns and villages in the country, where there were no banking facilities, to make payments to the families of the Yemeni workers who were in Saudi Arabia. Such activities would be difficult, maybe prohibited, today under anti-money laundering laws, since the bank certainly never knew the original remitters or the ultimate beneficiaries of the funds.

Another unusual piece of business was financing the export of raw cotton from Yemen, mainly to Germany at the time. Farmers grew cotton throughout much of the Tihama coastal plain between

Hodeidah and Mocha. A state-owned company that was responsible for dealing with the exports purchased the crop from the farmers. The bank provided finance to the state-owned company to bridge the time between their paying the farmers and receiving the sales proceeds under letters of credit opened in their favour by the foreign buyers. Since the bank related the amount that it was prepared to lend to the value of the cotton purchased for export, which was the security, it was necessary to check regularly the quantity of raw cotton held by the exporter. This raw cotton was stored in open fields in very high piles of bales of various shapes and sizes. We quickly realised that it was impossible to dismantle the mountains of bales and to weigh every one, so we established a method of calculating the total weight based on the volume and a sampling of the weight of a few bales. This seemed to work to everyone's satisfaction, and the results were close enough to reality when the exports actually took place.

Another important agricultural crop in Yemen was qat. This is a small evergreen shrub, similar in appearance to privet. It grows on terraced hillsides at the same altitude and in much the same conditions as coffee, once an important Yemeni export; it is widely cultivated, often at the expense of coffee as the qat can quickly be sold for cash and is usually used for chewing, especially during afternoon gatherings of merchants and businessmen. Qat is part of the national culture in Yemen; those who chew it claim that it aids business decisions, swallowing the qat juice having a mildly narcotic effect. Some qat was also exported (although not financed by the bank), especially to nearby countries such as Ethiopia and Djibouti. I once flew from Taiz to Djibouti in a DC3 aircraft of Yemen Airways on which sacks of qat filled half of the passenger cabin.

The Soviet Union had established its influence in Yemen during the civil war in the 1960s, and the country maintained a consulate in Hodeidah as well as the embassy in Sana'a. Among the Soviet-aid projects was the construction of a surfaced road from Hodeidah to Sana'a. At this time, foreign goods, especially consumer items, were virtually unavailable in the Soviet Union. Often the staff from the embassy and consulate would come to the bank in Hodeidah to make transfers to a mail-order company in West Germany in payment for items that were shipped to them in Yemen for eventual transfer back to their country or directly to their families in the Soviet Union.

At the time that the bank was establishing its branches in Yemen, the British Foreign and Commonwealth Office was establishing the first British embassy in the capital Sana'a, initially manned by a chargé d'affaires and a small staff. There was no diplomatic presence outside Sana'a at the time, although there is now a consulate in Hodeidah as well as the embassy in Sana'a. Since we were the *British* Bank of the Middle East, people sometimes thought that there was some connection with the government. This gave rise to one particularly macabre incident when the branch manager received a phone call one afternoon from the manager of the Al-Ikhwa Hotel, informing him that an Englishman had committed suicide in his room at the hotel and asking what the bank was going to do about this unfortunate incident. The branch manager and I proceeded to the hotel to verify the facts and then called the consul at the embassy in Sana'a for guidance. By this time, it was about 4:00 p.m. and although the drive from the capital would take at least four hours on the mountainous road, he said that he would set out immediately for Hodeidah. In the meantime, the branch manager was in touch with the police, who were anxious to see the matter closed as soon as possible. There was no Christian cemetery in the country and no facilities to store or embalm the body, so it was necessary for burial to take place quickly. The manager then called on the governor of Hodeidah to seek his assistance; he agreed that burial could take place on a patch of land adjacent to the Muslim cemetery. He issued appropriate instructions, and we showed a carpenter how to make a coffin. The consul, a former MECAS student and future director, duly arrived, accompanied by his wife, and they stayed overnight with the branch manager. Next morning, after calls on the police and the governor to complete formalities, we transported the body to the somewhat dusty and desolate burial site in a pickup truck, and the consul conducted a short funeral service. This was certainly not a typical twenty-four hours in the life of most bankers.

The three major cities in Yemen were Sana'a (the capital), Taiz and Hodeidah. Sana'a is situated in the mountains at an altitude of about 2,300 metres (7,500 ft); Taiz, about 250 kilometres to the south of the capital, is at about 1,500 metres (4,800 ft); and Hodeidah, the main port, is located on the coast in the Tihama plain. In 1971, the population of Sana'a was about 130,000 and Taiz and Hodeidah had around 90,000 each. When I arrived in Yemen, roads built by different aid donors linked the three main cities. The Soviet Union built the road from Hodeidah to the capital in 1961, and it was surfaced for its entire length. It passed through extremely difficult mountainous country, via Bajel and Manakhah, rising to over 3,000 metres (10,000 ft) at the highest point before descending to Sana'a. The 226-kilometre (142 miles) journey took between four and five hours, depending on the traffic. The Chinese built the road from Hodeidah to Taiz in the late 1960s. The first stretch of the 282 kilometre (162 mile) journey, across the Tihama plain through Zabid, was surfaced; but after that, when the road entered the mountains, it was still gravel. The journey usually took three to four hours, fording at least one un-bridged river on the way. There was a gravel road linking Sana'a and Taiz, a distance of 256 kilometres (159 miles), which passed through the towns of Damar, Yarim and Ibb as it wound through the mountains. It was originally built by the United States, and in 1974, the German government was funding its upgrade and surfacing. A joint venture between a British and a German contractor won the contract, and they chose to bank with BBME.

BBME Taiz branch, 1971
(HSBC Holdings Plc)

When BBME had first applied to the Central Bank of Yemen for permission to open branches in the country, it received three licences—for Hodeidah, Taiz and Sana'a. Even before Hodeidah opened, in September 1971, plans were underway for the branch in Taiz; and then, literally a few days before the Taiz branch was supposed to open, it seemed that disaster had struck. The Hodeidah manager received a letter from the central bank informing him that they had revoked the licences for Taiz and Sana'a, but giving no reasons. Both he and the chairman made immediate representations to the governor of the central bank, and they agreed that in view of the advanced stage of plans to open in Taiz, it could proceed; they never did relent on Sana'a. We always believed that the central bank attitude had been prompted by complaints from the only indigenous commercial bank, the Yemen Bank for Reconstruction and Development, which had a monopoly before BBME opened, that BBME was poaching too much of its business.

We moved quickly to finalise plans to open the branch in Taiz, which took place on December 17, 1971. Later the bank obtained permission to open a branch in Ibb, but subsequently, in the 1990s, decided to cease its operations in the country completely.

BBME Taiz branch opening, Dec 1971

In the 1970s, the standard tour of overseas duty with BBME was two years, followed by three months' home leave. The only exception was Saudi Arabia, where the tour was one year with six weeks leave, because the bank considered the country to be a hardship posting. After about a year in Yemen I decided, with the support of the manager, to suggest to the general manager that the terms of service in Yemen should be the same as in Saudi Arabia. Hodeidah seemed to us to be more of a hardship posting than Jeddah or al-Khobar. The general manager did not agree!

In his reply, making no mention of present-day Saudi Arabia, he reminded me of the hardships suffered in earlier years in most places that the bank operated.

In his letter, he wrote,

> Think for a moment about life in Bushire in 1947, with five other Europeans in the whole town, no air conditioning, no plumbing, kerosene fridge, water only off the ships, no beer, punkahs in the office, very little variety of food, no vegetables except 'ladies fingers' in the summer. Or think of Zahedan, where, in the winter, sufficient chipped potatoes had to be made and kept in tin biscuit boxes to last all through the summer, and no European company whatsoever, except, sometimes a Vice Consul. Is there nowhere in Taiz where there is a tennis court or an open-air badminton court or any little swimming bath or somewhere suitable for playing boules? As regards newspapers, you are really quite well off because when I was in Meshed the newspapers used to come in lots six weeks at a time and took three months to get to Meshed.

Obviously, in Yemen in 1972, where the London newspapers reached us by mail in about ten days, we had "never had it so good!"

However, the general manager did suggest that I take two weeks "local leave," with the bank paying my airfare. Therefore, in November 1972, I set out for my local leave in Kenya. To get there, I first had to drive the 282 kilometres from Hodeidah to Taiz from where I took an Air Djibouti DC3 to Djibouti. It was necessary to stay overnight there, which gave me the chance to see something of a French colony that was still very francophone; even the Foreign Legion was present. The next day I flew in another DC3, this time of Ethiopian Airlines, from Djibouti to Addis Ababa. On the way, we made a stop in Dire Dawa, where lunch was served to passengers in the airport restaurant. Another night stop was necessary in Addis Ababa, and on the third day after leaving Hodeidah, I finally reached Nairobi. During the flight from Addis to Nairobi, the plane crossed the equator, and the airline gave all passengers a certificate to commemorate this event.

My first visit in Kenya was to Treetops, a lodge not too far from Nairobi, at which Princess Elizabeth and the Duke of Edinburgh had been staying in February 1952 when she was informed that her father, King George VI, had died and that she was queen. Since the lodge first opened in 1932, other famous visitors have included Charlie Chaplin, Neville Chamberlain and Willy Brandt.

The owners of Treetops lodge built it, as the name suggests, on stilts among cape chestnut trees, and it had observation areas overlooking a floodlit watering hole that attracted a large variety of animals during the hours of darkness. Guests arrived in time for afternoon tea and stayed for dinner and overnight. Animals began arriving during the late afternoon, first waterbuck and warthog and later rhino and elephant, among many others. Although guests had rooms at the lodge for their overnight stay, they spent most of the time watching the nocturnal visitors to the water hole from the observation area. Quite early the next morning, the guests were transferred to a nearby hotel, owned by the same group, for breakfast before being driven back to Nairobi. My record of the visit shows that among the animals I saw were 114 elephant, 13 rhinoceros, 177 buffalo and 1 colobus monkey.

From Nairobi, I then travelled to Mombasa by road for a few days relaxation by the sea and returned to Nairobi by overnight train. The menu for dinner in the dining car included a wonderful reminder of my Paston School days: spotted dick and custard! The trip concluded with a tour by road to two of the game parks in northern Tanzania, Ngorongoro Crater and Lake Manyara, before returning to Nairobi from where I flew back to Taiz, this time via Addis Ababa and Assab.

Although I had been issued with a Chargex credit card when they were first issued while I worked for Toronto Dominion Bank in Canada, this was of little use outside Canada in the days before the Visa franchise became world-wide. In 1972, therefore, I decided to apply for the prestigious American Express card, with little hope that my application would be approved. Much to my surprise, it was, and I have been using the card ever since, having moved upwards in stages from the green card, through gold to platinum. I have recently declined an offer to receive the Centurion Card because its cost did not seem justified now that I am retired.

In February 1973, the bank transferred me from Hodeidah to become manager of the Taiz branch, and while I held the position, we received a visit from the London-based general manager of the bank. This was his first visit to the country, and as was customary during such visits, he called on various government and central bank officials and entertained them and the bank's customers in both Hodeidah and Taiz. In Taiz, I organised a dinner at the best hotel in town, the Ikhwa.

In June 1973, I was due to take home leave and travelled from Taiz via Hodeidah, Jeddah and Beirut to London. During my leave, I took a two-week cruise to the North Cape, the northernmost tip of Europe, on the *Queen Elizabeth 2*. The itinerary included calls at Hamburg, Copenhagen, Oslo, Bergen and Trondheim, as well as the North Cape. Cunard issued a certificate to each passenger certifying the date and time of crossing the Arctic Circle, which complemented the certificate issued by Ethiopian Airlines when I crossed the equator. One of my outstanding ambitions is to obtain a certificate of crossing the Antarctic Circle—to complete the set.

Chapter 9

LEBANON AGAIN AND MECAS

The year 1973 commenced with the United Kingdom, Ireland and Denmark entering the European Economic Community. During the year, the first mobile phone call was made in New York, the US dollar was devalued by 10 percent, and Israeli commandos, including future foreign minister and prime minister, Ehud Barak, raided Beirut and assassinated three PLO officials. In October, Egypt and Syria launched the Yom Kippur War during which the Arab oil embargo against countries which supported Israel commenced, causing an energy crisis.

In September 1973, I was due to start the ten month "long course" at the Middle East Centre for Arab Studies (MECAS) in Shemlan, a small village, with a population then of about four hundred fifty people, in the mountains at an altitude of about eight hundred metres, some thirty kilometres (20 miles) southeast of Beirut.

During leave in England prior to the start of the course, I took delivery of a new car, a Peugeot 504, with a plan to take it with me to Lebanon to use during my time there. At that time, there were regular sailings around the eastern Mediterranean Sea by passenger ships of the Italian Adriatica Line, which could also carry accompanied cars as cargo. The most convenient sailing to allow me to arrive in Beirut a few days before the course was to start was on the *Ausonia* from Venice. I therefore drove from England to Venice and embarked there, along with some fellow students from the British diplomatic service who were also taking their own cars to Lebanon. En route to Beirut, we called at Rhodes. On arrival at

Beirut port, I was met, by prior arrangement, by a clearing agent without whose help I would probably still be trying to get my car through the customs formalities. In order to take the car into Lebanon on a temporary basis, without having to pay customs duty, I had obtained a *carnet de*

The author meeting the captain of the Ausonia, August 1973

passages from the Automobile Association (AA) in England. This provided a guarantee that if I did not eventually re-export my car, the AA would pay the duty to the Lebanese authorities. The clearing agent eventually managed to get approval for the car to remain in Lebanon for just six months, whereas I was expecting to be there for almost eleven months. The agent assured me that it would be possible to extend this period in due course, but as we shall see, that process was not as straightforward as initially indicated.

Although the school provided accommodation in bed-sitting rooms for those who wanted to stay on the premises, I chose to live in a rented apartment in the neighbouring, predominantly Greek Orthodox, village of Souk al Gharb, about two kilometres from the school. The apartment was in a small three-storey building owned by the Attieh family, located on the side of a hill with magnificent views over the city of Beirut, the airport and the Mediterranean Sea. Two other students and their families were also living in the building. The only drawback was the somewhat ineffective central heating during the cold winter, when snow fell at that altitude, and low temperatures were usual for several months. Although living in the apartment, I decided to avail myself of the catering facilities offered at the school and took lunch and dinner there most of the time. The caterer, an elderly villager known as Abu Mousa, provided three meals a day for about US$3. The school also had a bar, named Thatcher's Club, not after the rising politician and future British prime minister, Margaret, but after the author of an Arabic grammar textbook, originally published in 1910, which was used in the early days of MECAS. The bar was open only from seven to eight each evening, except Saturday, and before lunch each Friday.

As soon as I arrived at MECAS, the administrator provided all students with copious notes, covering a multitude of possible situations, policies and procedures, including the availability and cost of domestic servants, where to do your banking (BBME, Saint George's Bay branch was favoured), and the cost of a seat in a shared "service" taxi from Shemlan to Beirut. There was also a warning not to try to bring firearms into the country and the information that cuts in the electricity supply often occurred, especially in winter. However, it was noted, the school had a standby generator and, in the last resort, Aladdin lamps. In respect of the electricity supply, nothing has changed for the better almost forty years later. Indeed the electricity situation is worse now.

The British government established MECAS originally in the Austrian hospice near the Via Dolorosa in Jerusalem in 1944 to teach Arabic to British military and civilian officers. The first director was Bertram Thomas, whose Middle East experience had started in 1916 and continued until his death, in Cairo, in 1950. His assistant, responsible for Arabic language instruction, was Abba Eban,[50] then an agent of SOE in Jerusalem and later the Israeli foreign minister from 1966 to 1974. As foreign minister, he played a significant part in the drafting of UN Security Council Resolutions 242 after the Six Day War in 1967 and 338, following the Yom Kippur War in 1973. He resigned from MECAS in 1946, following the attack on the King David Hotel in Jerusalem.

As the situation in Palestine became tenser, the government decided that MECAS should move to another location. In April 1947, students

---

[50]   Craig, Sir James, Shemlan, A History of the Middle East Centre for Arab Studies, 1998, MacMillan Press Limited, London

found themselves under canvas at an army camp near Amman while Bertram Thomas searched for a more permanent location. In September of that year, the school opened in Shemlan, where it was to continue to teach Arabic for another thirty years, not just to British diplomats and military officers but also to a wide range of other students from foreign diplomatic services and businessmen of many nationalities from many walks of life, including banking and the oil industry. The civil war in Lebanon forced its closure in 1978, and in spite of several suggestions, the school has never been replaced.

Over the years, MECAS gained a reputation, largely undeserved, as a spy school. It is true that among its students in 1967 was a man who was later to become head of the British Secret Intelligence Service (MI6) and who, during a posting at the embassy in Beirut as second secretary when I lived and worked there in 1970, had entertained me at his home. Conversely, the more infamous Kim Philby, the high-ranking British intelligence officer who defected to the Soviet Union from Beirut in 1963, was never at MECAS as a student, although he may have attended social events at the school while living in Beirut as a journalist prior to his defection. However, in 1971, Philby, in a newspaper interview given in Moscow shortly after the expulsion of 105 Soviet intelligence officers from the United Kingdom, did identify the MECAS student who had entertained me in Beirut and who was later to head the SIS as an MI6 officer.[51]

One spy, who did attend MECAS, was George Blake. A member of the British MI6, he was exposed as a Soviet double agent while studying Arabic in Shemlan in 1961 and recalled to London, where he was arrested and, after a trial held in camera, sentenced to forty-two years in jail. Kamal Jumblatt, the Druze leader, and a number of members of parliament used the publicity surrounding his arrest and trial to call for the closure of MECAS, alleging that the incident proved that the British government was using the school

---

[51]   http://www.telegraph.co.uk/news/obituaries/1309010/Sir-David-Spedding. html, accessed 14 Jan 2012

to train spies.[52] In spite of this campaign, the institution survived. In 1966, Blake escaped from Wormwood Scrubs prison and found his way to Moscow, where he still lives with the rank of a colonel in the KGB on a government pension. In 2010, on his eighty-eighth birthday, the former Soviet agent gave a rare interview to Izvestia in which he said he had no regrets and expressed no remorse for betraying Britain or its intelligence service. He went on to predict, "The American empire will disappear because everyone who lives by the sword dies from the sword."[53]

As well as the occasional spy, many students who went on to earn distinction later in their careers attended MECAS. One British diplomat who was on my course was Derek Plumbly (now Sir Derek). After serving in several senior posts, including ambassador to Saudi Arabia and Egypt, in January 2012 the UN secretary-general appointed him as the United Nations Special Coordinator for Lebanon,[54] an appointment that will surely test both his diplomatic and language skills.

When I first moved to the Middle East, in 1969, I had started taking Arabic lessons in Bahrain. There, BBME engaged a schoolteacher who taught from what may well have been the same books as he used when teaching Bahraini children—the Arabic equivalent of "*A* is for Apple, *B* is for Ball" and so on. This was also the approach used at MECAS in its early days.[55] By 1973, MECAS had a tried and well-tested method of teaching Arabic, sometimes described as a language in which it is possible to say nothing with great eloquence and one in which words derived from the same root could have one meaning and its complete opposite (as well as something to do with

52 Craig, Sir James, Shemlan, A History of the Middle East Centre for Arab Studies, 1998, MacMillan Press Limited, London
53 http://www.telegraph.co.uk/news/worldnews/europe/russia/8126815/British-double-agent-George-Blake-predicts-end-of-American-empire.html, accessed 14 Jan 2012
54 http://www.naharnet.com/stories/en/26559-derek-plumbly-appointed-u-n-special-coordinator-for-lebanon, accessed 21 Jan 2012
55 McLoughlin, Leslie, A Nest of Spies . . . ?, 1993, Alhani International Books Ltd, London

a camel!). During the early years, course material was developed by successive directors and principal instructors, especially James Craig (later Sir James) and Donald Maitland (later Sir Donald) in the 1950s; most of this was still in use until the school closed in 1978. There was the *MECAS Word List*, first used in 1957, which included some three thousand words, chosen for their frequency of occurrence, knowledge of which was considered necessary to claim a reasonable vocabulary in the Arabic language. Students were expected to learn 150 new words each week, and the proven method of doing this was to use cards about the same size as business cards, with the English word on one side and the Arabic on the other, flashing through the cards in almost every moment of spare time. *The Way Prepared*, a book containing reading passages, in which the new vocabulary supposed to have been learnt each week was introduced to the student in context, complemented this. In addition, we used the *MECAS Grammar of Modern Literary Arabic*, and I had equipped myself with copies of the *Oxford English-Arabic Dictionary* and *A Dictionary of Modern Written Arabic* compiled by a German, Hans Wehr.

In the period 1965-1968, the principal instructor was Leslie McLoughlin, who gradually introduced changes in teaching methods, in particular giving more emphasis to the spoken language from the beginning of the course. The main material used was simple dialogues developed by McLoughlin covering everyday situations.[56] After a break of two years, he returned to MECAS as principal instructor in 1970 and remained in that position until 1975, including the period when I was on the long course. During his second tenure, McLoughlin introduced further changes in teaching methods, including the use of a textbook new to MECAS called *Elementary Modern Standard Arabic* (EMSA) alongside the traditional materials. The Inter-University Committee for Near Eastern Languages at Ann Arbor, Michigan developed EMSA, first published in 1968. It had a major difference from the MECAS material in that it omitted short vowels from the text. In written Arabic, small marks above or below

---

[56]   McLoughlin, Leslie, A Nest of Spies . . . ?, 1993, Alhani International Books Ltd, London

the consonant may be used to indicate short vowels, but in general, this is not done.

From lesson 1, EMSA introduced the student to Arabic written in the way the student would have to read it in contemporary newspapers and books, without the short vowels. Many of the teachers, some of whom had been using the old teaching material for many years, were not enthusiastic about EMSA. The word list, grammar and EMSA were all used in the teaching of classical Arabic; but in addition, we had lessons in Lebanese colloquial Arabic, using material developed by the school, including a book called *The Spoken Arabic of the Levant*. While the written language is virtually the same throughout the Arab world, the spoken language differs greatly. Some critics describe Lebanese colloquial Arabic as the cockney version of the language and it certainly has a very distinctive sound.

There were about thirty-six students on my course, and it overlapped with the advanced course, on which there were another twelve students, all taught by about fifteen instructors. The two courses included people from the Australian, Canadian, German, Swiss and Japanese diplomatic services, the British Council, the Australian Trade Commission, a British officer in the Oman army, a representative of a major cigarette company and seven Japanese commercial students. They had the unenviable challenge of learning Arabic through the medium of English, a language in which not all of them were completely fluent. I was the only banker on the long course, but on the advanced course was a member of the family that gave its name to an old established British merchant bank

MECAS Class of 1974

established in 1782. This bank was to hit the headlines in a spectacular manner in 1995 when it collapsed following huge losses on unauthorised speculative trading in futures contracts. It was among the first victims of deregulation in banking, something that was destined to have even more serious consequences in later years. On the long course, the school divided students into "syndicates" of four people. The other members of my syndicate were a British diplomat, a Japanese businessman and the wife of a British Council director, who was also on the course. Lessons were from eight thirty to twelve

The author (front) with his syndicate members, MECAS 1974

thirty, consisting of five periods with a coffee break halfway through the morning. However, after lunch, it was necessary to devote considerable time to private study, especially learning the weekly allocation of new words from the word list.

Social life in Shemlan was limited, and in any case, there was not much spare time during the week after completing our studies each day. At weekends many students journeyed to Beirut for the bright lights and facilities available there. During the course, the school arranged for students to be entertained in the homes of villagers, where there was the opportunity to practice our MECAS Arabic, with which the inhabitants of Shemlan were well versed. On another occasion, I and some other students were invited to the home of former Egyptian Queen Farida, the first wife of King Farouk. After her divorce she lived for a time in Shemlan and there resumed painting, a pastime at which she was quite talented.

Just over a month after the start of the first term, on October 6, 1973, the fourth Arab-Israeli war began with a surprise coordinated attack on Israel by Egypt and Syria. At MECAS, all students and staff were avidly following the progress of the conflict, mainly on the BBC World Service radio news, although the only manifestations that we observed were occasional overflights by Israeli and Syrian military aircraft. One of the former jettisoned a fuel tank within our view, but it did no damage. The war and its aftermath totally changed MECAS as domestic Lebanese problems increased. In May 1976, events in Lebanon forced the evacuation of students and foreign staff by road to Damascus and Amman; although the school reopened in Shemlan in September 1977, its presence there lasted only until November 1978 when the final evacuation, by road to Damascus, took place.

During the winter of 1973-1974, I and several other students who were fond of skiing decided to rent a house in Faraya, where I had skied before while living in Beirut, for use at weekends during the skiing season. We located a suitable property in the village, a few kilometres below the ski slopes, and agreed terms. Like so many village houses in Lebanon, the front door opened into a central living room, leading off which were four bedrooms plus a kitchen and bathroom. That house must have been the coldest in Lebanon that winter. The only source of heat was an antiquated stove in the living room fuelled by *mazoot* (diesel fuel). It emitted an unpleasant smell and did not do much to increase the overall temperature inside the house. During one visit, I had the misfortune to slip on a patch of ice outside the house and injured my shoulder. One of the group drove me down to Beirut to the emergency department of the American University of Beirut hospital where, after they had made sure that I had cash to pay for treatment, I got an x-ray, and the arm was immobilised in a sling. Luckily, I had suffered no serious damage.

In January 1974, during the Christmas holiday at MECAS, I visited Cyprus again, this time with three fellow students. We stayed in Kyrenia, and it was the last time that I was able to visit that town for many years, as it fell within the occupied area of the island after the Turkish invasion in July that year. The following April, during the Easter break, a number of fellow students and I took a short trip to Crete.

While at MECAS, there were also opportunities to travel by car to the neighbouring countries. One such trip was to Damascus and northern Syria, including Hama, Homs and Aleppo and another to Amman, Petra and Aqaba in Jordan. When returning to Lebanon from a weekend trip to Damascus, a few weeks before the expiry of the time permitted in my *carnet de passages* for my car to remain in Lebanon, I encountered a problem with the customs at the Masna'a border crossing. Because of the short time remaining under the original permission, they decided that I could not take the car back into Lebanon. Negotiations in my best MECAS Arabic, a version of the language in which the customs official was not well versed, never having lived in Shemlan, produced only a compromise solution. The customs official allowed me to drive the car to Beirut port, accompanied by an officer, where it was impounded. A few days later, the same clearing agent who had assisted when I arrived in Beirut originally was able to arrange an extension of the expiry of the permit until after the end of my course, and I retrieved the car.

During the long course at MECAS, all students took a "language break" after they had had time to acquire a reasonable knowledge of the language, in order to put into practice what they had learned. During the course that I attended, the "language break" was in May 1974. In the early 1970s, the school reduced the duration from four to two weeks. In spite of the school's preference that students should not travel together[57] in preparation for the event, I had made plans for myself and two other students to spend the time in Yemen, through a friend living in Taiz and teaching English there. My friend had arranged that we would live with Yemeni families of his students. Unfortunately, just prior to our arrival, the families had had second thoughts about the presence of male foreigners in their homes, a problem that students also experienced elsewhere. We therefore stayed in a hotel in Taiz and still found plenty of opportunities to practice our Arabic in a country where, at the time, knowledge of English was far from common.

The course ended on July 26, and the following day, I left Beirut with my car, again on a ship of the Adriatica Line, via Alexandria to Naples. A fellow student from the Australian diplomatic service travelled with me. From Naples, we drove to England together, and

---

[57]   McLoughlin, Leslie, A Nest of Spies . . . ?, 1993, Alhani International Books Ltd, London

I had the opportunity to show him some of the sights in London before he headed off to his new posting in Amman. While we were in London, I decided to take him to Simpson's-in-the-Strand for a traditional English roast beef lunch. This was 1974 when this august establishment still enforced a strict dress code. Since neither of us was wearing a jacket and tie, we were politely told by the doorman that we could not be admitted because we were "not dressed." We lunched instead at Lyons Corner House, a little farther down the Strand, where the dress code was less formal and the food less expensive.

By the time that I reached London, I knew that I would be starting work with Toronto Dominion Bank in the Middle East in September. When this bank, for which I had worked in Toronto, decided to expand into the Middle East, they had tracked me down and persuaded me to rejoin them. In the meantime, I decided to visit friends from Yemen days who were holidaying in Switzerland. I travelled out from London by train to the small village of Rougemont in the canton of Vaud, in the French-speaking part of the country, and passed a pleasant ten days there riding up mountains in chairlifts, walking in the mountains and making a day trip to Geneva. That introduction to this part of Switzerland led to me buying a property there a few years later.

Chapter 10

United Arab Emirates

The year 1974 saw the end of the Arab oil embargo against the United States, Europe and Japan but not before the price of a barrel of oil had increased from US$1.81 in 1971 to US$3.00 in 1972 and to almost US$12.00 by the end of the embargo. In July, Turkey invaded Cyprus to prevent the country from declaring union with Greece following a coup d'état by Greek-led pro-*enosis* forces. Within a month, Turkey had occupied 37 percent of the island.

The price of crude oil continued to increase while I was living and working in the United Arab Emirates, reaching US$35.00 per barrel in 1981, still a long way from the heights that the price would reach in later years. The newfound wealth of Saudi Arabia and the other Gulf oil-producing countries, during these years and later, precipitated a mad rush by western banks and companies to establish a presence in the region and get their share of the business generated by the wealth and the demands of these countries for development. Dubai, especially, saw an influx of a variety of carpetbaggers offering everything imaginable to, sometimes, gullible buyers and searching for their pot of gold at the end of the Dubai rainbow. I particularly remember one, who was trying to sell prefabricated houses, constructed mainly from wood, and another peddling military uniforms and other more harmful items.

Dubai had always been a major trading port in the Gulf and aspired to maintain this position and become an important financial centre as well. However, in 1975 Bahrain, as part of a plan to diversify its economy, stole a march on Dubai by announcing plans to licence offshore banking units (OBUs). Essentially, OBUs could take three forms: locally incorporated with multiple shareholders, locally incorporated subsidiaries of foreign banks or branches of foreign banks. The huge income earned by the oil-exporting countries in the region since the increases in crude oil prices was attracting great interest among western banks and companies. The former were looking for ways to get their hands on the liquidity held by the oil exporters, and the latter were looking for ways to part the governments and citizens of the exporting countries from their wealth. Prior to the establishment of the OBU licencing scheme in Bahrain, it was difficult for a foreign bank to establish a presence in the Gulf; indeed, in Saudi Arabia and Kuwait it was impossible. If a foreign bank could obtain a licence, as in the UAE, it would have to be willing to take on local domestic business, which was not something that appealed to many of the major international banks. The opportunity to open an OBU in Bahrain did appeal to many international banks. Within four months of announcing the rules, the Bahrain Monetary Agency had received thirty-two applications, and the number of OBU's eventually peaked at over seventy. The main terms of the offshore licence were that the holders could do business with the government of Bahrain and its agencies, but not with other residents. They were free to deal with any non-resident. Lack of any reserve requirement was an added attraction. Names such as Manufacturers Hanover Trust Company (later merged with Chemical Bank that in turn was taken over by JPMorgan Chase Bank), Midland Bank (now HSBC Bank plc), Lloyds Bank and Credit Suisse were attracted.

Later, locally incorporated institutions, some such as Arab Banking Corporation and Gulf International Bank, owned by Arab governments, joined the community. All of the OBUs were attracted to establish in Bahrain because of the business-friendly law and the country's proximity to Saudi Arabia, the location of the greatest oil wealth in the region. Eventually, the UAE replicated the Bahrain initiative with a similar scheme, but very few banks took advantage of it; those that might have done so already had full domestic licences in the UAE or had already established OBUs in Bahrain and saw no need for a second offshore presence in the Gulf. The only names that I can recall that did establish OBUs in Dubai were Royal Bank of Canada and American Express Bank. Neither bank stayed for very long.

As oil wealth flowed to the region during the 1970s and companies and banks, notwithstanding the Bahrain OBU scheme, flocked to Dubai, the ruler, His Highness Sheikh Rashid bin Saeed Al Maktoum, initiated a number of major projects, the viability of which was doubted by many observers at the time. As well as a significant expansion of Port Rashid, in 1971 he conceived the idea of building an adjacent dry dock. Queen Elizabeth II formally opened it in 1979, and it became fully operational in 1983, at which time it had the capacity to accommodate vessels up to one million tons, larger than any hitherto built. Another such project was the Jebel Ali Free Zone. It is said, probably apocryphally, that one day in 1976 Sheikh Rashid drove down the coast towards the border between Dubai and Abu Dhabi and reached a point at which he stuck his camel stick into the desert and announced that this was to be the site of the new Jebel Ali port. The result was the construction of the largest port in the world, and in 1985, Dubai established a free zone at Jebel Ali, which is now home to over six thousand four hundred companies including one hundred twenty of the Fortune Global 500 enterprises.[58] Today the world's largest airport is under construction nearby, although since the recent economic downturn in Dubai and its financial problems, progress on this project seems to have slowed, and possibly, the government has scaled down the scope.

Another idea conceived in the 1970s was the Dubai World Trade Centre. This thirty-nine-story tower, the tallest in the region at the time, with adjacent hotel and apartment buildings, generated much

---

[58]   http://www.jafza.ae/en/about-us/jafza-facts-at-a-glance.html accessed 7 Dec 2012

criticism. It was considered to be too far from town, not commercially viable, and overambitious at a time when Sheikh Rashid was embarking on other major projects such as the dry dock and Jebel Ali port, which many influential citizens thought risky. The location was then a long way from the business centre of Dubai. Nevertheless, the project went ahead, designed by British architects and built by a British construction company. Queen Elizabeth II also opened this project during her visit in 1979. Today there are many skyscrapers lining Sheikh Zayed Road, including the tallest man-made structure in the world, the 104-floor Burj Khalifa, which is 829 metres (2,723 ft) tall, dwarfing the World Trade Centre.

Dubai World Trade Centre under construction, c1978 (HSBC Holdings Plc)

A project welcomed more generally during this period was the satellite earth station at Jebel Ali. Like its predecessor in Bahrain opened in 1970, Cable and Wireless built it for the UAE Ministry of Communications, and it had a capacity to handle over one thousand five hundred simultaneous telephone calls as well as television transmission. I was invited to the opening ceremony, performed by the UAE president and ruler of Abu Dhabi, His Highness Sheikh Zayed bin Sultan Al Nahayan on November 8, 1975, my thirty-second birthday.

Trade and commerce in Dubai was in the hands of a relatively small number of merchant families, many of whom were involved in "re-exporting" gold from Dubai to India in the 1960s and 1970s. This business, which was often said to be under the protection of influential Indian politicians as well as the ruler of Dubai, who was not above participating himself, was the foundation of many fortunes among the merchants of Dubai. Gold bullion was imported by airfreight, perfectly legally, from Switzerland, often on consignment to certain banks in Dubai. The agent bank would release the bullion to a merchant against payment, which was probably financed from the merchant's overdraft. The merchants often formed syndicates to spread the risk, as there was always the possibility that the Indian authorities could intercept a shipment. Almost anyone with the right contacts could buy a share in a shipment. Dhows, often equipped with surprisingly powerful engines to enable them to escape from Indian customs patrols, transported the cargo across the Arabian Sea to the west coast of India.

Dubai clock tower, 1976

One family business, established in the 1960s, makes an interesting case study. It was originally a partnership of three brothers; in the early days, they participated in a big way in the gold trade, and over time, their more legitimate business interests built up, financed in part from the profits of the gold trade but more by borrowings from banks. At the peak, they owned a car dealership, an engineering company, a construction company in joint venture with a Dutch contractor and an agency for an important American air-conditioning brand. They also owned the largest cinema in the UAE, a travel agency, a major five-star hotel, the franchise for an American ice cream brand, the first English language daily newspaper in the country and substantial property interests in Dubai and abroad. In 1970, they established a locally incorporated bank, in which they were the majority shareholders, but with small minority participations by three major banks from Switzerland, the United Kingdom and the United States. Over time, this bank established branches in Pakistan and participations in locally incorporated banks in Bangladesh and Nepal. In 1980, the brothers broke up their partnership. Two continued to run the existing businesses, and the third took his share in cash and immediately began to establish his own empire, including a five-star hotel complete with a revolving restaurant and an ice-skating rink, a car dealership and his own bank; he largely duplicated the businesses that the original family partnership had developed. Both empires were destined for disaster. During the 1980s, the business enterprises of both branches of the family got into serious financial difficulties. The brother who had separated from the others became involved with Nelson and William Hunt in an attempt to corner the market in silver bullion. They failed. The UAE Central Bank declared the two Dubai banks insolvent and closed them. They were merged eventually into a Dubai government-owned bank; depositors did not lose anything. The brothers agreed settlements with most major creditors on undisclosed terms.

The heirs of the brother who went it alone seem to have prospered since the death of their father, with business interests that now include real estate development, hospitality, gems and jewellery, automobiles and transport; it was recently reported that they had made a donation of US$ 5 million to the Dubai Harvard Foundation for Medical Research.[59] The heirs of the other two brothers do not seem to have fared so well. In October 2006, the Dubai courts ordered the restructuring of their companies, much reduced in size since the 1980s, to give the government of Dubai a 30 percent holding in exchange for debts owed to the government and companies controlled by the ruling family.[60]

One bank that decided to establish a presence in the Middle East during the boom years of the 1970s was Toronto Dominion Bank (TD), my former employer in Canada. They were, of course, aware that after I left them in 1969, I had lived and worked in the area and in mid-1974, they tracked me down while I was at MECAS. By then they had established a Middle East representative office in Beirut and bought a small Lebanese domestic bank, Banque des Cedres, which was renamed Toronto Dominion Bank (Middle East) SAL. TD had also applied for licences to open full commercial

---

[59]   http://www.dhfmr.hms.harvard.edu/news-and-events/news/
      dhfmr-receives-donation, accessed 18 Sep 2012
[60]   http://pranaygupte.blogspot.com/2006/10/dubai-govt-takes-30-stake-in-
      galadari.html, accessed 14 Jan 2012

branches in Abu Dhabi and Dubai, and the United Arab Emirates Currency Board, the predecessor of the central bank, had approved these applications. The bank was in the process of recruiting staff to establish and manage these branches and offered me the job in Dubai.

In August 1974, I spent some time in the London branch of the bank to become better acquainted with their international operations. While at the London branch, I had my introduction to the Eurodollar. Eurodollar refers to US dollars deposited with banks outside the United States and therefore outside the control of the Federal Reserve. The first known Eurodollar deposit occurred in 1957, when the Soviet Union, fearing a possible freeze of assets held in the United States, moved US$800,000 to Moscow Narodny Bank in London[61]. The volume of these deposits with UK and European banks grew quickly. Because they were free from reserve requirements and deposit insurance costs, interest rates were lower than in the United States. It was natural for banks to utilise these dollar deposits to fund international lending; London became the major centre for booking such loans and a market for syndicating large Eurodollar loans among a group of banks developed there. Around this time, London and other centres saw the establishment of consortium banks, often set up to specialise in international Eurodollar lending. One such institution was Midland and International Bank Ltd, the shareholders of which included TD as well as Midland Bank and others.

When I arrived in Beirut in September 1974, I worked from the representative office while making initial preparations for the establishment of the Dubai branch. Later that month, I made my first visit to Dubai and Abu Dhabi, accompanied by a colleague from Beirut who had already done some groundwork there. I made a second visit in October and in November moved permanently to Dubai.

Initially I stayed at the Ambassador Hotel on the Dubai side of the creek. This Indian owned and operated hotel was one of three in

---

[61]   http://en.wikipedia.org/wiki/Eurodollar, accessed 7 Dec 2012

Dubai that might have just managed a four-star rating at the time; in 1974, no five-star hotels existed. The accommodation was adequate, the menu acceptable, and the service very good. It was a distinct improvement on the Al-Ikhwa Hotel, at which I had stayed during my early days in Hodeidah.

Finding accommodation, both office premises and a house for me, was the next challenge. At the time, there was a large influx of companies and their expatriate staff to Dubai. Suitable offices and

The TD Bank manager's house,
Dubai, 1975

houses were in short supply. After a few weeks, I found a villa to rent in Jumeirah, the residential area favoured by expatriates. It was one of six built by one of the major merchants in Dubai; it was new and available immediately, and the bank agreed to take a five-year lease, paying the full rent for the period in advance. This was common practice then, and the amount must have more than covered the full cost of construction paid by the property owner. Add to that the fact that the ruler had probably given the land to him, and you can see that property development was a lucrative occupation for UAE citizens in a market where, at the time, ownership of real estate by foreigners was not permitted.

One of the first things that I did was to identify a suitable legal advisor for the bank in Dubai, and another banker introduced me to a Scottish lawyer established in the emirate for a few years. Soon after I met him, he asked about the bank's agreement with the ruler of Dubai, and I discovered, quite by chance, that although the UAE Currency Board, headquartered in Abu Dhabi, had granted a banking licence under the terms of federal law, this was not sufficient to open for business in Dubai. We would require an agreement with the ruler and a trade licence from Dubai municipality. The municipality would not issue the trade licence until the bank signed the agreement with the ruler. After consulting the regional office in Beirut, the head of which had been instrumental in obtaining the currency board licence, the bank's lawyer made approaches to the ruler's office and received a favourable response. In due course, a suitably senior person travelled from head office in Toronto to Dubai to sign the agreement with the ruler, which included a clause requiring the payment of 10 percent of the branch's annual profits to the ruler's office.

In 1974, the UAE was only three years old, and each of the member states still exercised a degree of independence from the federation and continue to do so, although less than at the beginning. This was one such example. Another was that in those days there was still a customs and immigration checkpoint on the road between Dubai and Abu Dhabi. Inspection of passports took place there, although they were not stamped again. On one occasion, an official stopped a friend at this checkpoint and did not allow him to continue into Abu Dhabi because he was wearing shorts!

I tried to find a suitable office location in Deira, but when that search failed to produce results, I started looking on the Dubai side of the creek. Eventually premises located in a busy commercial street were identified which could, with imagination, be converted into a small branch. The bank intended that this would eventually be supplemented by a bigger main office in Deira, as a presence on both sides of the creek was considered desirable. Once lease formalities were completed, including the payment of a substantial sum of "key money" to persuade the existing occupant, a pharmacy, to relocate, work began to convert the premises to a bank, including the not-so-easy task of obtaining the necessary telephone and telex lines. The large influx of new companies was causing an excess of demand over supply. By this time, a Canadian colleague who was to be the assistant manager had arrived in Dubai; together we took a temporary office in a building occupied by a Swedish-owned shipping agency. The managing director of the shipping company introduced me to an Englishwoman who was seeking a new job. She had been living in Dubai for several years and was well versed in local procedures. I employed her as my secretary, and together, the three of us worked on the preparations for the branch opening.

We had to decide on how to mechanise the branch accounting, as head office in Toronto was unable to provide any assistance in this matter. Naturally, NCR was present in Dubai and by this time were offering their Class 299 accounting machine, which had largely replaced the Class 32 as the workhorse for banks in the Gulf. This machine had a selectric type of letter ball, a core memory of 8K for a stored program and 8K for data. This was a significant advance on the Class 32 as it enabled storage of some customer data, including the name and address, and automatic calculation and posting of interest. This machine was our choice for the branch in Dubai.

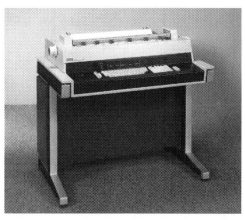

NCR Class 299 accounting machine (The NCR Archive at Dayton History)

In early April 1975, I visited the regional office in Beirut to discuss final plans for the Dubai opening. This was to be my last visit to Lebanon for many years.

A few days after I left, on April 13, gunmen attempted to assassinate the Maronite Christian Phalangist leader Pierre Gemayel, as he was leaving church after Mass. In retaliation, Phalangist gunmen ambushed a bus carrying Palestinians, most of them civilians, killing twenty-seven passengers. Clashes between Palestinian forces and Phalangist militia followed, generally said to mark the beginning of Lebanon's fifteen-year civil war. Other than a quick visit by sea from Cyprus to East Beirut in 1988, in a lull during the civil war, I was not to visit Lebanon again until 1993.

During my early days in Dubai, there was a debate in financial circles about the possibility of allowing foreign exchange and money market brokers to establish offices in the country. At the time, banks undertook interbank trading directly, one bank with another, at exchange or interest rates that they negotiated between themselves. A few London brokers had opened branches in Bahrain following the establishment of the offshore banking scheme there and had an interest in expanding their activities to the UAE. During this period, Toronto Dominion Bank's head of treasury in Toronto made a visit to the region, and while he was in Dubai, we called on the general manager of what, at the time, was one of the few locally incorporated banks. This man was an elderly Scot, who, before taking on his position with this local bank, had enjoyed a long career with a British overseas bank. He had a reputation for being conservative and parsimonious, as all Scottish bankers should be, and the balance sheet of the institution that he ran illustrated this: its customer lending in 1975 constituted only about 20 percent of the bank's assets, but it still produced a commendable return on capital for the shareholders. The subject of licensing brokers came up during our meeting, and this caused him to embark on a long and aggressive tirade against the idea, which, according to him, was unnecessary: he could see no good reason why he should pay them to deploy his substantial liquidity. Notwithstanding his opposition, the authorities eventually licenced brokers, which quickly established presences in Dubai and Abu Dhabi, but his bank still dealt directly with its limited number of regular counterparties. Toronto Dominion Bank became one beneficiary of his policy, often trading substantial amounts of foreign currency with the bank.

In March 1975, Dubai witnessed the opening of the emirate's first five-star hotel, the Intercontinental. One of the prominent merchant families owned the property, located on the creek side in Deira, close to what was then the main business district of Dubai. The ruler, Sheikh Rashid, performed the formal opening during the afternoon, which was a "dry" event. In the evening, there was a gala reception in the hotel, at which alcohol was served. As the only five-star hotel in the city, the Intercontinental became the preferred venue for just about any reception held in Dubai for a while. Eventually other major hotels opened, including the creek side Sheraton and the Hyatt Regency, with its revolving restaurant and ice-skating rink, and regulars on the cocktail circuit, including myself, were able to enjoy some variety in the canapés offered. The property remained under Intercontinental management for over thirty years; the owners recently transferred management to Radisson, and the hotel is now rebranded as a Radisson Blu.

Toronto Dominion Bank, Dubai branch, 1975

Eventually, in May 1975, the branch was ready to open. Since summer was approaching, we decided that the opening would be low-key and to hold the official celebrations in the autumn, by which time the Abu Dhabi branch would have opened and events could be held in both locations. The official ceremonies took place in Abu Dhabi on October 31 and in Dubai on November 1, with receptions at the long established Hilton Hotel in Abu Dhabi and at the recently opened Intercontinental Hotel in Dubai. The head of the bank's international division from Toronto, the regional general manager from Beirut and their wives attended these events. Meanwhile the search for premises in Deira had yielded results and the bank decided to open a main branch there, while still maintaining the small presence on the Dubai side of the creek.

After the opening of the TD branch in Dubai, it soon became apparent that the bank's policies, particularly in lending, would make it difficult for the branch to become viable. My colleague running the Abu Dhabi branch, a former Grindlays Bank man, came to the same conclusion. In 1975, the man who had opened the BBME branches in Yemen, with whom I had worked there, had joined a newly established locally incorporated bank in Abu Dhabi,

Khalij Commercial Bank (KCB), as general manager. The major shareholders were the private office of the ruler of Abu Dhabi and a Dubai incorporated bank largely owned by the members of the family business mentioned earlier in this chapter. After establishing the head office and branch in Abu Dhabi, he was actively planning to open a branch in Dubai. In the spring of 1976, he approached me to enquire if I would be interested in taking on this job. Given my increasing disillusionment with the prospects for TD in the region, I decided to accept his offer and joined KCB in July 1976. I was one of many bankers who had worked for British overseas banks, such as BBME, Grindlays, Chartered Bank, Ottoman Bank and Eastern Bank, who joined local banks during this time of great expansion in the Gulf. Our experiences were not always pleasant.

My Abu Dhabi colleague also left TD a few months later, to join ABN-AMRO Bank in Dubai. Eventually, the civil war forced TD to close its representative office in Beirut and the Lebanese subsidiary was sold to another local bank in 1981. The bank closed its branch in Abu Dhabi in 1985 and Dubai in 1986 and retreated to markets with which it was more familiar.

Working for a local bank was somewhat different from being with an international institution with a head office seven thousand miles (11,200 km) away. Lines of communication to the general manager and directors were short, local contacts were invaluable and decisions, maybe not always the correct ones, were made quickly. Suitable premises were located in Nasser Square (now AlIttihad Square) in central Deira and work to convert them into a branch proceeded quickly. By September 1976, we were ready to open for business. At the same time, I had to find alternative accommodation, as the new manager at TD Bank had taken over that house. Once again, local contacts came in useful; the ruler of Dubai had given a plot of land to one of the directors of KCB from Abu Dhabi, and he was building four villas on this plot. The bank soon agreed to take a five-year lease on one of the villas and build a swimming pool in the garden at its expense. Once again, I had to furnish and equip a new home, but this was quite quickly completed.

The bulk of KCB's customer base were Dubai merchants who often held exclusive agencies for many items and were importing them in increasing quantities as development in the emirate progressed with lightning speed. The bank usually financed these imports by opening letters of credit in favour of the suppliers, through its correspondent bank in the country where the supplier was located. The goods might be motor vehicles, building materials, electronic goods, or any of literally thousands of other items, many of which were destined for re-export from Dubai to neighbouring countries. I even recall hearing a maybe apocryphal story of one bank that opened a letter of credit in favour of a beneficiary in Pakistan covering the delivery of labourers for a construction company! I have explained the mechanics of how an LC works earlier, but it is worth noting here how attractive this business was, not just to the opening bank, but also to its correspondents who would advise and probably confirm the LC and later negotiate the documents. Each of these services attracted a fee, payable by either the importer or the exporter, depending on the agreement between them. KCB's correspondent banks with a presence in the countries from which Dubai merchants regularly sourced their purchases visited me regularly to solicit this business and often offered an arrangement whereby they would share their commissions with KCB.

Diverging from the traditional business of trade finance, in the late 1970s, KCB undertook the financing of two important new hotels in Dubai, the Sheraton, situated beside the creek in Deira, and the Trust House Forte property (now Le Meridien) opposite Dubai airport. As was usually the case, the hotel properties belonged to local investors, and the hotel companies provided management services, including marketing and worldwide reservation systems, in return for a fee. A prominent Dubai merchant, who was also a minister in the federal government, owned the Sheraton, and the Trust House belonged to the ruler himself. An American company had won the contract for this project. The terms of the contract included an advance payment of 25 percent of the contract amount and the opening of an LC by the ruler in favour of the contractor to cover the cost of the project. The general manager of the bank and I attended the ruler's office to deliver a bank guarantee covering the amount of the advance payment and collect the cheque and for the signing of the LC application. The contractor required part of the advance payment to enable payment of a commission to their local agent, who has assisted in obtaining the contract.

Another real estate-related transaction in which KCB became involved was acting as security agent for a syndicate of Bahrain OBUs that was to provide finance for a development of twenty-four villas in Jumeirah, then the prime residential areas for expatriates in Dubai. A customer of the bank owned the land; and a foreign company was to undertake the development, marketing, management and financing of the project. The lenders required a mortgage on the land as part of the security, but none of these banks had a presence in Dubai. They asked KCB to act as the security agent by becoming the mortgagee on behalf of the syndicate. This was a groundbreaking transaction in Dubai and gave the lawyers involved plenty of food for thought. In the end, all of the parties agreed the documentation, the mortgage was registered, and KCB received a fee for its services. The developer repaid the loan on schedule, so KCB was never required to take any action under the security agency agreement. This is probably just as well, as I was not convinced that the Dubai courts would have understood the nature of the transaction.

Among the perils facing a local bank in the region in the boom years of the 1970s was *name lending*, when banks would provide credit facilities to clients based on their perceived reputation in the market, rather than any serious analysis of their credit-worthiness or the feasibility of the project being financed. Requests to lend to prominent personalities, particularly members of the ruling families of the emirates or businesses in which they had an interest were difficult to refuse. KCB was no exception, being subject to both of these pressures.

One day the senior local manager in Dubai told me with great pride that he had persuaded one such person to open an account. We received the completed account opening forms, including a power of attorney in favour of the customer's secretary, allowing him to operate the account. An impressive cheque book, with the name of the account holder embossed on it in gold leaf, was prepared and presented with some ceremony. However, the account holder made no deposit to activate the account although he soon put the cheque book to good use. While the customer was spending the summer in London, cheques signed by his secretary for substantial amounts in favour of various businesses in which the customer was a shareholder were presented, in some cases representing his contribution to the initial capital of a new company. The bank had no alternative but to pay these, thus creating a large unsecured overdraft in the account. The general manager at the head office in Abu Dhabi and I both became concerned and decided that we would fly to London to call on the customer to ascertain whether or not he was aware of the situation and to enquire when the overdraft might be repaid. We duly presented ourselves at his residence in Mayfair where he received us cordially. He assured us that he was aware of the situation and that the bank had no cause for concern. While the frequency and value of the cheques issued then decreased and the customer made occasional deposits, subsequent events led me to believe that the customer had not known what his secretary had been doing. An overdraft remained outstanding at the time that I left the bank, although I understand that the bank and the customer eventually reached an agreement for repayment.

KCB quickly outgrew the premises in Nasser Square. As well as opening a branch in Fehedi Road on the Dubai side of the creek, I started to look for an alternative location for the main branch in Deira. At the time, one of the bank's directors was constructing a building next to the Intercontinental Hotel on the creek side, and in 1980, the bank agreed to take a long-term lease on part of the ground and second floors (the first was car parking) in which to

Khalij Commercial Bank,
Dubai banking hall, 1979

relocate our main Dubai office. This became a much more spacious and luxurious branch than we had had before and, at the time, was superior to the head office in Abu Dhabi. From the management offices on the second floor, we had an excellent view of the creek and the entire activity taking place there.

Dubai Creek, view from the author's office, 1976

When we opened KCB in Dubai we, as usual, looked to NCR for accounting machines and settled on the Class 299 machine, which TD had used. However, after two years the bank began to consider computerisation of its activities. I became a member of a steering committee created to review various banking systems available, make recommendations to the board, and, eventually, oversee the implementation. Initially, we reached the conclusion that a banking software package that ran on IBM hardware would be suitable for the bank's business. This choice would have been a major coup for IBM, which was trying to break into the Gulf market in competition with NCR at the time. NCR, concerned about the impact that a sale to an important local bank by IBM would have on its business, pulled out all the stops to try to identify a banking system that would run on their hardware. This led us to the unlikely destination of Baton Rouge, Louisiana. There was a bank in Baton Rouge that ran a computer services bureau, providing data processing services for itself and other banks in the area, and they used NCR hardware.

In July 1979, together with other members of the steering group, I travelled to Baton Rouge to review the system and evaluate the possibility of it being suitable for KCB. While much of the functionality would work or could be easily adapted, there were no modules to process two important aspects of KCB's business, letters of credit and treasury operations. After lengthy negotiations, NCR, the Baton Rouge bank and KCB agreed that they would work together to develop the modules required for these aspects of our business and such changes to the existing modules as might be required to make them suitable for use by the bank. The eventual aim was to produce an international version of the system used in Baton Rouge, which NCR could market in the Gulf at a time when many banks were considering computerising their records.

I was closely involved in the development work with colleagues from KCB and the Baton Rouge bank. The bank established a data centre in Abu Dhabi and linked this to all branches by leased lines. In 1980, we began to convert the branches to the computerised system: first Abu Dhabi, then Dubai and later Al Ain. KCB had the first online real-time banking system in the UAE, and this enabled the bank to install Automatic Teller Machines (ATMs), a first in the country and something of a novelty generally more than thirty years ago. NCR was very active in marketing the system, and KCB received frequent visitors from other banks in the region that were considering buying it. Some eventually did.

The Souk Al-Manakh crash in Kuwait in 1982 had an effect in the Emirates. In 1977, there had been a relatively minor crash in the official Kuwaiti stock market, the effects of which the government had mitigated with a bailout of investors who had lost money, followed by the imposition of more strict regulation of the official market. The Souk Al-Manakh then developed as an unofficial stock market trading shares in speculative high-risk companies, some established outside Kuwait, including in the UAE, especially the emirate of Ajman.

Investors conducted trading in a converted (but air-conditioned) parking garage.[62] Buyers of shares would pay sellers with post-dated cheques in the expectation that by the time the cheque was due for payment, they would be able to sell the shares purchased at a much higher price and pocket a large profit. For a while, this happened. As in all financial matters, the saying "If something looks too good to be true, it usually is" certainly applied to this fiasco. The beneficiaries of these post-dated cheques usually discounted them with their bank to obtain cash prior to the due date in order to make further share purchases or, more likely, cover other post-dated cheques that they themselves had issued. The crash came in August 1982 when a post-dated cheque was returned unpaid; this caused the house of cards to collapse as subsequently many other cheques bounced in a chain effect. The Kuwaiti Ministry of Finance initiated an investigation, which quantified the value of the outstanding post-dated cheques at US$94 billion, a total close to the amount of the recent Spanish banking bailout thirty years later. The affair involved some six thousand people, probably the biggest stock market bubble to burst in history. Many investors were effectively bankrupt, and all of the local banks in Kuwait, except National Bank of Kuwait, technically insolvent. They survived only with support from the central bank.

Since the crash affected virtually all of the prominent merchant families of the state, the government eventually intervened by setting up the Difficult Credit Facilities Resettlement Programme, a bailout in effect. Because some of the companies traded in the Souk Al-Manakh had UAE connections, UAE speculators naturally became involved and requests to discount related post-dated cheques were made by KCB's customers. We managed to avoid involvement!

One problem, which regularly raised its head in Dubai, was the application of Sharia law to banking transactions. Islamic law prohibits the payment and receipt of interest, but traditionally, the Dubai commercial courts took a pragmatic approach to this issue. They would generally uphold a written agreement stipulating

---

[62]   http://www.gold-eagle.com/gold_digest_98/veneroso060198.html Retrieved 14 Jan 2012

an agreed rate of interest on bank borrowings. In the absence of a written agreement, they often imposed a maximum of 9 percent per annum. KCB instituted legal proceedings in Canada against a customer who had left Dubai to return to his home country, leaving substantial debts behind him, and the bank asked me to appear as a witness for the bank in Toronto when the case came to trial, after I had left the bank.

The bank had security documentation incorporating an interest rate of 14 percent per annum on the overdraft of the borrower and subjecting the agreement to the jurisdiction of the civil court of Dubai. The absence of the word *exclusive* before the naming of the Dubai court was critical. In his judgment, the Canadian judge dismissed the defendant's claim that the Ontario courts had no jurisdiction in the matter, ruling that the failure to use the word *exclusive* allowed for jurisdiction in any other court before which the matter was properly brought. He concluded that the enforcement of a judgement of the Dubai courts would probably differ little from enforcement in Ontario and could, indeed, be much worse; it was then, and still is, common to imprison judgement debtors in Dubai until the debt is paid. In the end, the bank obtained judgement for the debt amount plus interest at 6 percent per annum, although the judge did not explain why he chose that rate. The judgement set something of a precedent in Ontario courts, and it is still cited in legal textbooks.

As well as having courts that would enforce the payment of interest in commercial contracts, Dubai also took a practical approach to the matter of consumption of alcohol. Non-Muslim residents could obtain a permit allowing them to purchase alcoholic drinks from the two authorised importers, although the permit restricted the amount that could be spent in a month. The standard monthly limit was AED 500.00 (about US$136), although I was able to obtain a higher limit of AED 2,000 (US$545) to cover the need to entertain. In addition, alcohol was freely available in hotel bars and restaurants, theoretically only to non-Muslims, a regulation regularly ignored.

Naturally, not all Muslims were teetotal. I remember one occasion when I was flying from London to Dubai. The head of protocol at the ruler's court was sitting next to me. After takeoff, he ordered a whisky; and when the steward served it, he asked if it was Black Label. The steward replied that it was Red Label and offered to change it, an offer that was accepted. From my seat, I could observe the steward in the galley although my neighbour could not. The steward placed the offending glass on the counter, waited a few minutes, put it back on his tray, and served it again to the passenger, who contentedly consumed it believing it to be Black Label.

In early 1976, my former colleague in Hodeidah, now the general manager of KCB in Abu Dhabi, introduced me to flying light aircraft. He had taken lessons in Abu Dhabi and had a private pilot licence. One day he flew up to Dubai in a Cessna 172, a high-wing single-engine monoplane. He picked me up, and together we flew on to Ras al-Khaimah and landed there. The airport had only recently opened, had very few scheduled flights, and we were the first light aircraft to land there.

We visited the airport office where they had some difficulty in deciding how much to charge for landing fees. Their tariff included prices for Concorde and the Boeing 747 but not a Cessna 172. In the end, we settled on AED 6.00 (about US$1.65).

Landing at Ras al Khaimah airport in the Cessna 172, 1976

Later in the year, after I had joined KCB in Dubai, my colleague and I flew the Cessna to Bahrain on a business trip. The routing, at an altitude of five thousand feet, took us over the Gulf to Doha, giving us a bird's eye view of the many offshore drilling rigs, and then across the Qatar peninsular and along the east cost of Bahrain to

Muharraq airport. The journey took us about four hours, compared to less than an hour on a scheduled jet flight, but when we arrived, the airport authorities at least knew what landing fees to charge!

These flights raised my interest in private flying, and I decided to start taking lessons myself. I began using the same instructor and aircraft at Abu Dhabi as my colleague, but later, when flight training became available at Dubai, I switched to an instructor there, using a Piper 28 low-wing monoplane. Undoubtedly, the most terrifying part of the lessons was the first time I had to put the aircraft into a spin and then recover from it. First, the instructor told me to climb to ten thousand feet over a tract of desert southeast of the World Trade Centre. This he considered high enough to allow plenty of time to complete the recovery before crashing into the ground. He then demonstrated how to deliberately stall the plane and recover from the resulting spin. That experience was bad enough, but then I had to climb again to ten thousand feet and do the exercise myself. I survived to tell the tale. After a few months, I completed the necessary flying hours, and on June 19, 1977, I made my first solo flight from Dubai—a fifteen-minute circuit of the airport. I followed this with further cross-country flights until my teacher judged me able to make a cross-country solo flight, a necessity to qualify for a licence. On November 11, 1977, I made this flight, from Dubai to Abu Dhabi, then to Sharjah and back to Dubai. I had to land in both Abu Dhabi and Sharjah and obtain a signed acknowledgement of this fact.

In March 1977, I had the opportunity to fly in quite another style. British Airways had brought the supersonic Concorde into service in January 1976, but initially the only route on which they were able to operate it was between London and Bahrain. It was not until May 1976 that they obtained permission to start transatlantic flights to Dulles airport, Washington, DC, and it was only in October 1977 that flights to Kennedy Airport in New York were allowed. On the Bahrain-London route, permission had been given to operate at supersonic speed over the desert of Saudi Arabia and the eastern Mediterranean and Adriatic seas, but the aircraft had to slow down to subsonic speed over Europe. Concorde reduced the flying time from Bahrain to London from about seven hours to around four hours. Unfortunately, to catch the morning departure from Bahrain, I travelled from Dubai the previous evening, staying overnight in Bahrain at British Airways expense. It would have been quicker to take a direct nonstop flight from Dubai to London, but then I would not have joined the relatively few passengers to fly supersonically at the time. The 2-2 seating arrangement, less legroom and seat recline than in first class on conventional aircraft, and a relatively restricted menu reflected the limited space and weight restrictions on Concorde, compared to first class on a Boeing 747. The menu offered caviar and prawns to start, but for the main course a choice of only two cold dishes, beef Wellington or breast of duckling. Champagne flowed freely throughout the flight.

Concorde certificate Bahrain-London, 2 March 1977

I flew on Concorde again in March 1981. I was accompanying a Dubai client on a business trip to the United States at his expense, and he insisted on the best of everything, including travelling on Concorde from London to New York. The flight, which took about three hours, had us arriving in New York earlier in the day local time than we had left London. British Airways much touted this as an opportunity to have a full day of business in the Big Apple and, theoretically, return to London the same evening. I personally found myself even more disorientated than usual after a flight crossing several time zones and took more time to adapt than after a longer flight at subsonic speed.

My client had negotiated his appointment as a distributor in Dubai for a major US-made truck; we were travelling to the head office of the company, which at the time was located in a small town in Pennsylvania, to sign the formal distribution agreement. In keeping with my client's desire to travel comfortably, we stayed at the luxurious Helmsley House Hotel in Manhattan. This was some time before the imprisonment for tax evasion and fraud of the owning company's president, Leona Helmsley.[63] On the day after our arrival, we set out for the company's office, a distance of about 145 kilometres (90 miles), in a typically New York stretched limousine. My client and the truck manufacturer signed the agency agreement, and I returned to Dubai at subsonic speed, leaving my client to enjoy the pleasures of New York for a while longer.

In 1977, I met two new members of the British expatriate community in Dubai, Don Revie and his wife Elsie. Don had just arrived to take up the post of coach of the United Arab Emirates' national football team. He had resigned as the England team manager to take up this appointment in somewhat controversial circumstances. On July 11th, 1977, the *Daily Mail* published the story before the Football Association had a chance to read his letter of resignation, which had been delivered after their office had closed the previous day. His reportedly lucrative contract in the UAE, £340,000 over four years[64], peanuts in comparison to the amounts paid to players and managers now, led to accusations of acting disloyally. The FA suspended him from football in England for ten years for bringing the game into disrepute, although he was successful in challenging this suspension in the English courts. After three years with the national team, Don went on to become manager of a Dubai club, Al-Nasr, in 1980 and then in 1984, Al-Ahli Club in Cairo.

---

[63] http://www.nytimes.com/2007/08/20/nyregion/20cnd-helmsley. html?pagewanted=print, accessed 21 Jan 2012

[64] http://en.wikipedia.org/wiki/Don_Revie, accessed 7 Dec 2012

In 1986, Don and Elsie moved to Scotland to retire. Unfortunately, he did not live to enjoy it for long. He was diagnosed with motor neuron disease in 1987 and died in May 1989. An indication of the acrimony surrounding his relationship with the Football Association was the absence of any representation from them at his funeral. However, he was still well regarded in Leeds, where he had played for and managed the team at Elland Road. After his death his widow, Elsie, and Lord Harewood, president of Leeds United, officially opened the Don Revie North Stand, which was part of a refurbishment of the ground, creating an all-seat stadium. His impact on English football was finally fully recognised in 2004 when he was inducted into the English Football Hall of Fame. More than twenty years after his death, his career and legacy are still being debated;[65] whatever the rights and wrongs, my personal experience of Don is of a friendly, kind man, generous to his extended family, and whom I am proud to have counted among my friends.

Around 1981 I acquired my first personal computer. My interest had started when I became involved in the KCB project to computerise its banking systems. During visits to Baton Rouge I had heard about Tandy (now Radio Shack), one of the companies that pioneered early personal computer development and had seen their products in the United States. In 1981 they appointed an agent in Dubai who began to import the Tandy TRS-80 and I decided to buy one, although to begin with I had no firm plan about the use to which it would be put. The cost was almost US$ 5,000.00 for the desk-top machine and a dot-matrix printer. The computer had just two floppy disc drives with a capacity that seems laughable today. I also bought a word-processing application, which, I recall had difficulty distinguishing between upper and lower case characters, and an accounting system. It was the beginning of a long-term interest in personal and, later, lap-top computers. I have owned one ever since, although as yet have not been able to persuade myself that it is time to acquire a tablet computer.

---

[65] http://www.guardian.co.uk/sport/2007/nov/25/football.newsstory, accessed 28 July 2012

Generally, officials and businessmen in the UAE at this time liked to develop long-term relationships with the many foreigners who flocked to their country to work. They would reward long and faithful service and profitable results. For example, throughout his time with the UAE national team and the Dubai club and during his legal battle with the English Football Association, Don Revie received the wholehearted support of a member of the Dubai ruling family, who had been instrumental in encouraging him to take up the UAE appointment in the first place.

Another long-term relationship was that of an Englishman who arrived in Dubai in the late 1950s to organise and run the customs department and became a trusted advisor to the then ruler, Sheikh Rashid bin Said Al Maktoum. In a similar way, a British brigadier who was commander of the Dubai Defence Force before it was merged into the UAE armed forces, at the time when Sheikh Mohammed bin Rashid was minister of defence, went on to become a long-time advisor to Sheikh Mohammed. He was involved for many years in everything from the ruling family's racing interests to the marketing of Dubai's oil output.

The most significant event ever in my personal life occurred while I was living in Dubai. It happened one Thursday evening, the start of the weekend in most Muslim countries, in October 1978. I was having a drink in the bar of the Intercontinental Hotel. At the other end of the bar, I saw a friend who worked for one of the airlines in Dubai. We joined up for a drink, and he introduced me to his companion, Maarouf.

Maarouf and I arranged to meet for lunch the next day at the Sheraton Hotel, where a lavish buffet was served every Friday. I was in the hotel lobby promptly at the agreed meeting time, one thirty. He kept me waiting for fifteen minutes, and when he arrived confessed that he had been unsure about how serious my invitation was. This was the beginning of a relationship, which, despite not being blessed by any religion and although it is not registered under any legislation, has survived until now.

As I discovered during our lunch, Maarouf was about six years younger than I was, was Lebanese, and at the time worked at Dubai airport for the Dubai National Air Travel Agency, better known as DNATA locally, in the airport manager's office. This company was the general sales agent for all airlines operating in Dubai at that time and handled all aspects of the airport management. During his work with DNATA, Maarouf was the only person employed at the airport who was fluent in Arabic and English and he was often borrowed by other organisations there, including International Aeradio Limited, the company providing air traffic control services and the Department of Civil Aviation. This brought him to the attention of the director of civil aviation, a member of the ruling family. This sheikh was also the patron of one of the four football clubs in Dubai, in fact the one that Don Review later managed. He persuaded Maarouf to work part-time in the club administration and in his private office. After some time, he resigned from DNATA and worked full-time for the club and the sheikh until leaving Dubai in 1984, not long after my departure from the UAE.

Maarouf will feature many times in the rest of this book.

Throughout my years in Dubai, I was to travel extensively, both on business and for pleasure. Shortly after my arrival in 1974, I made my first visit to India, a country that has always fascinated me, especially the history of the country during the days of the Raj. I flew to Bombay and then embarked on an Indian Ocean cruise that took me to Goa, Colombo and the Laccadive Islands over the Christmas and New Year holidays.

The next year I set out on a round-the-world trip that included visits to Delhi, Kathmandu, Bangkok, Hong Kong, Seoul, Tokyo, Vancouver and Toronto. Although mainly for pleasure, I took the opportunity to meet Toronto Dominion Bank's representatives in Hong Kong and Tokyo and to visit the head office in Toronto before returning to Dubai via London.

In the summer of 1976, I again visited India, this time mainly Kashmir and in 1977 made a trip to the Far East, including some time in Burma, then not generally on the tourist map. In October 1979, I made my third visit to Cyprus, together with Maarouf. It was his first visit to the island and my first since the Turkish invasion of 1974. This trip was the prelude to many that we have enjoyed together over the last thirty-five years. We had to fly to Larnaca, as the airport in Nicosia was in the United Nations buffer zone and unusable, and we stayed in Limassol, as Kyrenia and the northern part of the island were inaccessible.

In February 1976, my sister, Brenda, was married in Cromer to Peter Stibbons. I was part of the wedding party and so, for the first time, had to don a morning suit and grey top hat. After some years living in London and Suffolk, they returned to Norfolk and have lived in Cromer since 1992, where now I also now have a home.

During a trip to Europe in 1976, I spent some time in Switzerland as I was considering purchasing a property there. Although Swiss law relating to acquisition of property by foreigners was strict, there were certain areas and circumstances in which it was possible to buy a second home. One such region was the Canton of Vaud in the French-speaking part of the country, about 130 kilometres (80 miles) from Geneva. I had previously visited the area in 1974, after leaving MECAS, when I had stayed with friends who had an apartment in Rougemont, not far from the more famous resort of Gstaad. This time I saw similar apartments, eligible for sale to foreigners, in the neighbouring village of Châteaux-d'Oex. A mortgage in Swiss francs was easily available at a low interest rate from a local bank, and I decided to go ahead with the purchase, with a view to renting the property as a holiday home for part of the year to pay the mortgage. This proved easy to do, and the return, especially in the winter sports season, was good. When I eventually sold the property, some fourteen years later, although there was not a huge capital gain in low-inflation Switzerland, the substantial appreciation of the currency over that period meant a significant profit in dollar or sterling terms when I converted the proceeds.

During 1979 and 1980, there were several trips to Baton Rouge for discussions and work on the computer-banking package that the Louisiana bank was developing for KCB. During one of these visits, in February 1980, I went on afterwards to Fort Meyers, Florida. There, on the introduction of a broker in Dubai, I looked at a condominium development, the Landings, and ended up buying a house there. The intention again was to rent it. It took many months before the agent found a tenant, and even then, the rent was well below the level that the developer told me I could expect. There was the advantage that the lease was for one year, and in fact, the same tenants renewed four times before I decided to sell the property in 1985, as the return on the funds invested was not attractive.

In the summer of 1979, Maarouf and I took another trip together. We went first to Switzerland, where we stayed in my apartment in Château-d'Oex, and then to Marbella in Spain before ending in London. In July 1980, we decided to visit the United States and booked a holiday that included the outward journey from Southampton to New York on the *Queen Elizabeth 2*, car rental and hotels in the United States, and a return flight to London from Miami. After a few days in New York, we flew to Detroit, where Maarouf visited relatives while I drove to nearby Flint to see the Corbin family, American friends who had been stationed in Norfolk in the 1950s. We then went on to San Francisco and New Orleans before reaching Miami. While in Florida, we stayed for a few days in the house that I had bought in Fort Meyers, at that time still without a tenant, and drove through the Florida Keys to Key West. The return flight from Miami to London on British Airways was our first experience of their new product, Club Class. It was very different from the facilities offered in Club World today. There was no extra legroom, although the three abreast seating was changed to two abreast by an ingenious but uncomfortable method of adapting the economy seats and certainly no flatbeds. Really, it was little better than economy and did not justify the extra cost.

In October 1980, my parents celebrated their ruby wedding with a party at a hotel in Cromer, where they were living at the time. Maarouf and I attended. As well as friends and family from the area, my father's sister and brother-in-law came from Dublin, the first time that we had seen them for quite a long time. Another family event during this period was the birth of my sister's first daughter, my niece Bryony, in 1982.

In 1981, Maarouf and I decided to see how the other half lived and made a trip to the Soviet Union. Some of the places that we visited were to play an important part in my banking career later. Starting from London, we went first to Moscow; then to Bratsk, where the highlight of the visit was a tour of a dam and associated hydroelectric plant; and Irkutsk in Siberia, where we saw Lake Baikal, the largest freshwater lake in the world. After that, the tour took us to Tashkent and Bukhara in the Islamic area of the Soviet Union. Here, while having a drink in the hotel bar, Maarouf got into conversation with the barman, and on discovering that he was a Muslim, he gave him a small Koran, which he received with profuse thanks. The trip ended with some days in Leningrad (now Saint Petersburg).

In 1983, I was able to arrange for Maarouf's sister, Elham, who lived in a Lebanon that was still plagued by the civil war, to have an eye operation in London. I travelled there directly from Dubai to make the preliminary arrangements while Maarouf flew via Beirut and travelled on to London with his sister. After the successful operation, Elham flew back to Beirut while Maarouf and I took a trip to Scotland before returning to Dubai.

In Dubai in the mid-1970s, as now, there was a huge imbalance between the indigenous population and foreigners. In 1975, the census revealed the population of the emirate was 183,000; at the time, foreigners outnumbered citizens by four to one.

The 2005 census showed a population of 1.3 million, only 11 percent of whom were UAE citizens.[66] Today the estimated population is around 1.8 million, only 17 percent of whom are UAE nationals, and men outnumber women by almost five to one. Many of the foreigners arriving in Dubai in the '70s were labourers working in the construction industry on bachelor status, and that still prevails.

---

[66] http://www.uaestatistics.gov.ae/ReportDetailsEnglish/tabid/121/Default.asp x?ItemId=1869&PTID=104&MenuId=1, accessed 14 Jan 2012

Increasingly, with the opening of new hotels and shopping centres over the years, there has been a need to bring in even more foreign workers to staff these establishments, and the traditional sources such as India and Pakistan have been supplemented by Sri Lanka, the Philippines and almost every other country of the world. During my years with KCB, I made several trips to India, Pakistan and Sri Lanka to recruit staff for the bank, as it was difficult to find enough qualified local or foreign staff in the local market due to the increasing number of banks opening in the country.

In 1982, the majority shareholder of KCB decided to give a management contract to another institution in which it was a major shareholder, Bank of Credit and Commerce. This resulted in a

The author,
beside Dubai creek, 1980

significant change in the management style and philosophy, and the new general manager, a Pakistani, made it clear that he would not encourage any of the British management, of whom there were many, to remain, should they choose to leave. I hung on for a while in an increasingly difficult situation, and then in mid-1983, I decided to resign, although at that time I had not found alternative employment.

Around the time that I was preparing to leave Dubai, a Tanzanian singer, Sal Davies, swept to fame in the Emirate with his song "Back in Dubai." The chorus lines

Back in Dubai there's a sun and it shines there all the time.

Going home to the smiles on the faces of people reminds me Dubai is mine reflected the sentiments of many of the increasingly large expatriate population in the emirate at the time. They felt, as did I, that Dubai was home. However, after almost ten years it was time to move on. Cyprus beckoned.

Chapter 11

THE CYPRUS PROBLEM

Before I start to relate the story of my life and work in Cyprus, which spanned a period of twenty years, I think it is appropriate to provide some background information about the Cyprus problem. As with my chapter on the Middle East problem, I attempt this exercise with some trepidation, such are the firmly entrenched opinions with which most Cypriots, on both sides of the dividing line, view the present situation and the historical events that led to it.

In April 1984, my aunt and uncle from Dublin, Mary and Pearse O'Malley, came to visit me in Cyprus. They had lived for thirty years in Belfast before retiring to the Republic of Ireland and were well acquainted with inter-communal problems and violence, having been in Belfast throughout the "troubles" of the 1970s. Indeed, they themselves had been the target of an attempted assassination during that time.

During their stay, I gave a cocktail party, and among the guests was a man who had been the Cyprus foreign minister during the 1970s. When introduced, my aunt, always a forthright person, remarked to him, "You are a very handsome man. Where are you from?" He replied, "I am Greek."

That reply highlights at least part of the Cyprus problem, that both Greek and Turkish Cypriots consider themselves to be from their respective "mother countries" first and Cypriots second.

Background

The modern history of Cyprus began in 1878 when, following secret negotiations, Britain and the Ottoman Empire signed the Cyprus Convention, which gave control of the island to the United Kingdom. The exact wording of the relevant clause of the convention was "And in order to enable England to make necessary provision for executing her engagement, His Imperial Majesty the Sultan further consents to assign the Island of Cyprus to be occupied and administered by England." In return, Britain agreed to assist the Ottoman Empire in the event of Russian aggression. Effectively, Cyprus became part of the British Empire. After the Ottoman government decided to support Germany at the outbreak of World War I, Britain annexed Cyprus. In 1925, it was formally declared a Crown colony and remained so until being granted independence in 1960. At the time of the first British census, in 1881, the population of the island was 74 percent Greek Cypriot and 24 percent Turkish Cypriot, with about 2 percent comprising other minorities.[67] At the time of independence in 1960, the breakdown was about 81 percent Greek (including Armenians and Maronites, in accordance with the constitution) and 19 percent Turkish.[68] Greek Cypriot demands for union with Greece (*enosis*) began as early as the 1930s. In 1931, rioters burned down Government House in Nicosia, and protests gained momentum after the end of World War II. In 1948, King Paul of Greece said that the people of Cyprus desired union with Greece, and two years later, the future president Makarios, then bishop of Kition, organised a plebiscite, the result of which claimed that 96 percent of the Greek Cypriot population were in favour of *enosis*.[69]

---

[67] http://en.wikipedia.org/wiki/Modern_history_of_Cyprus, accessed 22 Jan 2012

[68] http://countrystudies.us/cyprus/21.htm, accessed 22 Jan 2012

[69] http://countrystudies.us/cyprus/10.htm, accessed22 Jan 2012

The EOKA Campaign

The National Organisation of Cypriot Fighters (EOKA), which was established in 1952 with the aim of achieving *enosis*, began a violent campaign against British rule on April 1, 1955. Gen. George Grivas led the organisation, with the support of the head of the Orthodox Church in Cyprus, Archbishop Makarios III, a fervent supporter of *enosis*. At the time, Britain had made it clear that it intended to remain in Cyprus indefinitely.

On July 28, 1954, the minister of state for the colonies, Henry Hopkinson, replied, somewhat ineptly for a former diplomat, to a debate in the House of Commons about Cyprus, that there were certain territories in the Commonwealth "which, owing to their particular circumstances, can never expect to be fully independent." After adding mysteriously that he would not go as far as that about Cyprus, he then promptly did go that far by recalling that he had already said "that the question of the abrogation of British sovereignty cannot arise, that British sovereignty will remain."[70] In late 1954, the government moved the British Middle East headquarters to the island from Egypt, and Cyprus became an important intelligence-gathering centre in the eastern Mediterranean.

Makarios' involvement with EOKA led to his exile to the Seychelles in 1956. Following his release, Britain still did not permit him to return to the island, and he settled temporarily in Athens. He returned to Cyprus in 1959, following the signing of the Zurich and London Agreements in February of that year, which laid the foundations for independence. In presidential elections in late 1959, Makarios received over 60 percent of the popular vote and took office as the first president of the Republic of Cyprus on August 16, 1960.

During the 1950s, when the EOKA campaign was in progress, Turkey and the Turkish Cypriots became very alarmed as the stated aim was *enosis*, and their calls for partition (*taksim*) started. To counter EOKA, the Turkish Resistance Organisation (TMT) was established;

---

[70]   http://www.cyprus-conflict.net/narrative-main.html, accessed 15 Jan 2012

one of its founders was Rauf Denktash, who was to lead the Turkish Cypriot community for many years and who became president of the Turkish Republic of Northern Cyprus (TRNC) after its unilateral declaration of independence in 1983. The creation of TMT played into the hands of the colonial government and their "divide and rule" policy, whereby the colonial power set the two groups against each other in an attempt to avoid combined action by both Greek and Turkish Cypriots against British rule. The establishment of the auxiliary police, comprising solely Turkish Cypriots, after the beginning of the EOKA campaign, is just one example of the British policies that contributed to the inter-communal hostilities.

Independence

In the run-up to independence, violence continued, not just against the British but also between the two communities; and there was increased interest and involvement from Greece and Turkey, by then both members of NATO. In 1958, in response to a British proposal for independence, Makarios took the position that he would only accept it as an alternative to *enosis* if the constitution of an independent Cyprus specifically excluded *enosis* or *taksim* in the future.

In September 1958, Britain outlined a proposed constitution for an independent Cyprus. Both of the Cypriot communities accepted it at a conference in Zurich in January 1959, at which neither Greece nor Turkey was represented. The terms included the following:

- the prohibition of both *taksim* and *enosis*
- a Greek and Turkish military presence in Cyprus in a 3:2 ratio
- the creation of two sovereign base areas to be used by Britain in perpetuity
- a Greek Cypriot president, elected by the Greek Cypriot community and a Turkish Cypriot vice president elected by his community
- a cabinet which included seven Greek Cypriots nominated by the president and three Turkish Cypriots nominated by

the vice president, with decisions requiring an absolute majority, but giving rights of veto to the president and the vice president
- The United Kingdom, Greece and Turkey to be guarantors of the constitution.[71]

Another conference in London in February 1959 confirmed the agreement, and on August 16, 1960, Cyprus became independent. Independence was enshrined in three treaties—the Treaty of Establishment, the Treaty of Alliance and the Treaty of Guarantee. Turkey invoked the Treaty of Guarantee in 1974 to justify its invasion.

The constitution of the Republic of Cyprus at the time of independence in 1960 made no mention of a national anthem; in 1966, following the withdrawal of Turkish Cypriots from the government, the council of ministers, then comprising only Greek Cypriots, adopted the Greek national anthem for use in Cyprus. Likewise, after the unilateral declaration of independence by the TRNC in 1983, that country, recognised only by Turkey, adopted the Turkish national anthem. [72]

While lacking an anthem, in 1960 the new Republic did have a national flag defined in its constitution. It was the result of a competition, judged by the president and vice president elect, and won by a Turkish Cypriot teacher, Ismet Güney. The design competition rules prohibited the use of blue or red (the predominant colours of the Greek and Turkish flags respectively), as well as the inclusion of a cross or a crescent.

Interestingly, article 4 of the Cyprus Constitution permits the flying of the Greek and Turkish flags in the following circumstances:

- The authorities of the republic and any public corporation or public utility body created by or under the laws of the

---

[71]   http://www.kypros.org/Constitution/treaty.htm, accessed 15 Jan 2012

[72]   http://www.nationalanthems.info/cy.htm, accessed 22 Jan 2012

republic shall fly the flag of the republic, and they shall have the right to fly on holidays together with the flag of the republic *both the Greek and the Turkish flags at the same time.*

- The communal authorities and institutions shall have the right to fly on holidays together with the flag of the republic *either the Greek or the Turkish flag at the same time.*
- Any citizen of the republic or any body, corporate or unincorporated, other than public, whose members are citizens of the republic, shall have the right to fly on their premises the flag of the republic *or the Greek or the Turkish flag without any restriction.* [73]

The lack of a national anthem and the authorisation in the constitution of the use of the flags of the two "motherlands" were certainly not conducive to the creation of a new nation or a feeling of national unity. It was also, in retrospect, a mistake that the head of the Cypriot Orthodox Church became the first president of the republic. He was a man viewed by the United States as "the Castro of the Mediterranean" and his pro-enosis views were well known; it was surely difficult for him to separate his religious and secular responsibilities.

Inter-communal Strife

Unfortunately, the constitution of the new Republic of Cyprus proved to be unworkable. It attempted to ensure that the Greek Cypriot majority would not disadvantage the Turkish Cypriot minority but failed to deliver on its promises. Among the terms of the constitution aimed at maintaining a balance between the two communities were significant veto powers given to the Greek Cypriot president and Turkish Cypriot vice president. After independence, the Greek Cypriots, through the Akritas plan,[74] tried to force the Turkish Cypriots from government, inter-communal violence continued and

---

[73] http://confinder.richmond.edu/admin/docs/cyprus.pdf, accessed 14 Dec 2012

[74] http://www.cyprus-conflict.net/akritas_plan.html, accessed 15 Jan 2012

Turkey threatened to intervene in the island. Despite the prohibition of *enosis* in the constitution, Makarios from time to time continued to speak in support of it as an eventual aim, and many Greek Cypriots saw independence as an interim measure until they could achieve *enosis*. Likewise, many Turkish Cypriots still favoured *taksim* as the eventual solution.[75] In November 1963, following deadlock in government caused by repeated vetoes by the Turkish Cypriots, in particular over the budget, Makarios proposed thirteen amendments to the constitution.[76] This was in spite of strong advice from both the Greek and Turkish governments not to try to change the constitution in any way. The amendments were intended to improve the efficiency of government but would have meant that the Turkish Cypriots would have to give up most of the protections built into the constitution to protect their minority interests, including the veto power of the vice president (although the president would also have lost this power). Following the outbreak of inter-communal violence and their rejection of the proposed constitutional changes, the Turkish Cypriots were forced to withdraw from the government and civil service.

At the time of independence, no part of the island was exclusively Greek or Turkish although there were areas where one or the other ethnic group predominated, such as Greek Cypriots in Kyrenia and Turkish Cypriot quarters in Larnaca and Paphos.

After 1963, some consolidation of the communities took place, and it was difficult for members of one community to travel through areas controlled by the other, as I discovered during my first visit to the island in 1970.

Inter-communal strife worsened following the withdrawal of Turkish Cypriots from government in late 1963, leading the three guarantors of the Treaty of Establishment—the United Kingdom, Greece and Turkey—to propose the establishment of a peacemaking force made

---

[75] Kerr-Lindsay, James, The Cyprus Problem: What Everyone Needs to Know, 2011, Oxford University Press, New York

[76] http://www.cyprus-conflict.net/13_points.html, accessed 15 Jan 2012

up from their military forces already based on the island under the treaty.[77] The government of Cyprus, in late December 1963, accepted this offer. A cease-fire was arranged along a line drawn in green across the map of the island by the British commander of the peacemaking force, thus establishing the term *Green Line* to describe what has now become the de facto border between the Greek Cypriot government-controlled areas and the self-declared TRNC. The agreement also included the establishment of a neutral buffer zone along the Green Line, patrolled by the peacemaking force and the holding of a conference in London attended by representatives of the three guarantor countries and the two communities in Cyprus. The conference met in London in January 1964 but failed to achieve any progress. The Cyprus government rejected the idea of a NATO peacekeeping force and demanded that the existing peacemaking force should become UN mandated. Makarios demanded the termination of the 1960 agreements as unworkable and their replacement by "unfettered independence"—a unitary government with freedom to amend the constitution. He offered the Turkish Cypriots minority rights, which they rejected out of hand. The Turks said that the December fighting proved the need to separate the two communities physically. Consequently they demanded a fully federal state of Cyprus with a border between Turkish and Greek provinces known as the Attila Line, which was not unlike the then existing cease-fire line or, failing that, "double enosis" which would impose a frontier across Cyprus between Greece and Turkey themselves, two solutions that would imply a population transfer. The London conference broke down with no chance of agreement.[78] Following the breakdown of the conference, the situation deteriorated rapidly. There was kidnapping and hostage taking, further separation of the two communities creating Turkish Cypriot refugees, failure of the government to control the situation and increasing fears of Greek and/or Turkish military intervention. The United States prevented Turkish intervention at that time by making it clear to Turkey that

---

[77] http://www.unficyp.org/nqcontent.cfm?a_id=1600&tt=graphic&lang=ll, accessed 23 Jan 2012

[78] http://www.cyprus-conflict.net/narrative-main-%203.html, accessed 15 Jan 2012

it would not intervene to assist them if an invasion of Cyprus led to conflict with the Soviet Union.

In February 1964, in response to urgent requests from the governments of the United Kingdom and Cyprus, the UN Security Council considered the situation in Cyprus. On March 4, the security council passed Resolution 186 calling, inter alia, for the establishment of a UN peacekeeping force in Cyprus (UNFICYP). Following the agreement of the Cyprus government, the force deployed in March, with a mandate to maintain security and prevent inter-communal fighting. That force is still on the island, albeit on a smaller scale than at its peak. Resolution 186 also provided for the appointment of a UN-appointed mediator. In 1965, the incumbent mediator was probably the first to accuse both sides of lacking a commitment to negotiate a settlement,[79] and many, myself included, would argue that in this respect, nothing has changed since then. In the ten-year period, 1964-1974, there were various attempts to resolve the Cyprus problem, without success, including lengthy inter-communal talks between the Greek Cypriot president of the House of Representatives Glafcos Clerides and Turkish Cypriot leader Rauf Denktash.

The Turkish Invasion

In early 1974, the military junta was in power in Greece, and an element of Greek Cypriot right-wing supporters started to plot *enosis*, leading to a coup d'état against the Greek Cypriot government of President Makarios on July 15, 1974. The coup was effected by the Cypriot National Guard led by Greek officers and EOKA-B and installed Nikos Sampson as president, with the stated aim of *enosis*. Makarios managed to escape from the presidential palace in Nicosia, went to Paphos, and eventually to RAF Akrotiri in one of the British sovereign base areas, from where the RAF flew him to England. Turkey could not stand by and let *enosis* happen. Following failure to enlist British support for intervention, Turkey invoked powers it claimed to have under the 1960 treaties of which the United Kingdom,

---

[79]   http://www.cyprus-conflict.net/galo_plaza_report.html, accessed 23 Jan 2012

Turkey and Greece were guarantors and invaded Cyprus on July 20. In fact, it is doubtful that Turkish intervention fell within the powers granted by the treaties, which required consultation on action among the three guarantors, and only if that failed, unilateral intervention by any of them, and that "with the sole aim of re-establishing the state of affairs created by the Treaties."[80] Turkey had not consulted Greece, perhaps understandably given that country's own domestic problems at the time, and it soon became apparent that Turkey was not aiming to re-establish the state of affairs hitherto prevailing. On July 23, three days after the start of the invasion, the Greek military junta in Athens fell and Nikos Sampson stood down as president of Cyprus. Talks in Geneva between the three guarantor powers and, later, involving the two communities, did not produce a result, and on August 14, Turkey resumed its military advance.

Within a month of the initial landings, Turkey had occupied some 37 percent of the island, including the important port of Famagusta and the tourist town of Kyrenia, both of which had substantial Greek Cypriot populations before the invasion. As the Turkish invasion took place many Greek Cypriots in the northern part of the island fled south and Turkish Cypriots in the south moved north. Most of those who did not move voluntarily were later encouraged or forced to do so, effectively creating two ethnically cleansed areas. The cease-fire established a line across the island, separating the two areas that was a modification of the Green Line created in 1963, in the process dividing the capital, Nicosia. It was (and still is) patrolled by an enhanced UN peacekeeping force and few people were able to cross from one area to the other. Since 1974, talks have taken place between the Greek and Turkish Cypriot leaders at many venues, sometimes with the participation of others, especially the UN. To date, the two parties have not found a solution for reunification acceptable to both of them. While the generally touted solution, as envisaged in the High Level Agreements between Makarios and Turkish Cypriot leader Rauf Denktash in 1977, is a

---

[80]   http://www.mfa.gov.cy/mfa/mfa2006.nsf/All/484B73E4F0736CFDC22571 BF00394F11/$file/Treaty%20of%20Guarantee.pdf, Clause IV, accessed 23 Jan 2012

"bi-zonal, bi-communal federation," each side has its own ideas about what this means in reality, and these are difficult to reconcile. In November 1983, not long after I arrived in Cyprus, the situation was further complicated when the Turkish Cypriot administration made a unilateral declaration of independence, establishing the Turkish Republic of Northern Cyprus, a country recognised, then and now, only by Turkey and completely dependent on the mother country for its political and economic existence.

European Union Membership and the Annan Plan

In 1990, the internationally recognised government of Cyprus applied for European Union membership. The EU expected that the process of accession negotiations would aid efforts to find a solution to the Cyprus problem, the implication being that the benefits of membership would cause the Turkish Cypriots to make concessions. Certainly, the Greek Cypriots saw EU membership as a means to a solution of the problem, mostly on their terms. Turkey and the Turkish Cypriots were very disturbed by the EU decision to open negotiations on Cyprus's membership, and they adopted a more hard-line position in subsequent talks. During the EU accession process, Turkish Cypriots were offered the opportunity to participate but did not accept.

In April 2003, in a surprise move, the TRNC, then led by Rauf Denktash, decided to open the "border" and permit free movement of people, vehicles and goods across the Green Line. This took the Greek Cypriot government by complete surprise, and there were hurried measures taken to control the flow of people in both directions. Within two weeks, more than two hundred thousand Greek Cypriots had crossed to the north, despite the government's opposition to them doing so. There were no serious incidents. One of the effects of the opening of the Green Line, unwelcomed by the Cypriot government, was that many Turkish Cypriots applied for Cypriot identity cards and passports issued by the internationally recognised government. Since it claimed sovereignty over the whole island, the government could not refuse these requests. The travel documents issued by the TRNC required holders to obtain visas to visit practically any country except Turkey. Even before EU accession, a Cypriot passport allowed visa free travel to many countries and, after accession, the right to travel, work and live in any EU country.

When the "border" opened, Cyprus was in the final stages of preparation for accession to the European Union, which took place a year later. During that time, in the face of international pressure, the Greek Cypriot and Turkish Cypriot leaders, Tassos Papadopoulos and Rauf Denktash, encouraged by the UN secretary-general Kofi Annan, agreed to restart talks, with the aim of finding a solution before Cyprus's EU accession, scheduled for May 1, 2004. In the absence of substantive progress, on March 31, 2004 Annan submitted a proposal for a solution, which was to be voted on in separate referenda in each community on April 24. The EU, United States and Turkey, quickly expressed their support for the Annan Plan. Although Denktash was not in favour, in the end, 65 percent of Turkish Cypriots voted for the plan in their referendum.

Among Greek Cypriots, President Papadopoulos led a vigorous campaign against the plan, even breaking down in tears during one television broadcast.[81] In their referendum, 72 percent of Greek Cypriot voters said an emphatic "no."

Notwithstanding the rejection of the Annan Plan, Cyprus joined the EU on May 1, 2004. At the time of accession, the Green Line regulations came into effect. These ensured free movement of EU citizens, including Greek and Turkish Cypriots and, in certain circumstances, third-country nationals, across the Green Line and set out the way in which the movement of goods was to be controlled.

Generally, after the rejection of the plan, Greek Cypriots were viewed negatively, especially within the EU, and the Turkish Cypriots received considerable sympathy. Whether or not the EU should have allowed Cyprus to join while the division of the island

---

[81]   http://mondediplo.com/2004/05/07cyprus, accessed 23 Jan 2012

continued is a matter that is still debated. The EU must surely regret importing the problem that also adds complications to the Turkish accession negotiations.

Since 2004, there have been further attempts to reach a negotiated solution. An agreement in 2006 achieved nothing of value. In presidential elections in 2008, Demetris Christofias, general secretary of the Progressive Party of the Working People (AKEL), a party based on the principles of Marxism-Leninism, replaced Tassos Papadopoulos and agreement was reached to recommence talks. The agreement envisaged a Cypriot-led process, with the "assistance" of the UN's special advisor on Cyprus, former Australian Foreign Minister Alexander Downer. These talks have now dragged on for over four years and, in spite of several prods from the UN secretary-general, have not produced the desired outcome. The UN seems to be concluding that a federal solution is not possible.

Conclusion

In his book *Echoes from the Dead Zone*, Yiannis Papadakis identifies probably more similarities than differences between the two communities in Cyprus.[82] Each educational system teaches hatred of the other community, and both communities continually emphasise the atrocities perpetrated on them by the other. Older people on both sides on the Green Line remember with affection friends from the other community with whom they lived side by side before the trouble began in 1963, and these same older people are reluctant to talk about the atrocities committed by their own community, although they admit that they occurred. His analysis is remarkably similar to the conclusions reached by Philip Mansel in his book *Levant*[83] about the attitudes of the Turkish and Greek populations of Smyrna (now Izmir), following the forced exchange of populations between Turkey and Greece in 1923.

---

[82]   Papadakis, Yiannis, Echoes from the Dead Zone, 2005, I B Tauris & Co Ltd, London

[83]   Mansel, Philip, Levant, 2010, John Murray, London

One would expect that the passing of time would heal the wounds. However, both communities in Cyprus continue to remind the younger generation of the alleged atrocities committed by the other, and successive governments from all sections of the political spectrum on both sides of the Green Line have prolonged negotiations and regularly tried to lay the blame for lack of a settlement on the other party.

The Cyprus problem has reached the point where even the United Nations secretary-general is losing patience with both communities, the European Union must certainly be regretting its decision to admit a divided island, and most Cypriots are sceptical that a solution acceptable to both communities will ever be found. Indeed, I suggest that many, perhaps a majority, could accept a permanent division of the island under certain conditions.

The division of Cyprus and the effective ethnic cleaning, which started in 1963 and was completed after the 1974 Turkish intervention, is without a doubt a tragedy. However, I would argue, the present status quo is a solution that both sides could accept if they were honest about their feelings. The Turkish Cypriots started calling for *taksim* in the 1950s; the Greek Cypriots who originally wanted *enosis* since the 1930s have generally prospered since 1974 and, if they are honest are, I believe, content to live separately from the island's Turkish Cypriot population in an independent country, a feeling that is undoubtedly reciprocated. For a long time the educational system of both communities has been very nationalistic, and even in colonial days, children of both communities generally attended separate schools at which the speech and culture of the "mother countries" and, more importantly, nationalistic stories and ethnic propaganda were taught. This did not change following independence, and since 1974, it has probably become even more extreme. Several generations of children from both communities have never met each other, and each has been taught that the other community is barbarous and committed atrocities against the other. This is true, but what has not been taught and is seldom, if ever, discussed in each community is its own guilt, the atrocities that their community committed.

If one accepts that the problem began soon after independence, rather than when Turkey intervened in 1974, attempts to solve the Cyprus problem have been going on for nearly half a century without result. The present good offices mission of the United Nations secretary-general seems to be going nowhere; indeed, the impression is that neither side is willing to make the concessions required to achieve what is the generally accepted objective of establishing a Cyprus united in a bi-zonal, bi-communal federal system. Each side has significantly differing views about what this solution would really mean in practice. At meetings with the UN secretary-general in January 2012, no practical progress could be reported, and one Cyprus English language newspaper talked of "partition step by step" and concluded that both sides "are drawing closer to a 'velvet divorce,' an outcome not indigestible to the international community."[84]

While it may be repugnant to some, especially those displaced by the conflict, what is wrong with accepting that neither a return to the status quo ante or reunification in a federation are possible and, instead, work towards a solution in which there are two independent states on the island? In doing so, some territorial adjustments could be made, and compensation should be paid to the refugees from both communities who were displaced between 1963 and 1975.

---

[84] http://www.cyprus-mail.com/greentree/partition-step-step/20120123, accessed 27 Jan 2012

Chapter 12

CYPRUS

In 1983, seatbelts for drivers and front-seat passengers became compulsory in the United Kingdom and US president Ronald Regan announced that the Global Positioning System (GPS) would be made available for civilian use. Among events that would influence my future life, a bombing at the US embassy in Beirut killed sixty-three people and suicide truck bombings destroyed the US and French barracks in Beirut, killing three hundred and five, most of them service personnel participating the Multi National Force.

In addition, an agreement was signed on Israeli withdrawal from Lebanon, and the Turkish occupied part of Cyprus unilaterally declared independence as the Turkish Republic of Northern Cyprus, a country recognised then and still only by Turkey.

I had visited Cyprus as a tourist on three previous occasions, in November 1969 while working in Bahrain, in January 1974 while attending MECAS and in October 1979 while living in Dubai. During the first two visits, prior to the Turkish invasion of July 1974, I had stayed in Kyrenia; the third visit was spent in Limassol. I arrived for the fourth time on October 30, 1983; this time I was arriving to live and work in Nicosia, the last (and still) divided capital in the world.

After the 1974 Turkish invasion of Cyprus, as one of several measures taken to stimulate the economy in the government-controlled areas of the country, Cyprus established a scheme to allow the incorporation of offshore companies in 1976 and later, offshore banking units (OBUs) in 1982. Essentially, an offshore company was a Cyprus limited liability company, 100 percent of which was beneficially owned by non-residents. Such companies enjoyed freedom from exchange control, and both the company and its expatriate employees enjoyed significant tax concessions. Companies were taxed at 4.25 percent on their operating profit and the employees at 50 percent of normal Cyprus personal tax rates, and that only for income relating to days actually spent in Cyprus. Income relating to days spent outside was not taxed in Cyprus. In addition, the company and its expatriate employees were exempt from customs duty on a range of items, including private motor vehicles. OBUs enjoyed the same tax breaks.

In 1977, in the early stages of the Lebanese civil war, Federal Bank of Lebanon, a relatively small family-owned bank in Beirut, established a representative office in Nicosia. It was the first such office to be licenced and opened. Subsequently, in 1980, the then deputy chairman of that bank proposed to the Central Bank of Cyprus that they should consider permitting the establishment of OBU's in the country and after due consideration the idea was approved and regulations were issued in 1982.

Central Bank of Cyprus officials followed the example of Bahrain in framing the regulations under which OBUs would operate. The banking licence did not allow an OBU to do business in the domestic currency (then the Cyprus pound) or, generally, with residents of the country. However, an OBU was permitted to provide banking services in foreign currency to the increasing number of offshore companies being established and their expatriate staff and to do business with companies and individuals elsewhere in the world. From time to time, the central bank would grant permission for an OBU to provide finance in foreign currency to a domestic borrower if the project was considered to be in the country's interest and would generate foreign currency income to service the loan.

During the years that have elapsed since the offshore company and offshore banking schemes were established, Cyprus has had to adapt to changing conditions and modify the rules, especially as a result of significantly increased anti-money laundering and "know your customer" (KYC) laws that were introduced from the 1990s onwards and after joining the European Union in 2004.

Since 1976, the terms *offshore company* and *OBU* have fallen out of favour because of the wrong perception that such vehicles were used for illegal activities, if only tax avoidance. In Cyprus, *international banking unit* replaced the term *offshore banking unit* in 2000 and now there is no distinctive designation. Additionally, as a consequence of joining the EU, the tax rules have changed. All companies, regardless of the nature of their ownership, are taxed at a uniform corporate tax rate, at present 10%, and all employees, Cypriot or foreign, at the same standard personal tax rates.

Over the years, the country has been able to benefit, as far as offshore business is concerned, from the civil war in Lebanon, the conflict in Yugoslavia and the breakup of the Soviet Union—all of which events became sources of business for the offshore industry, especially Cypriot accountants and lawyers, as well as the banks, both domestic and international.

In early 1983, I answered an advertisement in the *Financial Times* for a number of vacancies in a new offshore bank, Federal Bank of the Middle East (FBME), under establishment in Nicosia. FBME was the first OBU to be licenced under the new regulations and was 51% owned by Federal Bank of Lebanon, although the shareholding structure has changed since then. I applied for the position of operations manager. In due course, the deputy chairman and the general manager interviewed me in Dubai and later in London, but by that time another candidate had been offered the operations manager position. For the one and only time in my life, I decided to use *wasta*. This Arabic word can be loosely translated as "influence," from a root meaning "intervention" or "good offices."

As it happened, I had a friend in Dubai who, I knew, had been a colleague of the FBME general manager in another bank, and I asked him if he could assist. He may have spoken well of me because I was eventually offered the position of marketing manager; however, when I was reviewing this chapter with the present chairman of FBME, he assured me that *wasta* had not been necessary. He and the general manager had already decided that they wanted me to join the bank. I accepted, mainly because I had already given notice to Khalij Commercial Bank in Dubai and was keen not to join the ranks of the unemployed when the notice period expired. Although I was not convinced that I was the right person for a marketing position, I thought that it could provide a foot in the door in a new institution and prospects for advancement and a change of direction. This proved

to be the case as I was with the Federal Bank of the Middle East (renamed FBME Bank in 2005) for longer than any other institution in my banking career.

From the outset, the business plan of FBME was to develop business from the Middle East, especially Lebanon, which was still

The author (left) with General Manager, Geoffrey Sutcliffe, FBME Nicosia, 1983

suffering from the ongoing civil war, which had started in 1975 and was destined to continue until 1990. The bank's sister bank in Lebanon, Federal Bank of Lebanon, was expected to be a source of business introductions. In addition, as the civil war had dragged on in Lebanon, many Lebanese businessmen had moved to Cyprus and established offshore companies as vehicles for the continuation of their international activities, and these and their foreign staff were another potential source of business.

Among the international business conducted during the 1980s was the finance of the export of fertilizer from Romania to several destinations in the Middle East and Central America. In December 1986, I visited Bucharest for discussions on this business with the exporter, a state-owned company, and to meet with officials of several banks to discuss arrangements for handling the letters of credit that FBME would open in favour of the exporter. This was my first visit to a country that was to feature prominently later in my life. It took place during the days that Nicolae Ceauşescu ruled Romania with a very firm fist. In the 1970s, western banks and governments had made substantial loans to Romania to finance economic development. Ceauşescu did not realise that the funding terms were not always favourable, and in the end, the loans devastated the country's finances.

In 1982, he decided to repay all of Romania's foreign debt, and to accomplish this, he ordered that most of the country's agricultural and industrial production must be exported to provide foreign currency to fund the debt repayments.[85] The result was a dramatic decline in living standards in the country and the absence of many items from the domestic market. During my visit, I stayed at the Intercontinental Hotel in Bucharest, the only good hotel in the city, where there was no heating, intermittent electricity, the staff all wore overcoats inside the building and the offerings in the restaurant were very limited. The television in my room provided only the one Romanian state channel. Against this background, our interest in encouraging exports was well received, and the necessary arrangements for the letters of credit were quickly concluded with Frankfurt-Bucharest Bank. By the summer of 1989, shortly before his demise, Ceauşescu had succeeded in repaying all of the country's external debt, but this did not count for much among the long-suffering population when the revolution came a few months later.

A revealing experience during this visit to Romania occurred when I decided to attend a performance of Madame Butterfly at the state opera. I took a taxi to the theatre from the hotel, but after the performance, when the audience emerged, there was not a taxi in sight. I approached a man who had also been at the performance asked him if he spoke English and if he knew how I might find a taxi. He took one look at me and immediately ran away. At the time, the Romanian Department of State Security, generally referred to as the *Securitate*, was a much-feared organisation employing over five hundred

---

[85]   http://www.historyguide.org/europe/ceausescu.html, accessed 16 Jan 2012

thousand informers as well as eleven thousand agents.[86] It was one of the largest secret police organisations in Eastern Europe. Contact between Romanians and foreigners was not encouraged, and I suppose, the man I had approached was afraid that if an informer reported him talking to me, he would face problems. Luckily, I had taken note of the route on my way to the theatre, which was quite direct, so I walked back to the hotel, a distance of not much more than one kilometre.

Another unusual piece of business undertaken in 1987 was the banking arrangements for the export of Iraqi oil by truck through Turkey to Yugoslavia. At this time, the Iraq-Iran war, which had started in 1980, was ongoing, and Yugoslavia was still a united, socialist country; sanctions against both countries were yet to come. During the early years of the Iraq-Iran war, western companies, banks and governments had continued to supply goods to Iraq and grant credit.

However, by 1987, companies from countries such as India and Yugoslavia had been supplying goods and services to Iraq on more favourable terms, to fill the gap as western companies restricted further credit to the country.[87] Iraq concluded an agreement to repay debts owed to Yugoslavia by deliveries of oil from its northern oil fields. A Cyprus offshore company, a subsidiary of a Yugoslav state-owned trading company, was appointed to handle the logistics of transporting the oil to Yugoslavia. I accompanied representatives of the company to Istanbul to assist in setting up the payment arrangements for the transport costs with the Turkish contractor. Because of the political situation prevailing between Cyprus and Turkey, the transportation company was reluctant to accept the direct commitment of a bank in Cyprus. A solution was found by using a major Swiss bank, with which FBME had a strong relationship, as an intermediary.

The bank's involvement in Iraq in the 1980s pre-First Gulf War, pre-sanctions era, when Saddam Hussein was allowing the private

---

[86]   Smith, Craig "Eastern Europe Struggles to Purge Security Services", *The New York Times*, December 12, 2006

[87]   http://www.photius.com/countries/iraq/economy/iraq_economy_foreign_trade.html, accessed 22 Jan 2012

sector to import consumer goods, also included working with a Cyprus offshore company supplying major brands of cigarettes and whiskey to the country.

Another country, which generated significant business in the days before strict sanctions, was Libya. FBME had a client who supplied equipment for the country's oil industry through Libyan government-owned purchasing companies established in London and Düsseldorf. In the early 1990s, the managing director of the client company, who was naturalised Cypriot of Iranian origin, was the subject of a "sting" operation organised by the US Customs.

He was lured to the Bahamas, supposedly for a meeting with representatives of an American company. From there he was kidnapped, flown to West Palm Beach in Florida, and was arrested for violating unilateral US sanctions on Libya. President Reagan had implemented these sanctions in 1986. It was well known that they did not apply to non-US persons (which he and his company were), who were not present in the United States.

For that reason, until his kidnapping, he had never visited the country since the sanctions were imposed. The victim's book *In the Claw of the Eagle*[88] tells the full story and includes much detailed information on the history and background to US unilateral sanctions. The same author, who also conducted legal business with oil industry companies in Iran, has also written another book, this time about sanctions against Iran.[89]

FBME was able to take advantage of the concession permitting OBUs to provide finance to domestic companies, with central bank approval, on several occasions. The first occurred early in 1984 when the central bank permitted the bank to open letters of credit and provide short-term refinancing for the import into Cyprus of crude oil from Libya and Iraq. Permission for these transactions was

---

[88]   Alikhani, Hossein, In the Claw of the Eagle, 1995, Centre for Business Studies, London

[89]   Alikhani, Hossein, Sanctioning Iran, 2000, I B Tauris, London

granted by the central bank because, at that time, the domestic banks had reached the prudent limit for this type of business.

In 1987, one of the leading firms of maritime lawyers in Cyprus visited the bank, with a Cypriot client, regarding the possible financing of the acquisition of the first cruise ship by the client, a major tourism company in the country. Since tourism was so important to the island's economy, and because the vessel would generate foreign currency income, once more central bank permission was forthcoming, and the deal was arranged by FBME, in syndication with other banks. This was the first syndicated loan arranged by any bank in Cyprus. The ship was built in Finland in 1966, so it was already twenty years old, but furnished with full international trading certificates. The new owner renamed the ship *Princesa Marissa*, after the daughter of the chairman of the company and, after refurbishing, used it mainly for short cruises from Cyprus to Greece, Israel and Egypt, and, after the end of the civil war, Lebanon. There was a casino on board, operated by another client of the bank. The *Princesa Marissa* was the beginning of a fleet which in time became the most successful cruise business in the Mediterranean. Twenty years later, during the Israeli war on Lebanon in 2006, this ship again featured in my life when I was evacuated on it from Lebanon to Cyprus during the Israeli war, and in 2008 she was scrapped in India.

Egyptian foreign trade was also financed by FBME, including cotton yarn exports to the United States for a Nassau-based company and timber imports from Yugoslavia for a Cyprus offshore company, the latter prior to sanctions, of course. Another Egyptian export that featured in the bank's business was potatoes to the United Kingdom. When this business started, I went to Cairo to witness the start of the first transaction, involving the acquisition and packing of the potatoes for shipment by airfreight, and then flew to London to see the arrival and processing by the importer, located near Peterborough. I arrived in London on an overnight flight from Cairo early on October 16, 1987, the morning after the hurricane had struck southern England, causing extensive damage over a wide area of the country, but this did not prevent me keeping to my schedule.

When FBME was first established in 1982, it had become a shareholder in Arab Financial Services (AFS), a company promoted by the Union of Arab Banks and incorporated in Bahrain; all of the other shareholders were banks and financial institutions in the Middle East. The initial business of the company was primarily issuing travellers cheques under the Visa brand and distributing these for sale through banks in the region. FBME was one such bank. Later it started to undertake the issue of Visa credit and debit cards and the provision of card transaction processing and billing services for smaller banks, which wanted to offer their own cards to their clients but whose volumes could not justify the costs of setting up the systems to process the business. FBME utilised these services when it first started to issue its own payment cards.

FBME's deputy chairman was on the board of AFS and actively involved in the establishment of the company. He was a regular visitor to Bahrain for meetings and on one such visit, the general manager of AFS introduced him to the regional representative of ED & F Man Group. This led eventually to a new type of business for the bank; one of the activities of the Man Group was the management of closed-end collective investment schemes that invested in commodity futures and similar instruments and offered investors a guarantee of the return of their capital at the maturity date of the fund. They had recently launched one such fund for which the National Bank of Bahrain had provided the guarantee and underwritten the issue. After some negotiations, FBME agreed with the Man Group to launch a similar fund, FBME Mint Guaranteed Limited, of which I became a director. I was actively involved in all aspects of the project including setting up the legal structure and marketing the fund, especially to the bank's customers. FBME provided the guarantee to the investors that on the maturity date of the fund, their capital would be repaid; the guarantee was secured by the fund placing a deposit with FBME, which, with interest, would be sufficient to cover this obligation on the maturity date. The balance of the fund's assets was used to support trading with the Man Group. The fund was advertised extensively in publications circulating in the Middle East and attracted considerable attention, especially from expatriates in Saudi Arabia. During the selling period, I made a trip to Saudi Arabia to follow up on enquiries that had originated there, visiting Jeddah, Riyadh and al-Khobar. At the end of my stay in Saudi Arabia, I left via the then recently opened causeway to Bahrain, which proved to be a pleasant and hassle-free journey. This same causeway would be used most effectively to allow a contingent of Saudi security forces to enter Bahrain at the time of the uprising there in 2011.

During the marketing of FBME Mint Guaranteed, I also made a visit to Beirut with a Lebanese colleague to try to attract investment from banks and individuals there. This visit in 1988, during a lull in the civil war, was at the time that there were two governments in power in Lebanon, following the failure to elect a replacement for outgoing president Amine Gemayel. Michel Aoun was in power in East Beirut and Selim al-Hoss in West Beirut. I applied for a visa at the Lebanese embassy in Nicosia, and it was issued without question. At the time Beirut airport was closed so the only way to travel to Lebanon was to take the over-night ferry from Larnaca to Jounieh, a small port north of Beirut, overlooked by the famous Casino du Liban, in the area controlled by Michel Aoun. When I was boarding the ship, my passport was examined by officials representing the "government" in East Beirut, and in spite of the presence of the visa, I was asked to complete a form entitled Application to Visit, which was virtually identical to the embassy's visa application form. At the time, General Aoun did not recognise the authority of Lebanon's embassies abroad. On arrival, the stamp used in my passport was in the form always used in the past and since by the official government. The visit, confined to East Beirut, was uneventful, but we did not succeed in interesting many people there in the fund. No doubt they had other priorities.

When FBME first obtained its banking licence in Cyprus in 1982, one of the terms included was the permission to open numbered accounts, a feature that was common to all offshore banking licences granted then and for many years thereafter. It was FBME's then deputy chairman who had suggested this idea to the Central Bank when they were drafting the regulations and licence terms. Even in the early days, when "know your customer" (KYC) and anti-money laundering regulations were much less stringent than today, the bank required the same supporting documentation from holders of a numbered account as for a normal account. The only real difference was that in the records generally available to staff, a number rather than a name identified the customer, including on advices and statements. The actual identity of the account holder was on record in a register and files accessible only by a limited number of senior officers. These accounts were no different to the numbered accounts offered then and now by Swiss banks.

Numbered accounts were attractive to customers from a number of countries, especially the former Soviet states, who did not want to risk information about their accounts being revealed. Incoming payments to such accounts would usually only mention the number; outward payments would usually show the remitter as "One of Our Customers." Over the years, as KYC and anti-money laundering requirements became stricter, the Central Bank of Cyprus found it more difficult to defend its policy of allowing numbered accounts; initially permission to open new accounts was withdrawn in 2000; later in 2004, they required that all existing numbered accounts be converted to normal named accounts.

In 1999, the Cyprus stock market enjoyed an unprecedented boom, with the index soaring 700 percent. During this period, a number of family-owned businesses took advantage of the situation to make public offerings of shares, which were always grossly oversubscribed and made many of the original owners very wealthy. To the gullible public it seemed that the price of these shares could only go up. Many investors, who knew nothing about the workings of stock exchanges, rushed to participate in a market, which, in retrospect, can be seen to have been lacking in transparency and good governance. Often they used loans to finance their share purchases, and these shares then became the security for the loan; sometimes speculators mortgaged the family home. When the bubble burst, domestic banks were left with substantial loans for which there was often a significant shortfall in the collateral. As an OBU, FBME did not become a participant in this debacle.

At the time, a friend who had financial problems approached me; he was considering jumping on the bandwagon in an attempt to raise capital for his company. He showed me a report prepared by his accountants, a major international firm, which based on what I knew about the company was a marvellous work of fiction. If it was typical of information provided to potential investors in other share offerings, those who prepared such documents should have shouldered a lot of the blame for the subsequent crash of the market in 2000. My friend did not proceed with the idea.

In the late 1980s, FBME, looking to diversify its business, started to consider the Soviet Union. In 1987 the then deputy chairman and deputy general manager made the first pioneering visit to Moscow and in January 1991, I made my first visit with the deputy chairman of the bank and some American clients who were doing business in Russia. During this visit one of the clients was attracted to a lady who was sitting at the bar of the Mezdunarodnaya Hotel, where we were staying. The deputy chairman, who spoke Russian, acted as an intermediary and introduced the lady to our client. Not long after, they married! An unusual service for a banker to provide to his client.

This turned out to be the first of many visits to Russia and the other former Soviet states over the next five years as the business potential following the breakup of the Soviet Union developed. From 1991 onwards, these countries became an important source of business for the bank, and in 1993, FBME opened a representative office in Moscow to assist with business development in the region.

In the early days, travel around the former Soviet Union was not

always easy. Aeroflot still had a virtual monopoly of flights and was not the most reliable airline. The bank, therefore, often used a Russian Yak-40 executive jet to transport directors and management during their travels. Initially this was chartered, but later

FBME Bank Yak 40 at Vnukovo airport, Moscow (Stephan Karl)

FBME decided to buy its own aircraft, which was based at Vnukovo airport, Moscow, and used for most travel within the former Soviet Union for several years. Although an executive jet may sound an extravagance for what was then a relatively small bank, in fact it improved efficiency and productivity during a period when travel by any other means would have been difficult, unreliable, possibly dangerous and certainly time-consuming.

One of the earliest major deals relating to Russia was the establishment of escrow account arrangements for a barter deal involving the export of Russian coal, mainly to Scandinavia, the sale proceeds of which were to be used to finance the import from the United States and erection of prefabricated housing for the coal miners in the Kemerovo region.

In October 1992, I visited Washington with the Russian representative of the company organising the coal exports for discussions on the project and escrow and payment arrangements with the American exporter of the housing units. When the Russian exporter arranged sales, the foreign buyer would open a letter of credit advised through FBME, and after shipment of the goods and payment under the letter of credit, the proceeds would be deposited in the escrow account, from which, subject to the conditions of the agreement, payments could be made for shipments of the housing units.

An amusing event during the Washington visit was an encounter with a traffic police officer in rural Maryland. I was driving a rented car transporting some of the group to visit a construction site where houses similar to those to be supplied to Russia were being built. We stopped for coffee, and I parked the car in what seemed to be part of the recognised parking area. Before I had a chance to leave the car, a traffic police officer approached me and started to speak in an accent from the deep south of the United States. I asked him twice to repeat what he had said and then gave up trying to understand him. An American member of the party was called upon to translate!

The truth of the view, sometimes attributed to Winston Churchill but possibly originated by George Bernard Shaw, that England and

America were two countries divided by a common language was proved. It seemed that the police officer had set up a radar trap, and he was trying to tell me that I had parked in a position that blocked the line of sight of his equipment, preventing him from catching any offenders. I moved the car to a more acceptable location.

During the 1980s, Prof. Svyatoslav Fyodorov had pioneered groundbreaking procedures to treat many vision problems at the Moscow Institute of Eye Microsurgery, including the use of radial keratotomy and laser treatment to restore or improve vision in cases of cataracts, glaucoma and high degrees of myopia. The system was like a conveyor belt where patients would lie down on the bed; it would slide through a stainless steel door, and the patient would stop at the first surgeon under a microscope. Each surgeon performed a specific task, and then the conveyor belt brought around the next patient. A chief surgeon, occasionally Fyodorov himself, supervised from a video control. After Mikhail Gorbachev came to power in the Soviet Union and enacted economic reforms, Professor Fyodorov began to commercialise his techniques and is said to have become one of the first millionaires in post-Communist Russia. He chartered a passenger ship, *Peter I*, from the Black Sea Shipping Company, and converted it into a floating hospital. This ship first visited Dubai and then in 1992 it arrived in Larnaca in Cyprus where a Nicosia-based public relations company, which also worked for the bank, assisted in publicity and business development.[90] Among many thousands of others, the bank's chairman was treated. From Larnaca, the ship moved on to Gibraltar; while it was there, in 1993, I took my father for treatment that he could not obtain easily in England under the National Health Service.

During 1992, I made several visits to Ukraine. The bank at the time was considering ways in which it might increase its presence in Russia and other countries of the former Soviet Union and had received an introduction to a bank based in Odessa that was interested in having a foreign bank as a shareholder. During my first visit, I met the

---

[90]   http://russiapedia.rt.com/prominent-russians/science-and-technology/svyatoslav-fyodorov/, accessed 22 Jan 2012

chairman and senior management of the bank and obtained various information that FBME required before proceeding further.

The bank was located in a beautiful nineteenth century building in central Odessa, which once must have been a private residence. One unusual feature I was shown was a huge room on the first floor, maybe once the ballroom, which was full of busts of Lenin. These had been collected from many locations in the area after the fall of the Soviet Union and demise of Communism in Ukraine. I never did discover their fate, but as they were not included among the assets of the bank, this was not a problem!

I returned to Odessa a month later and then went on to Kiev to meet lawyers appointed to act for FBME and central bank officials to sound them out on their reaction to foreign investment in a domestic bank. In the end, FBME was unable to agree terms with the Ukrainian bank, although a correspondent banking relationship was established and normal bank-to-bank business conducted. In 2011, when on a holiday trip to Ukraine, I discovered that the bank was still in business in Odessa, in new and impressive premises.

From Kiev, I was to fly on to Vienna. During Soviet days, embassies abroad would issue visas for visitors that were a document separate from the passport and included a list of the cities to be visited and the order in which this would take place. Deviation from the itinerary was difficult.

In the early days after the breakup of the Soviet Union, the newly independent countries did not have their own embassies and so the Russian embassies, which had generally taken over Soviet embassy premises in most countries, including Cyprus, continued to issue visas in the same way as before covering most, if not all, former Soviet states. Thus, for this trip, as before, I had obtained a visa from the Russian embassy in Nicosia covering the route Moscow-Odessa-Kiev. It was duly stamped on entry into Russia at Sheremetyevo airport in Moscow, but when I left from Vnukovo, a domestic airport in Soviet days, there was no passport control. When I arrived in Odessa, a similar situation prevailed. My problem arose when I wanted to leave Ukraine from Kiev for Vienna. A very large and formidable lady immigration officer demanded to know why I did not have a Ukrainian visa and how I had managed to enter the country without one. I explained what had happened, and after she consulted senior colleagues, she allowed me to leave the country with strict instructions that I should obtain a Ukraine visa before any future visit.

I made a couple of further visits to Odessa and Kiev, armed with the correct visa and accompanied on each trip by a director of the bank. On one occasion, while we were having lunch in our hotel in Kiev, the director asked the waiter for some garlic to add to his food. The waiter replied that they had no garlic; my colleague persisted, telling him that he would tip him one dollar if he could find some garlic. The waiter responded that even for a million dollars, garlic was not available, and my colleague went without. The mighty dollar had failed to impress.

Another of the newly independent countries that I visited during this period was Armenia, where, during my first trip in January 1993, conditions were deplorable. I travelled to Yerevan from Moscow in the Yak-40, together with the deputy chairman of the bank and another director, arriving in the early evening. We had planned to spend three days in the Armenian capital.

On arrival at the airport, the temperature was twenty degrees below zero. At the hotel, said to be the best available, there was no electricity and no water flowed from the taps in the bathroom as the pipes were frozen. The temperature in my room was twenty-three degrees below zero; I slept in my clothes, including overcoat and Russian fur hat. The next day, after a meeting with the Central Bank of Armenia, we decided to curtail our visit and fly on to our next port of call, a warmer place in the Crimea, Simferopol. Unfortunately, because of the economic situation, there was no fuel available at Yerevan airport. Our pilot decided to take off anyway and then contacted various airports within his flying range with the available fuel and found that more was available at a small airport in southern Russia. We duly flew there, topped up the tanks, paid in cash from the suitcase that we carried for this purpose, and flew on to Simferopol.

The serious economic situation in Armenia following its declaration of independence from the Soviet Union in September 1991 was, in large part, due to the ongoing war with Azerbaijan over the disputed territory of Nagorno-Karabakh. Armenian victory in the war caused Azerbaijan and Turkey to close their borders and impose a blockade, which is maintained still, even though in October 2009 Turkey and Armenia signed a treaty to normalise relations. These events severely affected the economy of the new republic and closed off its main routes to Europe.

In the early days after the breakup of the Soviet Union, many new banks were established in Russia and the other newly independent states. FBME devoted considerable effort to get to know some of these banks and their shareholders and to develop correspondent relationships with them to enable such banks to conduct international business. Many established account relationships and arrangements for FBME to issue payment cards to their customers on a secured basis, which was one of the ways that FBME considerably expanded its card business at this time. I particularly remember one visit to a small bank in Moscow, the chairman of which had a retired Swiss banker as an adviser. The Swiss adviser received us in his office wearing carpet slippers; admittedly, the meeting was on a Saturday morning, but such informality was unusual. In spite of the carpet slippers, FBME did establish a business relationship with the bank, which was mutually beneficial.

One of the longest trips that I took in the former Soviet Union, in 1994, was in the Yak-40 to Yekaterinburg in the Ural Mountains, where Tsar Nicholas II and his family were murdered during the Russian revolution, Tyumen, in the oil-rich Ural Mountains area of Siberia, both in Russia and Almaty in Kazakhstan. By this time, FBME had increased its card business considerably and was looking to develop it further. Eventually, this aspect of its operations grew to such a size that it was transferred to a newly established, wholly owned subsidiary in Cyprus. The trip, with a colleague from the bank's card services department and the Moscow representative, was to visit banks with a view to promoting their use of FBME as an international correspondent and the issue of FBME payment cards to their clients who travelled abroad. At one bank in Almaty, I attended what must be the longest business meeting on record. My colleagues and I arrived at 10:00 a.m. and, with a break for lunch in the bank, finally finished at 9:30 p.m. However, this was not the end; the chairman of the bank that we were visiting then announced that we would proceed to the bank's private sauna in the basement of the head office. There a lavish buffet was laid out, with the usual abundance of vodka, cognac and champagne to accompany the food, in between sorties into the extreme heat of the sauna. We eventually got back to our hotel around 3:00 a.m. From Almaty, we were due to fly on to Tashkent in Uzbekistan the next morning, but when we arrived at the airport, the captain informed us that the Uzbek air traffic control would not grant permission for our flight, as they knew nothing about any visitors from Cyprus! So we returned to Moscow.

Accompanying us on this trip was Alexander Cooley, then a young undergraduate with an interest in central Asia, paying his first visit to Kazakhstan. His father was an old friend of the FBME Chairman, who, since we had a spare seat on the Yak 40, agreed to give Alex his first taste of the region. He is now a recognised expert on central Asia and is Tow Professor of Political Science at Barnard College, New York. Another unusual service provided by a banker.

I made my first visit to Beirut since the end of the civil war in November 1993. At that time, little had been done to start the rebuilding of the city centre that had been largely destroyed during the war. Solidaire, the company that was to undertake this work, was in the planning stages, but the company was not actually

BBME Bab Edris, Beirut, 1993

incorporated until May 1994. It was sad to see the damage that been inflicted on the city centre with trees and other vegetation growing wildly in areas that had been busy commercial streets. With some difficulty, I was able to find the British Bank of the Middle East office in Bab Idriss where I had worked in 1970-1971. The building itself was largely intact although surrounded by ruins. Today, that building is still unoccupied; why, I have no idea.

In July 1995, Arab Financial Services decided to hold a board meeting in Beirut, as a sign of support for the country and its effort to revive business and leisure tourism after the civil war. FBME and its sister bank in Lebanon, Federal Bank of Lebanon, hosted a reception for the board members attending the meeting and Lebanese officials and businessmen, including representatives of the Union of Arab Banks, at the Al Bustan Hotel in Broumana, just outside the city. Since there were a significant number of directors and management from FBME who had to travel between Cyprus and Beirut at different times and for different events, the bank decided to base its Yak-40 at Larnaca and use it to ferry people back and forth. The aircraft made so many trips over a few days that the authorities at Larnaca airport started asking questions, suspecting that an attempt was being made to establish a regular flight schedule on the route.

In February 1996, the firm of maritime lawyers who had acted for the owners of the *Princesa Marissa* in 1987 approached the bank to introduce a new client seeking ship finance. Their Romanian client had originally been a master mariner with a state-owned shipping company and head of its tanker division. Following the fall of Communism in Romania in 1990, he had taken advantage of opportunities to charter and operate vessels from state-owned companies and was building up an efficient ship management business based in Constanta. He then had the opportunity to buy his first vessel and required finance for part of the cost of upgrading it. The work was to be carried out at the then state-owned Constanta Shipyard. The ship was about seventeen years old, but with the planned upgrade, it was estimated that it would have a useful life, in compliance with all internationally accepted maritime standards, of at least ten years. I visited Constanta early in 1996, accompanied by one of the customer's legal advisors, to see the ship, the M/T *Libertatea*, which had been laid up for some time, and to discuss the plans with the shipyard and the owner. Following this inspection visit, the bank agreed to provide the required finance, and a year later, in February 1997, I was again in Constanta for the naming ceremony of the vessel, which had been renamed *Histria Prestige*.

This marked the beginning of a personal long-term friendship with the shipowner that continues to this day.

The author (right) with legal advisor, Maria Toumazi, inspecting the MT *Libertatae*, Constanta Shipyard, Romania, February 1996

In June 1996, on a business trip to the United States, I had another opportunity to fly Concorde from London to New York. At the time, the load factor on Concorde must have been low as British Airways was offering business class passengers from Cyprus to New York the opportunity to fly Concorde on one of the transatlantic sectors at no extra cost, and it fitted my schedule to take advantage of this offer. This turned out to be my last Concorde flight; largely because of a crash of an Air France Concorde at Charles de Gaulle Airport in Paris in 2000, both they and British Airways decided to withdraw the aircraft from service in 2003, and the era of supersonic passenger flight, in which I had participated three times, ended.

In 1996, with the millennium in mind, FBME decided to consider upgrading its banking software. The system implemented when the bank was set up in 1983 was suitable for the early operations, but something more sophisticated was required to cope with the developing business and increasing requirements of regulators; in addition, the old system would require upgrading to cope with date issues relating to the forthcoming millennium. I became leader of a steering group set up to investigate the options available.

After visits to London and Dublin to review banking packages developed by companies there, eventually we came down to a new banking package named Flexcube developed by an Indian company, Citicorp Information Technology Industries Limited (CITL) that was partly owned by the Citibank group. Therefore, on November 8, 1997, my fifty-fourth birthday, I and the other members of the team flew to Bangalore for discussions with the vendor on the functionality of the system and FBME's requirements. Technical and financial terms were quickly agreed, and on Christmas Eve 1997, representatives of the vendor were in Cyprus to sign the contract. FBME became the third bank to buy the system and the first outside India. The contract called for an eight-month implementation plan during 1998.

We started in February and went live on Flexcube on October 1, 1998, on time and within budget: unusual for an IT project. The system was newly developed and relatively untested in live situations. We realised when we decided to buy it that this would inevitably mean that problems would arise both during and after the implementation, and the licence fee reflected this possibility. We were not disappointed. CITL recognised the risk that the bank had taken in deciding to buy their system and support by the vendor for FBME, the first user outside India, was excellent, and our problems were usually fixed quickly. In the early days after implementation, CITL often used FBME as a reference bank, so we received regular visits from prospective users, including the Central Bank of Malta and Abu Dhabi Commercial Bank (which was a merger of three banks, including my former employer in Dubai, Khalij Commercial Bank). Since 1997, CITL has undergone several name changes; Citibank group is no longer a shareholder, and in 2006, the company became part of Oracle, who renamed it Oracle Financial Services Limited. In the years since FBME bought Flexcube, the system has developed beyond recognition, and it is now used by many major banks throughout the world, fully justifying FBME's decision to buy the new and relatively untried system in 1997.

In 2002, new approaches to banking regulation following the destruction of the World Trade Centre in New York had an unexpected effect on FBME. The bank was already incorporated and licensed in the Cayman Islands, but did not have a physical presence there, and operated in Cyprus as a branch of a Cayman bank, licensed by the Central Bank of Cyprus. At the time there were unprecedented concerns about so-called tax havens, money laundering, financing of terrorism and banking secrecy. These were accompanied by calls for greater control over banks established in locations such as the Cayman Islands resulting in changes to the banking law there. The regulator, the Cayman Islands Monetary Authority, decided that banks such as FBME should henceforth be required to have a physical presence in the Cayman Islands or cease to be registered there. The bank considered this and concluded that there would be no business advantage for it to have an office there. It therefore decided, with the agreement of both the Cayman and Cyprus regulators, to transfer its place of incorporation elsewhere and, after accomplishing this, to transfer the Cyprus OBU to the new entity and surrender its Cayman banking licence. The bank started a search for a suitable location; it considered a number of countries, including Romania and Latvia, both aspiring EU members at the time, as was Cyprus. I was actively involved in the discussions in each of the countries, where the acquisition of an existing local bank became a possibility. In the event, neither of the negotiations resulted in a deal, but then the bank identified another opportunity in Tanzania. The Bank of Tanzania (the central bank) had taken a local institution under its control and was seeking to sell parts of its assets and liabilities, including branch premises. FBME had experience in dealing in developing markets such as the Middle East, Eastern

FBME Bank, Nicosia, 1999
(FBME Bank Ltd)

Europe and the former Soviet Union; and the view of the directors was that a move into Africa made business sense. In due course, the bank reached an agreement with all relevant regulators, and the bank signed the purchase agreement in

June 2003. I will have more to say about my activities with FBME in Tanzania later.

As soon as I arrived in Nicosia in 1983, I started to look for accommodation as for the first time since I left Canada, my employer did not provide housing. Quite soon, I found an apartment in an area named Aglandjia, on a hilltop facing north towards the somewhat provocative Turkish and Turkish Cypriot flags carved in the side of the mountains in the northern part of the island. From my balcony, I could see part of the UN-patrolled Green Line and could watch planes from Istanbul, the only destination served from the north, landing at Ercan airport, just to the east of the city. I lived there until 1990 when I decided that the time had come to buy a home in Cyprus. It seemed likely that the rest of my working career would be there as it looked as though I would continue to work for FBME until it was time to retire.

At the time, the resale market for apartments and houses in Nicosia was limited. Most Cypriots tended to build or buy a house in which to live for life, and there was little labour mobility between cities to help create a secondary housing market. However, after a few months, a two-year-old two-story detached three-bedroom house was located in a suburban area called Lakatamia, about five kilometres (three miles) from the Nicosia city centre.

The author's house, Nicosia, October 2002

The house was acquired in early 1990. The first hurdle was for me, as a foreigner, to obtain the permission of the council of ministers to purchase the property, and while this was generally a formality, the wheels of Cypriot bureaucracy are slow to turn, and this took several months to obtain. Then there were the usual problems encountered in Cyprus regarding title deeds, which had to be overcome. Unusually, the seller had a title deed, but when I gave this to my lawyer, he pointed out that it covered only an empty plot of land; after the house was built, the owner had not bothered to have the title deed amended as, presumably, this would have cost him money.

The seller then had to get a certificate of completion from the municipality, which required him to complete construction of the pavement outside the house and have the title deed updated by the Lands Department, all of which took more time. At the time for the closing of the transaction and transfer of title, everything was in order, and I received the new title deed in my name within one week of signing the transfer deed. As anyone who has ever bought a property in Cyprus will understand, this was something of a record.

By 1993, I had sold my apartment in Châteaux-d'Oex, Switzerland and the house in Fort Meyers, Florida, and I began to consider purchasing a property in England, initially as an investment and to get on the property ladder, in case I ever decided to return there to live. After a search in London and the immediate area, I settled on a house in the "golden triangle" of central Windsor, about a four minute walk from the castle, which I purchased in May 1994. I located a letting agent who looked after the house as though it were her own, and she succeeded in finding good corporate tenants. This turned out to be the best of the various property investments I have made during my life. During the fifteen years that I owned it, it was rented for virtually the entire time and to excellent tenants, ranging from the general manager of the London branch of Bank of Tokyo to the Alitalia station manager at Heathrow. I sold it in 2009 when, in spite of the decline in property prices at the time, I realised a substantial capital gain.

A few months after my arrival in Nicosia in 1983, I was having a drink in a bar one evening when I got into conversation with another customer. It turned out that he had just come from a rehearsal for a play to be staged by a group called Anglo Cypriot Theatre (ACT). He mentioned that the group was in need of someone to undertake the lighting for the play, and when I spoke of my previous experience, he urged me to join the group. This I did for the production of *Ring Round the Moon* by Jean Anouilh—a play that I had lit for an outdoor production in Bahrain some fourteen years before. This time it was in the Chanticleer Theatre in Nicosia.

I went on to do the lighting for many productions over the next seven years, including Noel Coward's *Blithe Spirit* and *A Doll's House* by Henrik Ibsen, also in the Chanticleer Theatre, and open-air productions of Jean Anouilh's *Antigone* at Famagusta Gate in Nicosia and the Curium amphitheatre near Limassol. The next production was *A Man for All Seasons* by Robert Bolt in the gardens of the presidential palace in Nicosia and at the presidential summer home in the Troodos Mountains. The use of these locations was helped by the fact that the director of the play was the wife of the then foreign minister and because ACT agreed to donate the profits from the productions to a charity favoured by the president's wife. In between lighting, I occasionally appeared in small parts on stage, including as second priest in *Murder in the Cathedral,* Sir Oliver Martext in *As You Like It* and Francis Nurse in *The Crucible*. In

The author (left) as Sir Oliver Martext,
As You Like It, Nicosia, June 2001

1987, I became treasurer of the group, but by the early 1990s, pressure of work, in particular frequent travelling, caused me to drop out of productions, as I could never be certain that I would be available in Cyprus when needed. I continued, however, as treasurer of ACT for a total of fifteen years until the end of 2002, just prior to my departure from Cyprus.

In 1984, I made a trip to the northern part of the island with my aunt and uncle, Mary and Pearse O'Malley, who were visiting me from Dublin. At that time, there was one point at which it was possible to cross the Green Line, at the Ledra Palace Hotel in Nicosia, used by diplomats and other foreigners who had permission to cross. The Greek Cypriot authorities noted details of people departing for the north and it was the rule that one had to be back by 5:00 p.m. on the same day. I took my own car but had to purchase insurance cover for the day from a sales representative of a Turkish Cypriot insurance company, stationed at the Turkish Cypriot checkpoint. Otherwise, formalities on the Turkish Cypriot side of the Green Line were minimal, and in deference to the problems that it would cause to visitors, they refrained from stamping our passports. We first walked around northern Nicosia and then drove to Kyrenia on the north coast, stopping at Saint Hilarion Castle on the way. From the castle, there are commanding views of the north coast of the island. In the twelfth century, a fort was constructed on this site, where Richard the Lionheart was captured on his way to the Third Crusade. In the early 1960s, Turkish Cypriots successfully defended Saint Hilarion Castle against an attack by the Greek Cypriot National Guard. In Kyrenia, we stopped for lunch at a restaurant in the harbour area, which I found little changed from the time of my earlier visits in 1970 and 1974, prior to the invasion. Indeed, when compared to ten years before, most of what we saw of northern Cyprus during that 1984 visit was little changed. While the government-controlled areas had witnessed significant construction and a tourist boom, the occupied areas seemed to have been dozing in the Mediterranean sun.

Earlier in this book, I mentioned the kidnapping of Westerners in Beirut during the 1980s and one of the side effects of the Iran-Contra affair in Lebanon. One of the victims of kidnapping was Terry Waite, special envoy of the Archbishop of Canterbury; although many would say it was his own pride and stubbornness that led to his capture. In 1980, Waite had successfully negotiated the release of hostages in Iran and in 1984 in Libya. In 1985, he turned his attention to Lebanon, where he was successful initially in obtaining the release of Lawrence Jenco and David Jacobsen. Among my friends in Nicosia at the time was an American working at the United States embassy, whom I believed to be a CIA agent. This belief was strengthened when he had to cancel plans to attend a Christmas dinner, which Maarouf and I were hosting in 1988, following the bombing of Pan American Airways Flight 103 over Lockerbie in Scotland. Among the passengers on the flight were Matthew Gannon, the CIA's deputy station chief in Beirut and Maj. Chuck McKee, an army officer on secondment to the Defence Intelligence Agency in Beirut. Also on board were two diplomatic security service special agents, acting as bodyguards to Gannon and McKee, Ronald Lariviere, a security officer from the US embassy in Beirut and Daniel O'Connor, a security officer from the US embassy in Nicosia. They had flown together out of Cyprus that morning, connecting with PA 103 in Frankfurt.[91] Instead of dining with us, our friend spent his Christmas Day walking the countryside around Lockerbie searching for a suitcase. What it contained and whether or not he found it, I never discovered.

Our friend also spent a lot of time in Beirut, flying by helicopter directly to the embassy compound there, sometimes from Larnaca airport, but often from the British sovereign base at Akrotiri. On one occasion, he told me that Waite had stayed overnight at his house after arriving from London and that the next day he had flown him to Beirut carrying a suitcase containing US$2 million in cash. Some years later, a BBC television programme showed footage of our friend meeting Col. Oliver North, who had been deeply involved in the Iran-Contra affair in the mid-1980s, at Larnaca airport around the time that Waite was travelling to Lebanon. Waite became associated with North, and it was probably this association that was his downfall. When the Irangate scandal, which in part had involved the sale of US military equipment to Iran via Israel, became public

---

[91]   http://en.wikipedia.org/wiki/Pan_Am_Flight_103#cite_note-26, accessed 16 Jan 2012

knowledge, Waite felt it necessary to demonstrate his integrity and his commitment to the remaining hostages in Beirut.

On January 12, 1987 he flew, uninvited, to Beirut in the US helicopter. He was intending to negotiate with Islamic Jihad, the organisation that was thought to be holding the hostages, including Terry Anderson. Against the advice of the Druze leader Walid Jumblatt, who had provided security protection to Waite on previous visits, he agreed to a meeting with representatives of the kidnappers, who promised him safe conduct. He went alone. The group took him hostage and he remained in captivity until November 1991.

A family event on January 1, 1985, was the birth of my sister's second child, Alanna. Later during my time living in Cyprus, both of my parents died. My mother had had a stroke in 1991 which limited her mobility; later she developed lung cancer in 1995 and died the following May at the age of seventy-five. I was able to be present during the last few days of her life, a somewhat harrowing experience, given the ravages that the cancer had caused. My father survived her by four years, dying in July 2000 at the age of eighty-eight. I had planned a visit to him a week after his death, but he deteriorated rapidly during his last few days, and, sadly, I was not able to reach England before he died.

Cyprus was the venue for the Commonwealth Heads of Government meeting, attended by Her Majesty Queen Elizabeth II, in October 1993. For the duration of her visit, she stayed on the Royal yacht *Britannia*, moored at Larnaca. Among the social events during her visit was a reception for the British community given by the British high commissioner, to which I was invited.

In the gracious presence of Her Majesty The Queen
and
His Royal Highness The Duke of Edinburgh
The British High Commissioner and Mrs. David Dain
request the pleasure of the company of

Mr S.C.L. Hickey

at a Reception
on Tuesday, 19th October, 1993 at 5.30 p.m.
at 6 Philhellenon Street, Nicosia

A reply is requested on the enclosed card
by Wednesday, 6th October

Dress: Lounge Suit

Invitation to meet the Queen, Nicosia, 1993

236

All guests received written instructions on what to wear, what to do and when to do it. Ladies were informed that the wearing of hats was optional. Guests were instructed not to wear medals and told that cameras were not permitted. On arrival, officials divided guests into groups of about eight people, each with a "minder" from the high commission. Two rows of groups were arranged in the garden, on opposite sides of the lawn; after Her Majesty and the Duke of Edinburgh arrived, she set out down one line and the duke took the other. I was in the line meeting Her Majesty; when she reached our group, the "minder" introduced each of the guests. When I was introduced, the Queen asked me, "And what do you do in Cyprus?" I bowed (as instructed) and replied, "Banking, Your Majesty," to which her response was, "Oh, banking!" before moving on to the next group. I did not have the opportunity to discover what she thought of bankers then, but almost twenty years later with the world still suffering from the excesses of international bankers, her opinion may well be worse, if remarks that she and the Duke of Edinburgh made when they visited the Bank of England in December 2012 are anything to go by![92]

Another nonbanking activity in Cyprus, as in Bahrain, some twenty years previously, was my membership of the British Cemeteries Committee. This committee was formed after Cyprus gained independence from Britain in 1960 to administer the British cemeteries in Nicosia, Limassol and Larnaca, and, originally, Kyrenia as well. After the Turkish invasion in 1974, a separate committee in the north took over the administration of the Kyrenia cemetery. Members were appointed by the British high commissioner. The duties were not onerous. The committee met once a quarter and, after the December meeting, treated itself to lunch at the committee's expense.

Since the Greek Orthodox Church does not allow cremation, there is no such facility available in Cyprus, presumably because it would not be economically viable. This did not stop an enterprising Cypriot

---

[92] http://www.dailymail.co.uk/news/article-2247578/Queen-gives-Bank-chiefs-ticking-orf-crash-visits-vaults.html, retrieved 15 Dec 2012

living in England from proposing to us that the committee should acquire a used crematorium available in Cardiff, move it to Cyprus, and operate it there. The committee politely declined the offer.

At the time of independence, the right to use the then existing cemeteries had been granted to the committee in perpetuity. Having declined to establish a crematorium, the most significant issue that arose during my twelve years on the committee was how to solve the looming problem of a need for more burial space, particularly in Limassol, where the large aging British community was creating an increase in demand for burial plots. Money was not a problem; over the years, the committee had build up a sizeable surplus and could afford to buy land for a new cemetery if a suitable location could be found and necessary permission obtained from the authorities. We explored various options, including buying land adjacent to the existing Limassol cemetery. However, this did not materialise because of objections from residents in the area. Eventually, land was found near the villages of Erimi and Episkopi, just west of Limassol. It was in a rural area with no housing nearby, and we were able to obtain permission to change the use of the land from agricultural to a cemetery. By early 2002, the land had been purchased, a surrounding wall erected and sufficient space cleared of trees. The bishop of Cyprus and the Gulf, Clive Handford, consecrated the new cemetery in the spring of 2002 and the first burial took place on July 5 that year.

The author (left) at the consecration of the new
British cemetery near Limassol, April 2002

For much of the time that I lived in Nicosia, I was appointed by the British High Commission as warden for the area in which I lived. I was provided with an armband to wear; a document in Greek, Turkish and English confirming my appointment; and a list of the British subjects I might have to assist in the event of problems. At the time, and since, Cyprus was quiet and few people expected further hostilities that might necessitate any serious action by the wardens; this proved to be the case during my tenure. I understand that because of the lack of real need, the warden scheme no longer operates in Cyprus.

When I first moved to Cyprus in 1983, Maarouf initially stayed on in Dubai, but in 1984, he moved to Cairo. He lived there for about three years until I persuaded him to join me in Cyprus. While he was in Cairo and I was in Nicosia, we travelled back and forth regularly to visit each other and in that period, and after his move to Cyprus, took many vacation trips together. Among these were visits to Denmark and Sweden in 1984; Yugoslavia in 1988; the USA, for the second time, in 1991; China in 1992; Brazil in 1995; Morocco in 1999; India, Nepal, and Tibet in 2000; Cuba and Jordan, where we spent Christmas Day exploring Petra, in 2001; and Iran in 2002.

The author (right) and Maarouf Joudi,
Isfahan, Iran, 2002

In late 1999, with retirement in view, Maarouf and I decided to build a house in Lebanon to become our base after I ceased full-time work. Maarouf had bought a plot of land in an area called Cadmous, a few kilometres outside his home town of Tyre in southern Lebanon, about seventy kilometres south of Beirut, some twenty years earlier. It was in a very desirable location, on the top of a hillside at an altitude of about two hundred metres, with uninterrupted views to the south and west over the city of Tyre and the Mediterranean coastline. In December 1999, he signed the contract for the house construction, and this was completed over the following two years.

We took possession in early 2002.

Chapter 13

Lebanon Once More and I Become a Consultant in Tanzania

After almost twenty years with FBME in Cyprus and a banking career that by then had spanned forty years, I decided that it was time to retire. Early in 2002, I informed the bank that I intended to retire at the end of the year and did so on December 31, 2002. Immediately thereafter, at the request of the bank, I entered into a part-time consultancy agreement with them which, with minor interruptions, continued until the end of 2010.

Following my retirement, the plan to move from Cyprus to Lebanon came to fruition. The packers descended on the house in Nicosia in mid-January 2003 and managed to fill two containers—one forty and one twenty foot. The shipment left Cyprus in the last week of the month, and Maarouf and I, accompanied by our German Shepherd, Donna, flew from Larnaca to Beirut on January 31 to settle in the house that we had built in Tyre. The contractor had delivered the property about a year earlier, and we had stayed in it from time to time after that during visits to Lebanon, but there was still much work needed in decorating and organising it, especially after the shipment arrived from Cyprus. This I left largely to Maarouf, who is much more talented than I am in these matters.

Meanwhile, my consultancy work took me to Riga, Latvia, in January; Belgrade, Serbia, and Podgorica in Montenegro in March and several times to Bucharest. The bank was actively looking for new locations to establish a presence, and my visits to these places were to assess the possibilities. In both Latvia and Romania, the opportunity to acquire a small existing bank was identified. I assisted in drafting all of the necessary applications to the banking regulators, including compilation of supporting documentation, as well as in the discussions with the vendors. Unfortunately, in both cases, negotiations failed to end with an acceptable deal. Meanwhile, the opportunity earlier identified in Tanzania developed more promisingly, and in June, for the first time, I visited Dar es Salaam; my involvement with FBME in Tanzania continued throughout the term of my consultancy agreement until December 2010. Following a review of the accounts of the bank, control of which had been taken over by Bank of Tanzania, the central bank, FBME agreed to purchase some of the assets and liabilities and continue to employ 32 staff. In addition, FBME agreed to pay all interest due to depositors from the date the bank had closed. This undertaking was widely reported in the local newspapers and came as a surprise to the depositors; many of them turned up in the bank on the opening day to find out for themselves if the reports were really true. Under the terms of my consultancy agreement, the bank asked me to assist in the acquisition process and preparations for the opening for business. The purchase contract was signed in June 2003 and included taking on three branches—in Dar es Salaam, Mwanza and Zanzibar. A banking licence was issue on 11 July and FBME agreed with the Bank of Tanzania that it would open for business within three months. The work necessary before the bank was able to open for business was significant, including rebranding premises, printing stationery, integration of systems with Cyprus and staff training. I was involved in all aspects of the work and wrote the procedure manuals, which were a necessary precondition to the Bank of Tanzania granting approval to open for business. I also worked with local lawyers to review and, where necessary, adapt, all of the standard account opening and security documents used in Cyprus for use in Tanzania.

Initially, we had to commence operations in Tanzania using the banking software installed in the bank that had been acquired. This was partly because of time constraints and also lack of suitable communications facilities between Cyprus and Tanzania. In addition, a major Flexcube upgrade was planned to take place during 2004, and it was considered preferable to complete this in Cyprus before adding the Tanzanian branches to the system. Since the Tanzanian system could not be interfaced with Flexcube, the system in use in Cyprus since 1998, transactions between branches in the two countries and consolidation of reporting were among many issues for which solutions were required. Work-around solutions were devised for all issues, and in the remarkably short time of three months, the bank was ready to open for business in Tanzania on September 12, 2003, as had been agreed with the central bank when the purchase agreement was signed.

It was always the intention of the bank to put the Tanzanian branches on the same accounting platform as Cyprus, but this had to wait until after the completion of a Flexcube upgrade in Cyprus. During 2004, I was actively involved, as a member of the steering committee, with this upgrade in Cyprus and updating the manual of policies and procedures to reflect changes necessitated by the upgrade. Planning for the conversion of the Tanzanian branches, in which I was closely involved, started in late 2004 and implementation took place in 2005, the final cutover being on September 30. Because of the significant differences in the nature of the bank's business in Tanzania compared to Cyprus, there was a need for Tanzania-specific changes, including setting up new products to process the day-to-day customer transactions and apply the appropriate charges for this market. I took part in this aspect of the preparations for the conversion and, later, drafting additions to the bank's manual of policies and procedures to cover the new Tanzanian-related matters.

As well as my work in Tanzania, I also spent time at the bank in Cyprus on various matters. These included membership of a steering group established to oversee the implementation of policies and systems to ensure that the bank complied with the new capital adequacy requirements incorporating recommendations issued by the Basel

Committee on Banking Supervision in 2005, commonly known as Basel II. In this work, consultants from Ernst and Young assisted the steering group. Eventually the deliberations led to the purchase of a software package that could be interfaced with Flexcube to perform the various capital adequacy calculations required by the regulators and produce necessary reporting. The selection and implementation process took some time, but eventually we were ready for user acceptance testing in mid-2008, after which the system went live.

In 2006, work included drafting manuals of policies and procedures for two wholly owned subsidiaries of the bank in Tanzania, Tanpay Limited and Africa Precious Metals Limited (APM). Tanpay had been established to develop payment systems in Tanzania; the company became a principal member of both Visa and MasterCard, enabling it to issue internationally accepted payment cards billed in US dollars or Euros, as well as a domestic card, the Fedha Card, billed in Tanzanian shillings. It also was licenced to undertake merchant acquisition in Tanzania and was one of the first organisations in the country to offer this service, enabling merchants to accept both Visa and MasterCard in payment for goods and services. Tanpay also installed and operated ATMs for FBME as well as for other banks in Tanzania.

APM was established, with the encouragement of the Tanzanian authorities, with the objective of providing a facility to buy gold from artisan miners, refine it and export the metal. The company established a presence in several of the gold mining areas to act as collection and purchasing points and a refinery in the same building as the bank in Mwanza. Semi-refined gold was then exported under licence, usually to Dubai. I was involved from the inception of the idea in drafting policies and procedures covering the operations of the company and its relationships with the several different parties necessitated by the nature of its business. In order to gain an understanding of the business, I had to take several trips to the somewhat remote areas in which the company operated. These trips usually involved the use of small chartered aircraft that operated from Mwanza airport, itself not exactly the most modern in the world, to unsurfaced airstrips in the bush.

I mentioned earlier the financing that FBME had provided in 1996 to a Romanian shipowner to acquire his very first vessel. In 2005, after I had retired, I was surprised to receive a telephone call from his lead lawyer in Cyprus asking me if I would be prepared to become a director of a Cayman Islands holding company that his client was establishing to accommodate an ambitious newbuilding programme for ten new ships. Terms were agreed, and I was appointed chairman of the company. The ten new identical products tankers were to be built in Constanta Shipyard in Romania, which by then had been privatised, my shipowner friend, having become the majority shareholder. As each ship was ready for delivery, I was invited to the naming ceremonies at the shipyard, and on every occasion, the hospitality of the owner was abundant. On arrival at Bucharest airport, all foreign guests were transported to their seaside hotel near Constanta, sometimes by car, but often by chartered aircraft from Bucharest to Constanta airport. After one launching, all foreign guests were invited to spend the weekend at a lake-side hotel in the Danube Delta conservation area; and on another, we were given a

tour of the painted monasteries in the Bukovina region of Romania. We usually managed to hold a board meeting during these events, the most unusual location being in the rose garden of one of the monasteries.

The author (left) with Group Legal Advisor, Acis Montanios, Histria Tiger naming Ceremony, Constanta Shipyard, Romania, July 2008

After retirement, Maarouf and I continued to travel regularly for pleasure, in between the business travel necessitated by my consultancy work for FBME. In April 2003, we spent time in Tunisia that included a visit to the fringes of the Sahara desert, and in October 2003, to celebrate the twenty-fifth anniversary of our meeting each other in Dubai, we went to Istanbul. The next year, in June, we visited the three Baltic states—Estonia,

Lithuania and Latvia, newly admitted to the EU at the time; and in November and December, we took a long trip to Australia and New Zealand. The year 2005 was a busy one for consultancy work, and other than a visit to England, we did not undertake any other trips.

The author on a camel,
Tunisia, April 2003

In January 2006, South India was our destination and in June a long weekend in Lisbon.

Every summer, Lebanon enjoys many festivals of music and drama, the most famous being that held in the Roman ruins at Baalbek, which was first held in 1955. In the summer of 2003 Tyre decided to join the growing list of such festivals and included in its programme was Verdi's Aida, staged in the Roman hippodrome. Maarouf and I, together with a friend from Cyprus who was staying with us at the time attended the opening night. The performance was due to start at 9 p.m. but the late arrival of guests of honour, including the prime minister and the wife of the president, delayed it by almost an hour. Notwithstanding the late start, the audience enjoyed an excellent performance.

During this period, my sister and brother-in-law made two visits to stay with Maarouf and me in Lebanon. During the first, we were able to visit the border area with Israel, driving almost the entire length from Naqoura on the coast, where the UNIFIL headquarters is located, to Bint Jbeil and Khiam, location of an infamous prison where Israel and the SLA had held and tortured many Lebanese prisoners during the occupation of the area. On another occasion, we set out to try to locate the village of Joun, near Sidon, where Lady Hester Stanhope, British socialite and traveller, had lived and been buried in the early nineteenth century. We were pleased to discover a sign on the main coastal road near Sidon, indicating the way to the "Ruins of Lady Hester." Unfortunately, after that, there was an absence of further signs, but we were aided by somewhat vague instructions in a guidebook and eventually located the ruins of her house and what seemed to be her grave, both unmarked and overgrown.

During the period when I was providing consultancy services to FBME, I was spending roughly half of my time in Lebanon and half abroad. When the UN mandated investigation into the assassination of Rafic Hariri commenced, the first head of the investigation team was a senior German prosecutor, Detlev Mehlis. A number of people commented from time to time that he and I looked very much alike. This became a slight concern when an organisation called Jund al Sham threatened to assassinate Mehlis because of his alleged connections with Israel and the CIA. The similarity in our appearances was confirmed during an incident in 2005; I was driving from Tyre to Beirut when, as I was crossing the bridge over the Awali river just north of Sidon, my car developed a problem. Virtually all of the warning lights came on, and the engine simply stopped. I make no claim to any knowledge of the workings of the internal combustion engine, so I phoned Maarouf's nephew, Fadi, who owns a garage in Tyre and always looks after our cars. He said that he would come to me, and I settled down to wait. While I was waiting, a passing car transporter stopped, and the driver asked me if I required his services to move my car. I declined, informing him that help was on the way. In due course, Fadi arrived and decided that it would be necessary to transport the car to the garage, and he called a transporter whom he usually used. As I had to go on to Beirut to a meeting, we agreed that I would do so in his car while he accompanied mine back to the garage. After I had left, the driver who had offered me assistance returned to Fadi and once again tried to sell his services; he was, however, much more interested to know why Detlev Mehlis was driving around southern Lebanon by himself, without any security guards!

Chapter 14

The 2006 Israeli War on Lebanon

I will diverge from my usual format here to relate my experiences during the 2006 Israeli war on Lebanon, which, briefly, interrupted the established routine and caused me to leave the country for a short time. What follows is largely extracted from a diary that I maintained during this period, when I experienced my closest exposure to violence during all my years in what was, and still is, a volatile region.

About nine thirty on the morning of July 12, 2006, I was driving from my house in Cadmous, near Tyre, to the town, a journey of about eight kilometres (5 miles). As I left the house, I turned on the car radio to hear BBC World Service reporting that Hezbollah had kidnapped two Israeli soldiers on the Lebanon-Israel border. Almost simultaneously, there was a loud explosion somewhere to the north; it turned out to be the Israelis bombing the bridge over the Litani River at Qasmieh on the main coast road to Sidon and Beirut, about five kilometres (3 miles) north of the house. I decided to continue into town and do what I had to do. After this, I returned home, where we started monitoring the situation on various local and satellite news channels. Although there was Israeli bombing during the day, it was not in our immediate area. At about 8:30 p.m., following a bombing in the lemon orchards some two kilometres below the house, the mains power went off; it was not restored until ten days after the cease-fire. It turned out that the cut was because of damage to overhead power cables caused by the nearby bombing.

The next day, Thursday, July 13, we were awakened at about 1:00 a.m. by the sound of helicopters. Subsequently there were explosions inland, to the east of the house, and a small one in the orchards between the house and the sea. The air raid ceased within an hour, and the rest of the night was quiet. At 8:00 a.m., there was still no electricity, and we decided that we should ration the use of the generator to conserve fuel while still trying to keep the contents of the freezer frozen and enabling us to watch the news on television. Between generator sessions, we had a battery radio to keep us up to date on developments. The early morning news included the bombing of all three runways at Beirut airport and its subsequent closure.

I had planned to fly out the next day to Dubai and Dar es Salaam and contacted the airline, Emirates, which suggested that they could rebook me from Damascus on Saturday, assuming that it would be possible for me to get there by road on Friday. We decided to go into town to get money, petrol and groceries. Most shops were closed, including Al Janoub supermarket, but Spinney's supermarket was open and the shelves still well stocked. There were generally long queues outside bakeries and those food shops that were open. All the banks were closed and the ATM at our bank was not working. We were, however, able to get cash from an ATM at another bank and took as much as was allowed by the system limits. Throughout the afternoon, we could hear the sound of distant and sometimes not-so-distant aircraft, anti-aircraft fire and explosions.

Having received an e-mail from the Foreign and Commonwealth Office advising British citizens to keep in touch with the embassy, I phoned them to seek advice about travelling by road from Tyre to Damascus the next day. Their advice was not to try, as they expected the Beirut-Damascus road to be bombed. Two hours later, it was. The most severe damage was to a newly opened bridge carrying the highway over a deep valley near the highest point of the road over the mountains between the coast and the Bekaa valley. After the war, the United States government paid for repairs to this bridge, making good the damage caused by the weapons that they, no doubt, had supplied to Israel to destroy it. During the evening news on a local television station, there was film of a Lebanese cabinet meeting. I could not help noticing that one of the members had a solitaire game open on the computer screen in front of him!

On the third day, Friday, July 14, from about 7:00 a.m. there was the continual sound of planes overhead, but quite high, and we could see Israeli warships offshore, presumably to enforce the naval blockade that they had introduced. Between 9:30 a.m. and 10:30 a.m., three missiles landed in the area, two in the lemon orchards, about two kilometres below the house and one in a valley behind the house. The missiles that landed below us left a small crater in the road and burned a few trees, but the road remained passable. We went to town when the situation was quiet and found more shops open than on the previous day. The queues outside the bakeries were shorter, and there were quite a few people on the streets. We were able to get more cash from an ATM, increasing our supply in case it would be required for expenses or evacuation.

During the afternoon, there was the continued noise of aircraft overhead and repeated antiaircraft fire from a Lebanese army camp nearby which was, as usual, totally ineffective. During the evening, Hezbollah managed to damage quite seriously an Israeli warship that was shelling Beirut airport, with the loss of four members of the crew. This was achieved using Iranian-supplied Noor missiles, a weapon not previously used by the group. After that, we never again saw an Israeli warship off Tyre. Presumably, they kept out of range of the shore-based missile launchers.

On Saturday, July 15, the fourth day, the sound of aircraft, presumably on their way farther north, kept us awake during the night from about 1:00 a.m. to 6:00 a.m. There was still some bombing activity in the area in the morning, but this seemed to be very much targeted and not heavy. Once again, we went into town during the morning. It was very quiet; there were only a few shops open—those that were had only limited goods on the shelves. By lunchtime, it seemed that activity by both sides had reduced, and there was no more anti-aircraft fire from the Lebanese army camp. However, hopes that the lull was a prelude to a cease-fire proved wrong. If anything, the situation started to get worse later in the day, with bombings on the outskirts of Tyre and at Jounieh port, north of Beirut. Although various embassies were talking about evacuation of their citizens, there was little, at that time, they could do to move them out because of the Israeli naval blockade and the serious risks involved in travelling by road. Syria seemed to be letting in anyone who could reach the border, regardless of nationality or visa rules; but getting to the border involved a difficult, dangerous and expensive journey. One of Maarouf's nieces, who worked in Dubai and was on vacation in Lebanon when the war started, did leave by shared taxi to Damascus, from where she flew back to Dubai: the cost for the seat in the taxi was US$200, ten times the usual rate.

It was becoming clear that there was not going to be a quick solution, and we had to take stock of our food and fuel situation. At the start of hostilities, we had a well-stocked freezer and almost a full tank of generator fuel. As there had been no mains electricity since the first day, we had been rationing our use of the generator and now decided to reduce further its use until we could find a source of fuel. That day, we drank the last bottle of red wine. We still had several bottles of white in stock and no shortage of gin.

On day 5, Sunday, July 16, after enjoying a quiet night, things warmed up during the morning. We thought that Hezbollah fired missiles, the first to hit Haifa, from a lemon orchard at the bottom of the hill, about two kilometres from the house. There was a very rapid response, with four Israeli missiles hitting the location, but by then the crew must have moved the missile launcher elsewhere, following Hezbollah's "shoot and scoot" strategy.[93] Anticipating more reprisals, we took refuge for a while in a neighbour's basement, which was in a less prominent position on the hillside than our house. We returned home early in the afternoon when things were generally

---

[93]   Blanford, Nicholas, Warriors of God, 2011, Random House, New York

quiet. Israel started to issue warnings to people in the south to go north of the Litani River, as they were planning retaliation against Hezbollah for rocket attacks on Haifa. A number of people we knew in Tyre decided to take this advice and went to Sidon, the Chouf area, and even Beirut. We decided to stay. In the middle of war, we still had advertisements during the evening local TV news promoting the speed with which LibanPost would deliver your mail and the merits of Dewar's whisky.

On Monday, July 17, the sixth day of the war, the telephone landlines ceased to work because, as we later discovered, bomb blasts had brought down the overhead cables. This meant that there was no longer an Internet connection, and I was unable to send out my usual daily e-mail bulletin to friends and family. We went into Tyre about 9:30 a.m. and while there, I managed to use a friend's telephone line to establish an Internet connection. The telephone company only repaired the landline at the house two weeks after the end of the war, but the two mobile networks managed to maintain service throughout the conflict. Once again, there were very few people around and only a few small shops open. We were able to buy more supplies for some of our neighbours as well as for ourselves. News reports of the bombing of the road just south of Sidon seemed to be substantiated by ambulances heading that way from Tyre as we returned to the house. People continued to leave Tyre, often with no clear idea of where they were going. The bombing of the road seemed to confirm that staying put was the best thing to do, especially as a seat in a service taxi from Tyre to Beirut, usually about US$5, was by then costing US$100. The British embassy advised that Royal Navy vessels were on the way to Beirut; however, a decision on evacuation, especially from the south, depended on security guarantees from both sides in the conflict.

On day 7, Tuesday, July 18, we were awakened about 3:30 a.m. by an extremely loud explosion that seemed to be very close. When we went downstairs, we found the front door blown in as well as one air conditioning grill from the ceiling now on the floor. We retreated to the basement until daylight. We were unable to see where the bomb had fallen; later news suggested in a village about one kilometre south of the house. During the morning, with the help of a neighbour, we were able to make emergency repairs to the front door, but it remained unusable for the duration. Because of the lack of an Internet connection at the house, I sent a text message about the situation to my brother-in-law, and we arranged that I should do this daily and that he would pass it on by e-mail to the various family and friends who were on the distribution list of my earlier e-mailed situation reports.

Maarouf needed medication under a regular prescription, so he called the pharmacist that he normally uses at her home. She sent someone to the shop to get the required medicine, delivered it to Maarouf's nephew who lives near to it, and refused to take money in case he might need it for other things. This is just one small example of how the Lebanese were helping each other during the crisis.

A truck loaded with medical supplies from the UAE was bombed by Israel en-route to the south. In the meantime, people continued to leave Tyre, some in buses sent there from Sidon by Bahia Hariri, sister of the assassinated former prime minister, Rafic Hariri, and the first UK citizens were evacuated from Beirut to Cyprus on HMS *Gloucester*. UN attempts to negotiate a cease-fire received a cool reception in Tel Aviv. The United States and Israel seemed to have a plan and the time had not yet arrived for this gesture. Although it was a quiet evening, after the experience of the previous night, we decided to sleep in the basement and continued to do so every night.

On Wednesday, July 19, the eighth day of the war, after a relatively quiet night, things continued generally quiet throughout the country. The Israeli emphasis seemed to be very much on Hezbollah sites in the south, close to the border, some distance from Tyre. It was reported that the security council would meet the next day to receive a report from its delegation that had been in the area and that the US secretary of state, Condoleezza Rice, might travel to the region on Friday. Attacks on the orchards below us continued throughout the morning until about 2:30 p.m. After that, there was hardly a sound of aircraft. What we had seen seemed to confirm Israeli statements that they were now targeting Hezbollah locations and supply routes only. We suspected that Hezbollah were using agricultural roads through the orchards below us to move missile launchers. A local radio station reported that the electricity authority bill collectors were working in Jounieh and were threatening to cut off supplies if bills were not paid. They were lucky to have a supply to cut! We continued to spend most of our time in the basement and sleep there. I passed the time reading a biography of Adolf Hitler. It seemed appropriate somehow.

On the ninth day of the war, Sunday, July 20, there were some bombings in the orchards between 3:00 a.m. and 5:00 a.m., after which it was quiet. We could see a ship coming to Tyre, which turned out to be a Louis Cruise Lines ship from Cyprus, chartered by the UN. At that time, we did not know whom it was there to evacuate, and I had not been informed about the sailing by the British embassy. It later transpired that as well as UN civilian staff and dependents, it had taken out other foreigners, including some UK citizens. We went into town while the ship was lying offshore. The coast road to Tyre was obstructed by two large craters caused by Israeli bombings, but we were able to pass them. The town was very quiet. Some small shops and bakeries were open, and we were able to get bread, which was rationed to two bags per person; even I, a foreigner, got my allocation. The wine merchant was closed, so we were unable to replenish our red wine stocks! We returned home by 11:00 a.m., and shortly after, bombing of the orchards began again and lasted until 1:00 p.m. The evening news on one of the local TV stations was still interrupted by LibanPost advertisements. We continued to sleep in the basement.

On day ten, Friday, July 21, there was still occasional bombing around us early in the morning but less than before. Israel was ignoring attempts to arrange a cease-fire, but they did agree to set up a "humanitarian corridor" from Cyprus. How and when was not clear. An announcement on BBC World Service radio for British citizens in Lebanon said that the government was trying to arrange safe evacuation from south Lebanon. I called the British embassy to get advice. They knew no more than I did from the BBC news report but took my number and said they would call back. They never did. It was not clear why they did not coordinate with the UN, who had chartered a ship to come to Tyre the previous day.

Throughout the morning, there were regular bombings in a valley behind the house. Local television reports that Israeli military chiefs admitted that they had not broken the will or ability of Hezbollah seemed to be supported by continuing attacks on the same locations. The possibility of a large-scale Israeli invasion of the border area was raised again. Bombings continued in the afternoon until about 4:00 p.m. Jim Muir, reporting from Tyre on the 9:00 p.m. BBC World Service TV news, spoke of a mass burial in Tyre—but the bodies had actually been gathered from all over the south and were not exclusively from Tyre itself. In addition, there were reports of leaflets dropped on Tyre by Israeli planes, telling those left in south Lebanon to move north of the Litani River. Our local information was that people arriving from other villages in the south, closer to the border, had brought the leaflets to Tyre.

At 9:00 p.m., Al Jazeera TV reported Hassan Nasrallah saying that Hezbollah would let the Lebanese government decide about handing over the two soldiers they had kidnapped. We slept in the basement again. There were regular targeted bombings around us during the night; the blast from one of which set off the Pajero car alarm. The front door of the house succumbed to the repeated blasts again, and we had to nail wooden bars across the inside to keep it shut.

The next day, July 22, the eleventh day of the war, we went into town about 11:30 a.m. Abu George, the wine merchant, was open, so we stocked up on red wine and tonic as well as cigarettes, vegetables and bread, but very few shops were open. We spent another night in the basement.

Next morning, Sunday, July 23, the twelfth day of the war, local TV reported that an evacuation ship, *Princesa Marissa*, would be in Tyre on Monday morning. Later, when I was able to check e-mail, I found a message from the foreign office advising that a ship chartered by the German government would be in Tyre on Monday and would take any EU nationals wishing to leave to Cyprus. It advised those who wanted to leave to contact the embassy. I phoned the embassy, who knew nothing about it. This time they did call back within an hour to confirm and give me contact details of the warden in Tyre who was coordinating the arrangements with the German embassy. While in town during the morning, we received some fuel for the generator sent on a bus by a friend in Sidon. This gave us about five hundred litres in the generator fuel tank, but we sent the containers back for another shipment as, with no mains electricity, we were dependent on the generator for power. The Tyre warden called and confirmed that my name was on the list of those to be evacuated the next day. I was instructed to be at the Rest House Hotel at 7:00 a.m. Monday, although the sailing time was unknown. I spent the last night in the basement.

Maarouf, who has dual Lebanese and Cypriot nationality, could also have left on the same ship but adamantly refused to do so. He was obviously concerned about his family who remained in Tyre and elsewhere in the country and afraid that looters would steal things from the house if left empty. After considerable debate, I made the difficult decision that I would leave alone on the *Princesa Marissa* the next day, especially as I had work to do in Tanzania and in fact, should have been in Dar es Salaam two weeks earlier.

On the thirteenth day of the war, Monday, July 24, Maarouf drove me to the Rest House, where I arrived at 7:15 a.m. On the way, there was a lone road sweeper at work; otherwise, the streets of Tyre were virtually deserted, although the quantity of laundry drying on balconies seemed to indicate that more people had remained in the city than was generally estimated. There were already quite a number of people waiting at the Rest House, almost entirely Lebanese with dual nationality, mainly German. Many of the evacuees lived abroad and had been visiting family in south Lebanon when the war broke out. Designer jeans and T-shirts were noticeable among the men, but most of the women wore head scarves and long dresses. No one seemed to be organising anything, and I learned from a German TV reporter that the departure of the ship from Cyprus had been delayed, and that it was now expected to arrive in Tyre at 11:00 a.m.

instead of 8:00 a.m. and leave at 5:00 p.m. There seemed to be more journalists than potential evacuees at the Rest House at times; and since there were only two real foreigners amongst the evacuees, an English teacher at the evangelical school in Tyre and I, they gravitated to us. I was interviewed for BBC TV and Radio, ITN, Channel 4, and Sky News, plus the *Daily Telegraph*, *Sun*, *Mirror* and *Mail*. In its inimitable fashion, the *Sun*'s version of the story was the most sensational. Their reporter, Nick Parker, wrote, on July 24:

> Went back into Tyre today after hearing that the last of the Brits trapped in the south were being rescued by ship. Myself, photographer Roger and driver Peter ran the now familiar gauntlet of the "Highway of Death" between Sidon and Tyre. And we found two of the pluckiest Brits you'll meet in a hotel waiting to be evacuated. Peter Hayes—a 62-year-old teacher resplendent in a straw hat—absolutely refused to say he'd been scared by the hail of bombs wrecking the city. But top marks went to Sean Hickey—a banker who chose to **RETIRE** to one of the most dangerous and strife-torn areas on earth. Calm, smiling Sean told us how he'd sipped gin and tonic as Hezbollah rushed into a lemon grove and fired off two rockets right in front of him. Then the Israelis hit back with bombs and missiles at the launch site near Tyre. Sean appeared totally unruffled as he recounted the war drama and said he'd be coming back as soon as a cease-fire was declared. He boarded a rescue ship for Cyprus and gave us a cheery little wave as the lifeboat took him out of port. I'm presuming he'll be heading on to Somalia to chill out properly.[94]

There is a considerable degree of journalistic licence in Nick Parker's version of events. By the way, I never made it to Somalia, but I did return to Lebanon!

The ship finally arrived about 11:30 a.m. but had to unload humanitarian aid first. Finally, we left the Rest House in buses

---

[94]   http://www.thesun.co.uk/sol/homepage/56769/Hello-from-Lebanon.html

escorted by the Lebanese army, who also transported some people in their trucks. They even had their own video camera operator recording the event, no doubt for PR purposes. On arrival at the port, we discovered that the *Princesa Marissa* was lying offshore and that we would be taken out to her in the ship's lifeboats. There was some Lebanese bureaucracy to deal with while our passports were checked against the lists of each nationality, and we were given a voucher stamped by the official, but no exit stamp in our passports, for some reason. The voucher got us through the barrier and handed over to the German embassy staff, who were assisted by representatives of the Canadian and Australian governments.

An Australian consular officer, who had been sent hurriedly from Moscow to Nicosia to assist with evacuees from Lebanon, dealt with the British citizens, and we were quickly into a lifeboat and on the way to the ship. Transferring to the ship was a bit difficult, but there were plenty of willing hands to help, especially with the luggage, children and older people. Representatives of the German Red Cross were on hand to deal with medical problems. There were at least two wheelchair cases and two children with severe burns.

By 2:00 p.m., I was on board and in my cabin. Since the boat could carry eight hundred passengers and the number of evacuees was not much more than two hundred, there was no problem with space. Shortly after boarding, I went to the bar and had a pint of Cypriot Keo lager to cool me down. Lunch was soon offered, and the ship sailed on time at 5:00 p.m. Before we were out of range of the Lebanese mobile phone network, I received a telephone call from a reporter on the *Eastern Daily Press*, the local newspaper published in Norwich and covering my home area of north Norfolk. We talked at length about the war and evacuation, and he subsequently published an article in more sober terms than the *Sun*.

It was very appropriate that my evacuation from Lebanon was on the *Princesa Marissa*; this was a ship, finance for the purchase of which had been provided by FBME not long after I joined that bank in Cyprus.

During the war, all the banks in Tyre were closed, but I was still able to access my accounts using Internet banking, and I could see that direct debits for some utility bills were still being processed. This, I presumed, was because, for some years, the central bank had required all banks in Lebanon to have real-time online systems; therefore, head offices of banks could process these transactions centrally in Beirut, where banks were operating normally. I realised that I needed to get funds into my current account to cover such payments, so I decided to try a small transfer from Cyprus and see if this would be credited. In spite of the closure of the branch, it was. Therefore, there were sufficient funds to cover the bills until the banks reopened in Tyre after the cease-fire.

At last, on Monday, August 14, 2006, the fighting ceased, but not before more than one thousand Lebanese civilians had been killed, hundreds of thousands left homeless and crippling damage had been inflicted on the country's infrastructure. As usual, the Israeli response to the original incident had been totally disproportionate. When the cease-fire came into effect, I was in Dar es Salaam for some consultancy work, and it was not until ten days later that I was able to contemplate returning to Tyre. Due to the continuation of the Israeli sea and air blockade, the only possible air route in was via Amman, from where Middle East Airlines and Royal Jordanian Airlines were allowed by the Israelis to operate a shuttle service to Beirut. In theory, the Jordanian authorities were supposed to be checking all aircraft to ensure that nothing was shipped into Beirut for Hezbollah, but I did not notice any more security than usual. Therefore, on August 26, I set out from Dar es Salaam, via Dubai and Amman to Beirut. Maarouf met me at the airport, from where the journey to the house, which had generally taken fifty minutes before the war, took nearly three hours because of diversions, usually unsigned, around the damage to roads and bridges. The house had suffered no damage other than the front door, but an apartment building about seven hundred metres away had been bombed and several buildings in the city had been destroyed.

After I left for Cyprus on the *Princesa Marissa* midway through the war and Maarouf had stayed on in Tyre, the food situation had become more difficult. He found himself in the position of unofficial coordinator in the area, organising collection of supplies from various donor sources when such became available and purchase of any available foodstuffs from any other sources. He organised the distribution of the supplies, the preparation of meals by various ladies in the area, and delivery of the food to all who required it.

A few days after the end of the war, the secretary-general of Hezbollah, Sayyed Hassan Nasrallah, commented that had he known what the consequences would be, he would never have agreed to the event that started the war.[95] Notwithstanding that statement, no one doubts that Hezbollah has increased its stock of weapons since then, including some much more sophisticated than it had in 2006, although the border has been mostly quiet since the end of the war, with no significant incidents that can be attributed to the group.

---

[95]   http://www.guardian.co.uk/world/2006/aug/28/syria.israel, accessed 27 Jan 2012

Chapter 15

RETURN TO LEBANON AND TANZANIA

After the 2006 war, life quickly settled back into the usual routine. During 2007 and 2008, my consultancy work continued in both Cyprus and Tanzania, including ongoing work to update the MOPP, necessitated by the introduction of new banking laws and regulations in both jurisdictions and changes in the bank's business, including the introduction of new products and services. In particular, this included policies and procedures for two new departments, a recovery unit and a risk management unit. The former was established to take over the management of problem borrowing accounts from the credit department, and the latter was necessitated by the application of Basel II within the bank. One of my last projects, or so I thought, in October and November 2008, was a complete review of the bank's operations in Tanzania, working on this with several of the senior management of the bank.

In mid-2008, I had agreed with the bank that the consultancy agreement would be terminated at the end of the year, thus enabling me to retire for the second time. It was not to be; in January 2009, Maarouf and I took a trip to South Africa; and in February, some ten days after getting home, I received a telephone call from the deputy chairman of the bank asking me if I would like to go on safari for eighteen months. We agreed to meet in Cyprus a few days later at which time he explained that he wanted me to provide a coordinating role for the bank in Tanzania. Because of the review of the bank's operations there, in which I had participated a few months earlier, the board had decided that it would be necessary to make changes in the senior management and implement changes and improvements in systems and procedures. In the end, we signed a contract for an initial period of six months, later extended three times and finally ending on December 31, 2010, at which time I retired for the third time.

During the twenty-one months from April 2009 to December 2010, I spent much of my time in Tanzania, involved in a multitude of issues. These included working with the bank's lawyers to correct errors in the information held in the records of the Registrar of Companies. Despite the fact that the bank had filed the correct annual returns since its incorporation in 2003, when I requested various certificates from the registrar, it turned out that their records were not accurate or up to date. The department records were not computerised, and the manual filing system left much to be desired. However, after eight months of effort, we did manage to correct their errors and produce accurate certificates of capital, shareholders and directors, etc. I was also involved in documenting and implementing many changes to operational procedures and policies, which led to more efficiency in the processing of transactions such as domestic cheque clearing, treasury settlements and domestic interbank payments. In addition, I worked with the bank's external legal advisors on the introduction of standard forms of facility letter and security documentation such as mortgages and charges. Another major piece of work, also involving external lawyers, was the introduction of updated account opening documentation, including revised general terms and conditions and the resulting need to inform all existing customers of the changes.

I was also involved in the review of credit department procedures and the implementation of improvements. In the course of this work, I had a need to meet some of the bank's borrowing customers; one such meeting involved a visit to a farm situated in the southern highlands of Tanzania, some six hundred kilometres (375 miles) from Dar es Salaam. An agricultural expert from the University of Essex, engaged by the bank to advise it on the businesses of farming customers, accompanied me. Because of the distance involved, poor roads and the limited time available, we flew to the farm in a small chartered Cessna 206 single-engine aircraft. We landed at the main farm, which was situated at an altitude of about one thousand eight hundred meters (5,850 ft) to collect the owner and then flew on to a remote part of his property, located some 230 kilometres away on a plateau at an altitude of three thousand metres (9,750 ft). As is often the case in Tanzania, we used dirt landing strips at both farms but completed the journey without mishap. A few weeks later, other visitors to the remote farm were not so lucky; travelling in the same aircraft that I had used, but with a different pilot, the plane ran off the landing strip and ended up on its back. Luckily, everyone got out alive, but the owner of the farm suffered neck injuries that necessitated his going to South Africa for treatment. Such are the risks associated with providing banking services to customers in the African bush.

In early 2010, a new general manager for the Bank in Tanzania took up his position. He requested my continuing assistance during the period in which he became familiar with the bank, and my contract was extended to the end of the year, but with a gradually decreasing time commitment. The new general manager had considerable experience in banking in Africa, having started his career in the continent with one of the major British overseas banks, and had spent some time in Tanzania previously. Therefore, at the end of 2010, I was able to retire for the third time, and so far, this retirement has not been interrupted.

During my time in Tanzania, Maarouf visited me in Dar es Salaam a number of times. During his visits we were able to tour some of the game reserves in the country, including Serengeti, and spend some time relaxing on the beach in Zanzibar. He was also able to visit a niece who lives in Dar es Salaam. My work in Tanzania did not prevent Maarouf and me from travelling elsewhere for pleasure. In November 2006, we went to Vietnam, Cambodia and Laos, with a stop in Bangkok on the way. November and December 2007 found us in Argentina and Chile, March 2008 in Oman and October 2008 in northern India and Bhutan. In January 2009, we went to South Africa and April 2010 took a river cruise across Europe from

Budapest to Amsterdam. This trip was complicated initially by the Icelandic ash cloud; this prevented us from getting to London to join the tour, but we were able to fly directly from Beirut to Budapest instead and meet the group there. In a way we were better off than some of the passengers travelling from London; only half of them were able to fly, the remainder travelling by bus across the continent, with a night stop in Cologne, to join the ship in Budapest. However, this was not the end of the problems. When we reached Regensberg in southern Germany, we were delayed for three days as a lock on the Rhine-Main-Danube Canal was jammed, and all traffic on the river system had been brought to a halt. In December 2010, we finally managed a Nile cruise to visit to Upper Egypt, somewhere long on our list of places to visit. During this trip, we saw the Aswan High Dam, finance for the construction of which had been a factor in the second Arab-Israel war.

From l to r the author, niece Bryony Stibbons and sister Brenda Stibbons, August 2007

Family milestones were passed during this period. In August 2007, my younger niece, Alanna, now a qualified nurse, was married to policeman Matthew Forrester in Mattishall, Norfolk; and in June 2009, my sister, Brenda, celebrated her sixtieth birthday and retirement by renting a villa in Italy for a weeklong family gathering. Maarouf and I attended both events, adding some extra time in Italy to visit Rome again and to go to Pompeii.

In 2011, when I began to spend more time in Lebanon following my final retirement, the British embassy appointed me as deputy warden for South Lebanon. I had previously been a warden in Nicosia, where the likelihood of any need for action was limited. Lebanon was a slightly different situation, as there was a continuing tense situation along the border with Israel as well as the worsening situation in Syria that, it was felt, could spread to Lebanon.

In September 2011, Maarouf and I made our second visit to China. We had first visited that country in 1992, when their experiment with economic freedom was in its early stages. Now, twenty years later the transformation is dramatic. Modern buildings abound everywhere. In all the cities that we visited, the streets were wide and straight and traffic, of which there was an abundance, flowed freely. One negative aspect of this modernisation is the loss of much of the old parts of cities, which seem to have been demolished to make way for the new, without regard to the possibility of preservation for future generations.

From Beijing, we made a five-day side trip to North Korea. For a long time I had been curious about this last bastion of Stalinist communism and wanted to see what it was really like. Having visited the Soviet Union before its breakup, I suppose that we were expecting something similar. In some ways, it was similar, but much more extreme. We were escorted everywhere by two guides and a driver and at no time allowed to wander off alone. To prevent us doing so after the guides had left us, we and most foreign visitors were accommodated in a hotel on an island in the Taedong River; the bridge across the river was well guarded! Of course, the guides showed us what the government wanted us to see: there is no doubt that we saw the best that the country has to offer. Our visit coincided with the annual Arirang Games, held each year in the May Day Stadium in Pyongyang. The performance involves over one hundred thousand performers, including those in the seats on the opposite side of the stadium to the audience, who each held up different coloured cards to form various mosaic picture displays. The choreography, synchronisation and intricacy of acrobatic performances must be seen to be believed.

Contact with North Koreans was restricted to our guides and hotel staff, no doubt carefully selected for their jobs because of their reliability. I was surprised to learn that the authorities had allowed our senior guide to travel abroad, to attend a conference in South

Africa, and on the way, she had visited Dubai. How she reconciled the differences between Pyongyang and Dubai, I did not discover; she was reticent about talking on the subject.

However, it was in North Korea that I finally realised that I really had reached the age when it was time to retire. The younger and less experienced of our two lady guides insisted on offering me a helping hand each time that I entered or exited via the couple of steps at the door of our minibus.

I can best describe the year 2012, with apologies to Her Majesty the Queen, as an "annus horibilis." In January, Maarouf fell downstairs, suffering a severe cut on his head and concussion. In February, the automatic transmission on our GMC Acadia disintegrated into several thousand pieces, and in March, we had a fire in the house in Tyre. Luckily, we were at home at the time the fire started, and the emergency services responded very quickly, much to my amazement. The actual fire damage was limited to a small area, but the consequent smoke and water damage was infinitely worse. After a month of cleaning up, we were almost back to normal. As if all of this was not enough, in June, after a routine blood test and further investigations, I discovered that I had prostate cancer. Fortunately, it was at an early stage and still confined to the prostate. After consultations with doctors in Lebanon and

Inspecting the fire damage, Tyre, March 2012. The author (second from right) and Maarouf Joudi (third from right) (Ya Sour.org)

England, none of whom would tell me what they considered the best course of action, I had a list of three types of surgery or four types of radiotherapy from which to make my choice. After some research, including talking to friends who had been in similar situations, I decided on brachytherapy, a procedure that involves implanting radioactive seeds into the prostate, where they destroy the cancer over several months. I identified one of the leading consultants in this field, and he carried out the operation in September 2012; initial indications are that it will be successful.

Throughout all of these upheavals, work continued on this book, although more slowly that I had planned.

Chapter 16

RETURN TO MY ROOTS IN INTERESTING TIMES

It is often said that the expression "may you live in interesting times" is a translation of part of an ancient Chinese curse, the other two parts of which are "may you come to the attention of important people" and "may you find what you are looking for." Others say that its origins are ancient Egyptian or early Scottish. As far as I am aware, no one has ever been able to produce the Chinese language original of this curse, and its origin is more likely to be twentieth-century England, the earliest English use seemingly dating from the 1930s. Whatever the origin, I have certainly lived in interesting times and occasionally come to the attention of important people, although I am not sure that I have found what I have been looking for. Indeed, did I ever define what I was looking for?

Following the Israeli attacks on Lebanon in 2006, I decided that it was time to start thinking about establishing a bolt-hole in England. As mentioned earlier, I had owned a house in Windsor since 1994, but this had been rented ever since the purchase. In any case, I did not consider it suitable to be my eventual home in retirement, should I decide to live in England again. I therefore sold this house in early 2009 and, in spite of the financial crisis and downturn in property prices, realised a sizeable capital gain. I then started to look around at property in Norwich and north Norfolk and, in May

2009, settled on the purchase of an apartment in Cromer, just a couple of miles from my birthplace. I had reached the end of a long, scenic route from West Runton to Cromer that had taken me via Canada, Bahrain, Lebanon, the Yemen Arabic Republic (as it was then known), Lebanon for a second time, the United Arab Emirates, Cyprus, Tanzania and Lebanon yet again.

At various times in my life many people have asked me if I would ever return to England to live, and I have always replied with a categorical "no." However, as I grew older and especially after I gave up full-time work and began to experience some health problems that come to most of us with age, the idea became more of a possibility, although it is still not a reality. I divide my time between Lebanon and England, in between travels to many places, but my main base is still Lebanon and is likely to remain so for the near future.

In late May 2012, as I was working on this book, I was staying at the apartment in Cromer over a particularly pleasant weekend. On the Sunday morning, I decided to take a walk and made my way through the Warren Woods to the cliff path, down the slope to the east promenade and from there to the western end of the promenade and back home through the town. Such was the sunshine that I also decided that I would wear shorts and a T-shirt for this expedition, something that I have not done in Cromer for many a year. It struck me that not a lot had changed since I used to spend summer days on the beach in the 1940s and 1950s. A different type of beach hut, maybe a few more stones on the sand, more modern fishing boats, but in essence, the atmosphere was the same. Cafés selling fish and chips were well patronised, and I even saw three people in the sea, albeit two of them wearing wet suits! My nostalgic thoughts were brought down to earth when I passed the lifeguard station, itself an innovation that had not existed when I was a child. A notice board outside announced that the air temperature was 18°C and the water temperature 12°C; as a child, did I really play in the sand and swim in the sea when temperatures were at that level? So many years living in hot climates have caused me to shudder at such temperatures.

During the same stay in Cromer, I attended a performance in the theatre on the pier. This theatre, which has been in existence since 1905, just three years after the present pier was built, is home to the last "end of pier" variety show in England every summer. However, every May the Cromer and Sheringham Operatic and Dramatic Society presents a musical production there. In 2012, it was *Me and My Girl*. This was the first time that I had attended one of their productions for many years. I was astounded when, after the conductor mounted the podium in front of the orchestra, the first thing that they played was the national anthem. This must be the last place in Britain where this custom continues.

Two seemingly intractable problems have started during my lifetime and had an impact on it: the Israel-Palestinian problem began in 1948 and the Cyprus problem in 1963. Both seem likely to continue after I die.

Green Lines have featured in both problems as well as in Lebanon. Moshe Dayan, then head of the Israeli delegation to the Arab-Israeli armistice talks, drew the 1949 armistice line between Israel and Lebanon in green on a map; he went on to become chief of staff of the Israel Defence Forces, defence minister and foreign minister. In 1964, Maj. Gen. Peter Young, the British general officer commanding Cyprus District, drew a green line across a map of Cyprus, delineating Greek and Turkish Cypriot areas; he later became director of infantry at the Ministry of Defence, before retiring from the British army in 1968. In 1975, the dividing line between West and East Beirut came to be known as the Green Line; this was not because anyone drew a line in that colour on a map, rather because of the colour of the vegetation that had grown wildly after the area, separating mainly Christian East and predominantly Muslim West Beirut, had been deserted.[96] Now, more than twenty years after the end of the civil war, the company Solidaire, which was established in 1994 to undertake the restoration of central Beirut, has largely rebuilt this area. There is not much greenery now.

---

[96] http://en.wikipedia.org/wiki/Green_Line_%28Lebanon%29, accessed 16 Jan 2012

Much of my life and career has been spent living in or involved with the Middle East. As I wrote this book during 2011 and 2012, the region was going through a tumultuous period, which has come to be known as the Arab Spring and has yet to run its course. It started with the people's revolution in Tunisia when, on December 18, 2010, a young man, Mohamed Bouazizi, set fire to himself in protest after police confiscated the fruit and vegetables he was selling from a street stall. Within a month, Pres. Zine El Abidine Ben Ali has fled his country after continuous mass protests culminated in a victory for people power over one of the Arab world's more repressive regimes. Ben Ali, who had been president for twenty-three years, took refuge in Saudi Arabia. At present, this is the only one of the revolutions that appears to have been successful. After several interim governments had come and gone, elections for a constituent assembly took place in October 2011, and there has been a relatively peaceful transfer of power.

On January 17, 2011, emulating the Tunisian vegetable seller, an Egyptian, the owner of a small restaurant in Cairo, set himself on fire in an apparent attempt to highlight poor living standards in the country. Within a few days, thousands of Egyptians gathered in Tahrir Square in central Cairo, calling for the overthrow of the government of Hosni Mubarak, who had been president for three decades. They eventually got their way, and following his resignation on February 11, a timetable for transformation was announced. However, the country remained effectively under the control of the old guard, the Supreme Council of the Armed Forces, a generation of army officers who are contemporaries of Mubarak. Although parliamentary elections took place in May 2012, the constitutional court has ruled them invalid and stated that new elections must be held. This prompted the military council to dissolve Egypt's first freely elected parliament and to give themselves extensive powers.

Meanwhile, the candidate favoured by the Muslim Brotherhood, Mohammed Mursi, won the presidential elections in June 2012, although the result was not without controversy Although the military council handed over some powers to the new president, many doubted that the army would ever relinquish all power. One of Mursi's first actions was to recall parliament in defiance of the military council's decision to dissolve it. Parliament in turn formed a constitutional assembly, tasked with drafting a new constitution. The situation remained confused following Mursi's assumption of legislative powers and the ousting of the military council in August 2012 and decisions of the supreme administrative court, which theoretically rendered all of Mursi's actions unconstitutional. In November 2012 Mursi's decision to issue a decree giving him dictatorial powers resulted in further mass protests. It was soon followed by the hurried finalisation of the new constitution, which many found unacceptable. Demonstrations again took place in Tahrir Square and elsewhere, leading Mursi to rescind his decree, but stick to an early date for a referendum on the new constitution. Egyptians are impatient for faster progress, fearing that the military will intervene again. The future remains uncertain. It is interesting to note that in Egypt in 1952, after the revolution that saw the end of the monarchy and the installation of a military government by the "free officers," they abolished the constitution and promised Egyptians free elections. They were still waiting for this to happen at the time of the 2011 revolution, fifty-nine years later. Meanwhile a seemingly ailing Mubarak has been convicted and sentenced to life imprisonment for ordering the murder of protesters and corruption, although it does not seem that his life has much longer to run.

At the same time as the start of protests in Egypt, it was reported that at least four Algerians had set themselves alight in an echo of the suicide that triggered the unrest that brought down the leader of neighbouring Tunisia. The only tangible outcome of the relatively mild protests in Algeria has been the lifting of a state of emergency that had been in force for nineteen years; the country has been calm since April 2011.

Protests started in many towns in Yemen in mid-January 2011. To begin with, these were against the government's proposals to modify the constitution of Yemen, unemployment, economic conditions and corruption; but the demands soon included a call for the resignation of Pres. Ali Abdullah Saleh, who was in power since 1978. From late April 2011 onwards, Saleh signed several Gulf Cooperation

Council-sponsored agreements to resign and leave the country but reneged at the last minute. Then in June 2011, he was seriously injured in an attack on the presidential palace and was taken to Saudi Arabia for medical treatment. The vice president took over power as acting president. Shortly thereafter, the government refused to consider the idea of a transitional council as a prelude to democratic elections. Although Saleh left hospital in early August, he did not return to Yemen until late September, after increased fighting between government troops and demonstrators and dissidents loyal to some of the tribal chiefs who had sided with the protest movement. On November 23, Saleh signed another agreement, by which he would quit and leave the country. This he did finally in late January 2012, but only after parliament had passed a law granting him immunity from prosecution for actions during his time in office. It has been reported that he has been granted a visa to visit the United States for further medical treatment, but it seems unlikely that he will be allowed to remain there permanently. Perhaps he too will seek refuge in Saudi Arabia. The outcome of the Yemeni revolution is still far from certain, but developments in Syria have forced it from the headlines

Protests in Syria started on January 26, 2011, originally calling for political reforms and the reinstatement of civil rights, as well as an end to the state of emergency, which had been in place since the Ba'athist regime came to power in 1963.

More recently, demands have included calls for the resignation of Pres. Bashar al-Assad. Violent protests are continuing, and the government has responded with harsh security clampdowns and military operations, resulting in thousands of civilian deaths. Syria, a secular country, is perhaps the last place in which one could have expected a revolution. The country was ruled from 1970 to 2000 by Hafez al-Assad, self-proclaimed president after a coup d'état in 1970, and since his death in 2000, by his son, Bashar al-Assad, members of the minority Allawite sect of Shia Islam. Hafez governed under an emergency law that gave virtually unlimited powers of arrest and imprisonment to the security forces and had brutally suppressed an uprising in Homs in 1982.

Since the summer of 2011, there were increasing numbers of demonstrations in many parts of the country, and defectors from the army and security services have formed the Free Syrian Army to support the demonstrators. While some concessions were made by the government since the demonstrations started, including the lifting of the emergency law in April and the drafting of a new law to allow the creating of new political parties in July 2011, these seem to have had little practical effect and are generally considered to be too little too late. The opposition boycotted parliamentary elections in April 2012. In spite of sanctions imposed by the United States, the European Union and the Arab League, the suppression of the uprising continues, and it has become even more violent. In November 2011, the Arab League took the unprecedented step of suspending Syria's membership. Eventually, in late December, an Arab League monitoring group was finally allowed into the country, in theory to oversee the implementation of an agreement to end the bloodshed and initiate talks between the government and the opposition. Their mission was not a success and has been suspended.

The problem moved from the Arab League to the UN Security Council. Former UN secretary-general Kofi Annan was appointed to represent both organisations in trying to negotiate a solution with the Syrian government. An agreement was made, which included joint UN/Arab League monitors, but it was largely ignored by both the government and the opposition, and the monitors were unable to carry out their tasks. By mid-2012, the situation had deteriorated into civil war, although not everyone seemed prepared to call a spade a spade. Persistent predictions by pundits on various news channels that the government's days were numbered have passed with the Assad regime still in power. Russia and China, no doubt recalling the wide powers invoked by NATO countries after the passing of a resolution regarding Libya, have used their veto to thwart attempts by Western powers to get resolutions on Syria passed by the UN Security Council. In any case, there is a marked reluctance on the part of the West to become involved militarily in Syria. Annan resigned as joint UN/Arab League envoy in August 2012 and his replacement is Lakhdar Brahimi, a veteran Algerian diplomat who, to date, does not seem to have made any progress. Violence continues unabated;

it is estimated by the UN that more than 60,000 people have been killed and it is impossible to predict the outcome.

Protests began in Bahrain on February 14, 2011 and, initially, were largely peaceful, until a raid by police three days later against protestors sleeping at the Pearl Roundabout in Manama, resulting in the death of three protesters. On February 18, government forces opened fire on protesters, mourners and journalists prompting protesters to begin calling for the overthrow of the Bahraini monarchy and the government, headed by Prime Minister Khalifa bin Salman Al Khalifa, who had held the post since I lived in Bahrain in 1969. What happened in Bahrain was different to the revolutions elsewhere; essentially, it was protests by a Shia Muslim majority, probably encouraged and supported by Iran, against perceived injustices imposed by a ruling Sunni Muslim minority. Moreover, the result was different; the government suppressed the protests in Bahrain firmly, with the assistance of security forces from other Gulf Cooperation Council states, many of whom entered Bahrain on March 14, 2011, across the causeway from Saudi Arabia over which I had travelled several times. A few days later, the protesters' camp at the Pearl Roundabout was demolished and the iconic pearl monument torn down. In spite of well-documented stories of atrocities, including torture, by the Bahraini security forces, international reaction has been much more muted than in the case of other revolutions during the Arab Spring. Attempts by King Hamad to promote national reconciliation have taken place, and the country has been generally quiet since March 2011.

Next in line for a revolution was Libya, where Col. Muammar Gaddafi had led the country, in his somewhat eccentric way, since 1969. Anti-government protests began on February 15, 2011. Within a few days, the opposition controlled most of Benghazi, the country's second-largest city, and by February 20, protests had spread to the capital Tripoli. On March 17, at the request of the Arab League, the United Nations Security Council authorised a no-fly zone over Libya and "all necessary measures" to protect civilians. Two days later, France, the United States and the United Kingdom intervened in Libya with a bombing campaign against pro-Gaddafi forces. A coalition of seventeen states from Europe and the Middle East soon joined the intervention, and NATO agreed to take over the enforcement of the no-fly zone, the first and, so far, the only, overt international action in the events of the Arab Spring. By August, the rebels had taken Tripoli and controlled most of the country, an exception being Sirte, Gaddafi's hometown. In October, Sirte finally fell to the rebels, and Muammar Gaddafi was killed, probably murdered. His eldest son, Saif, was captured in mid-November, although little has been heard of him since his arrest. The National Transitional Council, which was running the country, declared the liberation of the county on October 23, 2011, and began to plan for the appointment of an interim government, promising elections for a constitutional assembly within eight months, followed by presidential and parliamentary elections a year later. Elections for the General National Congress were held in July 2012; it is tasked with forming a new government to take over from the Transitional National Council. The job of drafting a new constitution has been given to a sixty-member panel, which is to be elected separately. The official end of the war has not meant a cessation of violence. Disagreements between various militia and tribes and the government have led to bombings and fighting on several occasions, and it is doubtful that the government has full control of the entire country.

Since the events in Tunisia in December 2010, demonstrations have also taken place in Jordan, leading to economic concessions by King Abdulla; in Oman, where Sultan Qaboos has granted lawmaking powers to the elected assembly, dismissed ministers and made economic concessions and Morocco, where King Mohammed VI has permitted a referendum on constitutional reforms and vowed to end corruption. Even in ultraconservative Saudi Arabia, King Abdulla has announced that women will be permitted to vote and be elected in 2015 municipal elections and to be nominated to the Shura Council. Perhaps fearing that they may suffer the fate of other leaders, President Bashir of Sudan and Prime Minister Maliki of Iraq have said that they will not run for office again when their present terms end.

What it will lead to is anyone's guess. However, during more than forty years of involvement in such interesting times in the region, I have naturally formed some opinions. The "revolutions" in Tunisia, Egypt, Yemen, Libya and Syria have had one thing in common: the desire to bring to an end the rule of leaders who had long outlived their useful lives. The demonstrations that preceded the departure of the dictators and their regimes were not anti-Western; they were not anti-Israel, and they were not started by Islamic extremists (although in some cases they have joined the battle later). They were prompted by poverty, unemployment, inflation, corruption and lack of political and other freedoms. For the most part, the demonstrations involved the younger generation. However, one of the outcomes has been that Islamic parties have gained the majority of seats in the Tunisian parliament and did the same in the election in Egypt. An exception has been Libya, where the National Forces Alliance, led by the former head of the Transitional National Council Mahmoud Jibril won decisively, despite earlier predictions that Islamist parties would prevail. Whatever the outcome of the Arab Spring, it will not necessarily be the same in each country. I have my doubts that the average man in the street in Tunis or Cairo, Sana'a or Tripoli will be any better off under whatever government eventually succeeds the ousted one. Recent events in Egypt are beginning to support that view. Bearing in mind what happened in Palestine when Hamas won parliamentary elections, it will be interesting to see how Western governments will react to Islamic parties winning free elections and coming to power in some of these countries.

The double standards in all matters relating to the Middle East displayed by, in particular, the United States and European Union countries are exemplified in the differing attitudes to the uprisings in Libya and Bahrain. In the case of the former, NATO airpower was used, at the request of the Arab League and under a UN Security Council resolution, to attack government forces in support of the rebels. In Bahrain, the suppression of the revolution with the assistance of other GCC countries has passed without any condemning UN resolution and with no Western action. Prior to the Arab Spring, western powers had been keen supporters of the now-deposed leaders of Egypt and Tunisia and, in recent years, welcomed Gaddafi back into the fold. There has also been a lack of understanding of the nature of the tribal societies in Libya and

Yemen, which is a continuation of the ignorance displayed by the administrations of both George Bush Sr. and his son over Iraq. Libya, Yemen and Iraq needed a leader with a strong personality and the determination to hold the country together. While I am no supporter of Saddam Hussein, we have seen the consequences of his deposition in Iraq; will there be similar events in Syria, Yemen and Libya? There are worrying signs that this is possible. The actions of the government in Syria have exceeded those in any of the other countries in which revolutions have taken place. Although there have been many condemnations of these actions by many countries, there is a most notable reluctance on the part of Western nations to intervene with military action, as happened in Libya. Qatar has recently raised the idea of an Arab force to separate the protesters and the government forces, but it may take the Arab League a long time to consider this idea. However, double standards are not confined to Western countries. In Lebanon, Hezbollah was outspoken in its criticism of the Bahraini government but has publicly supported the Assad regime in Syria, leading to anti-Hezbollah demonstrations there.

Meanwhile, Lebanon has been a haven of relative peace throughout the Arab Spring. The country is not without political leaders who have been in power for a long time; the speaker of parliament, Nabih Berri, has held the post since 1991, and most of the political groups pass leadership from father to son. Naturally, the situation in Syria is the one that causes the greatest concern in Lebanon; both sides in that conflict having their supporters, both among the politicians and tribal leaders and the public. There has been some fallout in the form of refugees fleeing to Lebanon to escape the violence across the border and sometimes related incursions by the Syrian security forces pursuing alleged rebels. Tripoli, in northern Lebanon, has witnessed fighting between Allawite supporters of the Syrian regime and Sunni Muslims. The biggest question is the potential impact on Hezbollah should, as seems likely, the Assad regime eventually fall from power. Opinions are divided, but undoubtedly, loss of Syrian support and the use of that country as a transit point for supplies from Iran, would seriously affect the organisation's military capability. In spite of the relative calm on the surface, the situation in Lebanon remains, as it has been for most of the country's existence—fragile. The quantity of arms and ammunition in private hands, not to mention Hezbollah, is huge. There are stories in the local media almost every day about use of arms to settle personal disputes, often ending in fatalities. Generally, these go unremarked, and they are soon forgotten. Always a people ready to avail themselves of a commercial opportunity, Lebanese intermediaries have been active in supplying weapons and ammunition to Syrians, increasing the black market prices in Beirut significantly. Over the past year, the price of an AK-47 rifle has jumped from US$1,100 to over US$2,000, and a Glock 9mm pistol now costs more than US$3,000 compared to US$2000.[97]

However, let us get back to banking. Operationally, during my banking career, I have moved from handwritten ledgers at Barclays Bank in Sheringham and the British Bank of the Middle East in Hodeidah, through NCR Class 32 accounting machines in Bahrain and Beirut. Later, NCR Class 299 machines and an early computer-based banking system in Dubai and finally, to what is currently one of the most sophisticated online real-time banking systems in Cyprus and Tanzania.

The nature of the banking business has also changed dramatically over this time. To take just one example, when I started my career in London, the sterling area and exchange control existed, and banks undertook foreign exchange trading virtually exclusively to cover customer requirements for approved transactions. Now no controls exist, and banks trade trillions of dollars every business day, the vast majority of the deals being for speculative purposes.

The "Big Bang" in London financial markets in 1986 and the later abolition of the Glass-Steagall Act in the United States heralded major changes in banking on both sides of the Atlantic. Reduced regulation and the ability of banks to mix commercial and investment banking activities enabled them to use customer's deposits to, effectively, gamble. In the last twenty years, bankers have become increasingly

---

[97]   http://www.thetimes.co.uk/tto/news/world/middleeast/article3013538.ece, accessed 16 Jan 2012

ingenious in devising instruments, initially structured to hedge risk, into risky business themselves. The deregulation of derivatives by the US Commodity Futures Modernisation Act of 2000 enabled banks to create, among other things, instruments based on "subprime" mortgages. In 2001, while with FBME, I met a representative from a major American investment bank who tried to persuade me that the bank should invest his institution's collateralised debt obligations. I resisted the attraction of the seemingly generous yields, in no small part because I did not understand the nature of the instruments. In 2003, Warren Buffett described derivatives as "financial weapons of mass destruction" and suggested that they "appeared to have been devised by a madman" and "that they could harm the whole economic system."[98] It is a great pity that bankers and their regulators as well as the rating agencies did not heed his comments. Seldom did the bankers or regulators discuss the activities of those involved in this business, which started in the 1990s, in public. Was this because the bankers considered the subject to be beyond the ability of others to understand? Was it because the regulators failed to understand just what the bankers were doing?

A major factor that has contributed to the current banking crisis is the nature of the bonus system in banking, particularly for so-called investment bankers. In general, banks calculated annual bonuses on the profits made during a single year and not related to the long-term benefit obtained by the institution. Only very recently has a banker been asked to forgo part of a bonus awarded earlier when the business that generated it turned sour, and this is still far from usual—this largely the result of pressure from shareholders.

The result of the casino-like activities of some banks was the banking crisis which started in 2008 and which has not yet fully run its course. The solution has to be more regulation and the separation of "high street banking" from the much riskier activities of the so-called investment banks. At the time of the start of the present banking crisis, the industry thought JP Morgan Chase to be a relative paragon when compared to its peers. However, in May 2012 its fallibility

---

[98]   http://news.bbc.co.uk/1/hi/2817995.stm, accessed 25 Sept 2012

was displayed for all to see when the bank announced losses of more than US$2 billion from derivatives trading. This estimated figure was later increased to US$5.8 billion, with a possibility that it could reach US$7 billion.[99] The claims of this bank that bankers knew their business and did not need more government regulation sounded somewhat hollow after this revelation. In remarks published prior to attending senate hearings on the matter in June 2012, Chase CEO, Jamie Dimon, admitted that the transactions leading to the losses were not properly analysed and that "risks controls were generally ineffective" in challenging the decisions made by the chief investment officer. Risk committees in place at JPMorgan Chase, he said, "were not as formal or robust as they should have been."[100]

The most recent banking scandals to come to light, the fixing of LIBOR rates involving, among others, Barclays Bank and Union Bank of Switzerland, and gross failures in the compliance function at Standard Chartered Bank and HSBC have further affected the reputation of banks and bankers at the most senior level. Heads have rolled and more should follow.

Throughout my banking career, I have been what might be called a generalist. I have acquired substantial knowledge of many aspects of the business, from simple cash transactions to letters of credit, compliance and foreign exchange trading, to name but a few. In large part, this is because I worked for many years with small banks and had to know what was going on in all departments.

Today, most people entering the banking industry tend to specialise in one aspect of the business and acquire little knowledge of the rest. Similarly, staff seems to be trained to respond in fixed, structured ways to customer enquiries. I recently sent an e-mail to the Isle of Man subsidiary of one of the UK high street banks, where I have an account, querying the delay in processing a payment I had instructed.

---

[99]   http://www.huffingtonpost.com/2012/07/13/jpmorgan-chase-q02-earnings-2012_n_1670629.html accessed 12 Dec 2012

[100]   http://www.miamiherald.com/2012/06/12/2846350/jpmorgans-jamie-dimon-releases.html#storylink=cpy, accessed 13 June 2012

In response, I received a telephone call in which the relationship manager informed me that she had been instructed that all she could do was to read to me from a script on her computer screen. This she proceeded to do. When I cut her off in midstream, she was a little upset, but being able to read between the lines, I was not interested in hearing the rest of her speech; it was obvious to me that the bank considered me to be a "high risk" customer, based on my country of residence. Eventually the payment was processed.

In January 2011, the governor of the Central Bank of Nigeria, Mallam Lamido Aminu Sanusi, was named as central bank governor of the year for 2010 by the *Banker* magazine in recognition of his achievements in salvaging the crumbling Nigerian financial system. Shortly thereafter, I heard him talking in an interview on the BBC World Service; he spoke of the need for bankers to cease their reckless behaviour, to go back to basics, and to remember that most of the money that they used to finance their activities was not theirs to use for speculation. His remarks reminded me of those made by the chairman of FBME, the late Michel Saab, in the mid-1980s. The bank was arranging the first syndicated loan in the Cyprus banking market, and at the signing ceremony, he said to the chairman of the borrowing company, "Remember, this is my depositors' money that I am lending you. You must repay it so that I will be able to repay them." This was good advice that many investment bankers today would do well to heed.

In November 2011, the governor of the Bank of England, Mervyn King, appeared before a joint parliamentary committee in London considering plans to create a new subsidiary of the central bank, the Prudential Regulatory Authority. He commented that banks had been buying and selling financial products that were "riskier than they (i.e. the regulators) had been lead to believe" and that the rigid, "rules-based" approach by regulators in the past had allowed the financial sector to take on huge liabilities, with regulators largely unaware of their activities. Sir Mervyn said the new authority should be able to tell banks, "Look, frankly, we don't understand why your organisation needs to be so complex. We can't work out what you are doing, so you're going to have to change it. You haven't broken a rule, but too bad, you've got to change it."

These remarks, I think, sum up what banking should be about. The business started in a very simple way—with bankers, who usually had unlimited personal liability borrowing from one group of people, their depositors, and lending part of those deposits to others. Today it has become such a complicated business, staffed by highly rewarded specialists, most of whom do not understand the entire business of their institutions. Equally to blame are senior management and directors who often do not understand the risks that their institutions are taking. From Sir Mervyn's remarks, it seems that regulators may have had the same problem. I am not embarrassed to admit that I still do not understand the derivative products and derivatives of derivates that caused the financial crisis that began in 2008. Alas, in spite of the near meltdown of the international financial system in the first decade of the twenty-first century, bankers do not seem to have learned any lessons.

Index